contents

KU-032-778

INTRODUCTION

AS Psychology: The Study Guide

Authors: Nigel Holt and Rob Lewis

Nigel Holt has a PhD in psychology, is a Senior Lecturer in Psychology at Bath Spa University and is a team leader examiner at AS and A2 with a major examination board. In addition to teaching and examining, he spends time researching the use of e-learning and podcasting in psychology and the perception of sound. He talks regularly to A-level students at conferences around the UK, and is also the author of university-level research and psychology textbooks.

Rob Lewis has been teaching for over 20 years, and presently lectures in psychology and maintains interests in neuro and anomalistic psychology. His primary focus has been A/AS level Psychology but he has also taught at both undergraduate and postgraduate levels and has most recently been involved in initial teacher training. He is an extremely experienced examiner, having held senior examining posts with several exam boards. He continues to be involved in specification development, delivering INSET and examining at a senior level.

ACKNOWLEDGEMENTS

Nigel and Rob would like to thank Kate and Nicola – this book would simply not have been finished without their continued good humour, patience and support. Thanks go to Caroline for her work in designing the study guide and making sense of our many requests. Thanks also go to Nicola Taylor, Head of Social Science at Monmouth Comprehensive School, for her help in thinking up fun and useful questions and for allowing us to share her mind maps with you.

WHO IS THE STUDY GUIDE FOR?

We can see how this book will be useful for teachers and psychologists but we've really written it for students. However much teaching and instruction students get, when it comes to the exam it is all down to them.

WHY HAVE WE WRITTEN HIS BOOK?

We're both very interested in researching and teaching psychology. That's an understatement, really. It sounds odd but it's what we do most of the time. When we are not teaching or examining psychology we talk about psychology, and think about how best to investigate it and how best to teach it. The study guide gives us the chance to do all of these things, and pass on some of our knowledge and experience to those who will benefit most – students.

Our work as examiners has shown us that it is not just remembering the information that counts, it is understanding how to answer the questions. Sometimes the hardest exam papers to mark are those that clearly are written by capable students who have answered the questions in ways that make it difficult or impossible for us to give them marks! A little knowledge about how to approach exam questions can go a very long way, and we've included more than a little advice on that in this study guide.

It doesn't matter which textbook you've used in studying psychology, or even if you've not used one at all. We've written the study guide so that it is carefully focused on the AQA(A) AS specification and will be extremely useful for anybody taking that examination.

FURTHER HELP

We've included a good summary of the information you'll need to revise for the examination, but we know that some students like additional support, and some really like to stretch themselves. For more detailed information and for any clarification you think you may need, we've written *The Student's Textbook* (ISBN: 978-184590093-9).

KEY FEATURES OF THE BOOK

Each chapter covers a section of the specification and contains a summary of the key information needed for success in the exam. It is presented in a clear, concise and highly visual format.

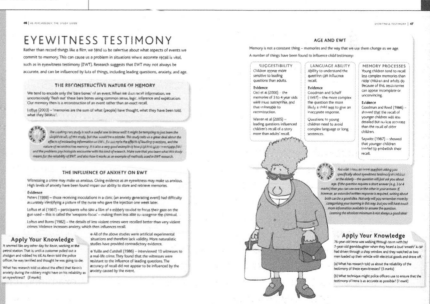

APPLY YOUR KNOWLEDGE

One of the most challenging aspects of the examination is those questions that require you to apply your knowledge of psychology to novel situations. There is no rote learning this – you really do have to *understand* what you learn in order to do well. Of course, practice in these analysis and application questions will do you a load of good and because of this we've written lots of questions that give you a chance to try out your knowledge and develop question-answering skills.

Apply Your Knowledge

The athletes at the start of the race take their marks and prepare for the sound of the starter's pistol. 'BANG!' they're off!

(a) Identify one physical feeling that tells the athletes that they are feeling stressed. (*1 mark*)

(b) Explain how the physical feeling you identified in part (a) was generated by the body's response to stress. (*4 marks*)

ASK AN EXAMINER

These green boxes appear all over the place. The phrase 'Ask an Examiner' is used because we know that an expert perspective can be invaluable, especially during revision. They are directed at the learner, and are often responses we, as examiners, have given to questions from students and teachers. A few hints and tips here and there can go a long way towards making examinations a less painful experience!

This is a correlational design. Alarm bells should be ringing! What can you conclude? Does maths ability cause pool playing ability, or the other way around? Of course, you can't conclude either, only that they are positively related.

HOW SCIENCE WORKS

Psychology is a science and one of the important goals of this AS level course is to develop an understanding of how psychologists scientifically investigate human behaviour. The first chapter provides an underpinning knowledge of psychological research methods, but how science works is more than this – it is about how psychologists go about solving scientific problems.

Throughout the book we have provided opportunities for you to engage in practical activities in order to develop these skills, as well as ones that deepen your understanding of research methods.

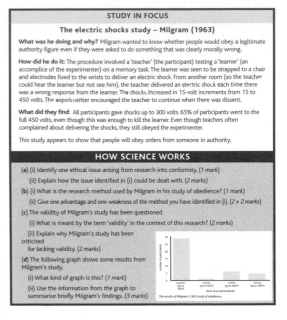

STUDY IN FOCUS

The electric shocks study – Milgram (1963)

What was he doing and why? Milgram wanted to know whether people would obey a legitimate authority figure even if they were asked to do something that was clearly morally wrong.

How did he do it: The procedure involved a 'teacher' (the participant) testing a 'learner' (an accomplice of the experimenter) on a memory task. The learner was seen to be strapped to a chair and electrodes fixed to the wrists to deliver an electric shock. From another room (so the teacher could hear the learner but not see him), the teacher delivered an electric shock each time there was a wrong response from the learner. The shocks increased in 15-volt increments from 15 to 450 volts. The experimenter encouraged the teacher to continue when there was dissent.

What did they find: All participants gave shocks up to 300 volts. 65% of participants went to the full 450 volts, even though this was enough to kill the learner. Even though teachers often complained about delivering the shocks, they still obeyed the experimenter.

This study appears to show that people will obey orders from someone in authority.

HOW SCIENCE WORKS

(a) (i) Identify one ethical issue arising from research into conformity. (*1 mark*)

(ii) Explain how the issue identified in (i) could be dealt with. (*2 marks*)

(b) (i) What is the research method used by Milgram in his study of obedience? (*1 mark*)

(ii) Give one advantage and one weakness of the method you have identified in (i). (*2 + 2 marks*)

(c) The validity of Milgram's study has been questioned.

(i) What is meant by the term 'validity' in the context of this research? (*2 marks*)

(ii) Explain why Milgram's study has been criticised for lacking validity. (*2 marks*)

(d) The following graph shows some results from Milgram's study.

(i) What kind of graph is this? (*1 mark*)

(ii) Use the information from the graph to summarise briefly Milgram's findings. (*3 marks*)

The results of Milgram's 1963 study of obedience.

MIND MAPS™

We think mind maps™ are extremely useful in organising your thinking and really visualising how different areas fit together, so we've included a number of them in the study guide. These are only examples of mind maps – the real value of them is making your own!

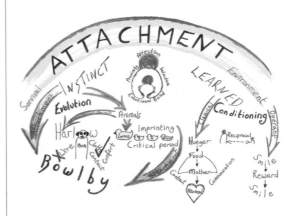

IN THE NEWS

Psychology gets into the news all the time. We've included a number of examples of how newspapers from around the world have described some of the ideas you are learning about. We've also included 'stretch and challenge' questions that *really* make you think about what you'll read in each article, and relate the issues raised to what you've learned in psychology. They are not always easy questions – but then, that's why they are called *stretch and challenge*!

THE EXTENDED WRITTEN RESPONSE

Writing longer extended answers can be a little tricky, and it is often difficult to see how best to include description and evaluation. For this reason we have included a number of answers to extended written response questions to give you an idea of what to aim for in your own answers. We've also added lots of comments about the content of the answers to give you an understanding of the thinking that went into it and what examiners will be looking for. You will also find some other (unanswered!) questions for you to practise.

CHECK YOUR KNOWLEDGE

There is a set of exam-style short-answer questions to test your knowledge of the content of each chapter. Your answers can be checked against the chapter content for accuracy.

THE EXTENDED WRITTEN RESPONSE – ADDITIONAL QUESTIONS

1 Discuss the biological approach to psychopathology. (*12 marks*)

2 Outline and evaluate two definitions of psychological abnormality. (*12 marks*)

3 Describe and evaluate one or more psychological therapies used to treat abnormality. (*12 marks*)

Example answers to these questions can be found at www.askanexaminer.com

USEFUL WEBSITES

http://www.freudfile.org/
The life and work of one of the most influential psychologists in history, Sigmund Freud.

http://www.makingthemodernworld.org.uk/learning_modules/psychology/02.TU.04/
This is a fantastic site. Have a poke about here and see what you can find out and learn about psychology and mental health. There are interactive components where techniques are explained and your opinions of them are recorded. There is a lot to do here, and a good deal of it is relevant to your examination.

http://neurophilosophy.wordpress.com/2006/12/04/the-incredible-case-of-phineas-gage/
The amazing story of Phineas Gage, whose abnormality was brought about by physical damage, a terrible accident at work, where a metal spike was driven through his head. Read all about it here.

http://www.youtube.com/watch?v=OmkiMlvLKto
This film tells the story of Clive Wearing, whose abnormality came about as a result of an infection.

http://www.apa.org/monitor/mar02/genetic.html
Here we find that whether someone suffers with anorexia is down to both their psychology and their physical

http://www.rcpsych
Some questions an
electroconvulsive t

http://www.nhsdir
Here, the National

http://www.socybe
In this site, the ste

GET TO KNOW YOUR EXAM | 161

SECTION A – COGNITIVE PSYCHOLOGY AND RESEARCH METHODS

Total marks for this question: 4 marks

1 (a) Tick **two** of the boxes below to indicate which of the following concepts relate to the multi-store model of memory:

Sensory memory
Articulatory loop
Chunking
Visuo-spatial sketchpad

(2 marks)

1 (b) According to the multi-store model, what is the **capacity** and **duration** of short-term memory?

(2 marks)

Total marks for this question: 15 marks

2 It has been suggested that humans are not constantly vigilant and often simply don't remember details of events happening around them. To test this, psychology students conducted a study in a nearby town centre. Working in pairs, one student approached a passer-by and asked for the time. A few minutes later the second student approached the same passer-by and asked him or her to describe the person who had just asked the time.

u expect the

(3 marks)

GLOSSARY

A

Acronym
A method of improving a memory for something that takes the first letters of items to be recalled and forms them into an *acronym*. An example is ROYGBIV for the colours of the rainbow: red, orange, yellow, green, blue, indigo, violet.

Age of witness
The accuracy of the memory of an event (the *eyewitness testimony*) may be influenced by the age of the witness. The accuracy of the elderly or children may be questionable.

Agency theory
Milgram's theory for why people obey authority figures. It includes descriptions of *autonomous state* and *agentic state*.

Agentic state
Part of *agency theory*. The *agentic state* is where individuals feel that they have diminished responsibilities for their actions because they are the 'agents' of others.

Aggression
Intentional or unintentional harm directed towards others. Whether *day care* generates an increase in aggressive behaviour in children is unclear.

Aims
The aims of a *research* project describe the reason for carrying out the research. They indicate what the research intends to investigate or find out.

Ainsworth
Mary Ainsworth is a major thinker in the area of *attachment*. She was instrumental in designing the *Strange Situation*, an experimental technique for investigating attachment type in children.

Antidepressant
Drugs used to treat mood disorders, particularly depression.

Antipsychotic
Drugs used to treat symptoms of psychotic disorders such as schizophrenia, including hallucinations and disturbed thinking.

Anxiety
The physical tension associated with feeling stressed. A factor that may influence the accuracy of an eyewitness.

Anxiolytic
Drugs used to treat feelings of anxiety, common examples of which are benzodiazepines.

Anxious/avoidant attachment
A type of *insecure attachment*. Children explore less, show little distress on separation and are not very nervous around strangers. Also known as Type A.

Anxious/resistant attachment
A type of *insecure attachment*. Children show great distress when separated from the caregiver and ambivalence on reunion.

Articulatory loop
Part of the *working memory model*. Often referred to as the 'inner voice', it is the verbal rehearsal system in the memory.

Attachment
An emotional bond between the child and the principle caregiver.

Autokinetic effect
An optical illusion used by Sherif (1936). If you stare at a spot of light in a darkened room it will appear to move. He had participants in groups estimate how far they thought the spot had moved in an investigation of *conformity*.

WEBSITES

There is a wealth of information about psychology on the internet. There is so much of it in fact that it is really easy to quickly get bogged down with material and surf into many dead-ends and less than useful sites. At the end of each chapter we provide you with a few suggestions for websites that we have found useful ourselves. If you wish to you can use these as starting points for you own web searches. But beware! There is no guarantee that what you find in websites is accurate, up-to-date or truly helpful.

GET TO KNOW YOUR EXAM

We've included a chapter called 'Get To Know Your Exam'. Our aim with this is to familiarise you with the examination, including advice on the kinds of skills that are being assessed and how you will be assessed. We have also included a full examination paper for you to practise – that is, an exam for Unit 1 and Unit 2. Answers are also provided in the Example Answers appendix. This chapter also provides you with useful advice and ideas to help your revision.

EXAMPLE ANSWERS

We have provided example answers for all the Apply Your Knowledge questions in the book. This section also provides answers to the examination papers. We haven't gone down the route of providing examples of poor, average and good answers – all the answers we give would, in our opinion, get you maximum marks in an examination. We believe that this is the most useful way of using example answers to develop examination skills and self-confidence. Note, however, the use of the term *example* answers – these are not *model* answers, nor are they the *absolute* answers to questions. There are many ways of achieving maximum marks.

GLOSSARY

These things are really useful. A glossary is a tailor-made dictionary. We've included all the

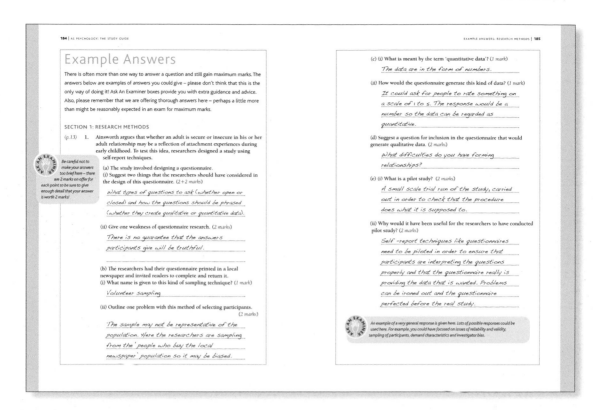

terms you will need to be aware of, or might need to look up quickly during your revision. A good glossary saves a lot of time and can really make a difference when you don't have long to find information you really need.

NOTE TO TEACHERS

Hello! We didn't write this book for you but we know you are out there … It would please us enormously if you found this study guide helpful to you in your teaching. We are always happy to hear from and to talk to fellow teachers, so if you have any questions or comments on the content of this book please feel free to contact us. Some of you might meet us in the real world and are formally invited to engage in old-fashioned communication – a chat. If you prefer electronic forms of communication, you can e-mail us at teachers@askanexaminer.com. Either way, good luck in your teaching.

Section 1

Research Methods

WHAT YOU NEED TO KNOW

Research Methods is in Unit 1 of the specification. As you learn you are expected to develop your knowledge and understanding of Research Methods. You also need to develop the skills of analysis, evaluation and application. Rather than just recall and reproduce information, you are expected to be able to apply a knowledge and understanding of Research Methods to all areas of the specification. The subject content is split into three parts:

Methods and techniques

- Research methods in psychology, including experimental methods, and non-experimental methods such as observation, self-report, correlation and case study
- Advantages and weaknesses associated with these various research methods

Investigation design

- Designing and conducting psychological research

Data analysis and presentation

- Analysis, presentation and interpretation of psychological research findings

DOING PSYCHOLOGICAL RESEARCH

Psychology is a science and relies on research for its accumulated knowledge. To appreciate psychology fully it is necessary to understand how psychologists conduct research.

AIMS

Ask yourself the question 'Why were the researchers carrying out their project?' The answer might begin with the phrase 'They wanted to find out whether...' or 'They wanted to look for the relationship between ...'. This answer describes the *aims* of the research.

The AIM: 'The researchers wanted to investigate the relationship between potato eating and sleeping.'

HYPOTHESIS

The hypothesis turns the aim into a statement that can be tested. If we are doing an experiment it is called the experimental hypothesis (H_1). If doing any other kind of research it is known as the alternative hypothesis (H_A) and it comes in two different forms.

Directional

'Eating more potatoes makes people sleep more.'

A specific direction is predicted – more potatoes lead to more sleep. Choose a directional hypothesis if you have an idea of what might happen, perhaps from previous research.

Non-Directional

'Eating potatoes changes the amount people sleep.'

No specific direction is predicted – people might sleep more or they might sleep less. Choose a non-directional hypothesis if you are not sure what might happen, perhaps if you are beginning your investigation with pilot research.

TEST YOUR HYPOTHESIS!

Design your research to test your hypothesis. This means that the hypothesis will either be supported or rejected by your findings.

ASK AN EXAMINER

You may be asked to write a hypothesis. When you do, remember to include the independent and dependent variables and also make it clear whether it is directional or non-directional.

VARIABLES

Variables are things that change in the research. They may change on their own, or you may change them. They may also change because you have changed something. Example: 'Carrying more bags of sugar makes you run slower.'

Independent Variables (IV)

The researcher changes these. The number of bags the researcher gives the person to carry.

Dependent Variables (DV)

This is what the researchers measure, what they write down or record. The time taken to do the running.

Extraneous and Confounding Variables

Anything other than the independent variable that may influence the dependent variable is an extraneous variable; for instance, the temperature when running. We need to predict these and control them. If the dependent variable is influenced then the extraneous variable has become a confounding variable.

DON'T FORGET TO OPERATIONALISE!

This basically means writing your hypothesis in a way that makes it clear how the dependent variable will be measured.

Get to grips with the idea of operationalising – you will almost certainly be expected to know about it in your exam. For example, you might be asked to write a hypothesis, in which case the examiner will expect it written in an operationalised form.

Apply Your Knowledge

Ainsworth argues that whether an adult is secure or insecure in his or her adult relationship may be a reflection of attachment experiences during early childhood. To test this idea, researchers designed a study using self-report techniques.

(a) The study involved designing a questionnaire.
  (i) Suggest two things that the researchers should have considered in the design of this questionnaire. (*2 + 2 marks*)
  (ii) Give one weakness of questionnaire research. (*2 marks*)

(b) The researchers had their questionnaire printed in a local newspaper and invited readers to complete and return it.
  (i) What name is given to this kind of sampling technique? (*1 mark*)
  (ii) Outline one problem with this method of selecting participants. (*2 marks*)

(c) (i) What is meant by the term 'quantitative data'? (*1 mark*)
  (ii) How would the questionnaire generate this kind of data? (*1 mark*)

(d) Suggest a question for inclusion in the questionnaire that would generate qualitative data. (*2 marks*)

(e) (i) What is a pilot study? (*2 marks*)
  (ii) Why would it have been useful for the researchers to have conducted a pilot study? (*2 marks*)

SAMPLING

We select a sample of participants from a population. Avoid sample bias, i.e. where participants are not representative of the population. For example, when investigating a community of mixed ethnicity, choosing a sample of all white participants is not 'representative' and results may be biased. There are three methods of sampling, and each has its problems. The number of participants should reflect the population.

RANDOM SAMPLING

Where everyone in a population has an equal chance of being selected.

'Names from a hat' is one way of doing this, or random names generated by a computer.

Bad because: relies on all participants being available to participate. If they are not, then sampling is not truly random. And purely by chance you may get a biased sample, e.g. 10 rugby players may pop up at random, biasing your sample.

OPPORTUNITY SAMPLING

Ask anyone you can find to participate.

Bad because: most of the population is excluded, not everyone will stroll past you when selecting. The experimenter may have unconscious biases to selecting certain types of people. What if you are attracted to that person? Some people may like helping and will say yes because of this, possibly biasing your sample.

VOLUNTEER SAMPLING

Advertise for people to help you, e.g. for a small fee.

Bad because: you may get a bias from 'helpful' or 'interested' people so your sample will not reflect the population from which you are sampling. If you advertise for volunteers you may get a bias depending on where you advertised, i.e. adverts in a psychology department draw abnormally large numbers of psychologists!

DEMAND CHARACTERISTICS

Features of the research may cause participants to change their behaviour, e.g. participants might find clues as to what the study is about.

Demand characteristics can be reduced with a single-blind procedure where only the experimenter knows the details of the procedure. This involves some deception which may raise ethical concerns.

INVESTIGATOR EFFECTS

The age, gender, ethnicity or behaviour of the researcher may influence the participant. The researcher may also subconsciously interpret behaviours as favourable to his or her hypotheses.

A double-blind procedure where neither participant nor researcher knows the aims of the procedure can assist in eliminating investigator effects.

RELIABILITY

This refers to the consistency of the research. Can the research be replicated? i.e. if it were carried out again would you find the same things? Or, if two researchers observed the same thing, would it be rated similarly? The more reliable the research, the more confidence we can have in its findings.

VALIDITY

Does the test or research actually do what it claims to? If it does, we say it is valid. For example, a thermometer is a valid measurer of temperature but an egg timer is not. Tests for intelligence include Intelligence Quotient (IQ) tests, which have questionable validity as researchers regularly debate whether they really do test intelligence.

Reliability and validity are core ideas in psychology, and you can expect to have to apply and use these concepts everywhere.

PILOT STUDIES

A pilot study is a small-scale version of the investigation. It is useful because it checks to see if the procedure does what it is supposed to, allowing problems to be 'ironed out'.

It reveals issues of reliability and validity, whether extraneous variables have been controlled, provides a check on the operationalisation of variables, demand characteristics and investigator bias, and gives insight into the experience of participants.

Apply Your Knowledge

The Great Holtodo has a world-renowned memory. He really is something special, and can remember the order of up to 500 cards that have been professionally shuffled. Holtodo claims that the key to his superb memory is taking regular exercise and drinking water derived only from melted Welsh snow. For some time now psychologists have been closely investigating Holtodo's amazing talents and claims.

(a) (i) What kind of study is this? (*1 mark*)

(ii) State one weakness of the research method identified in (a). (*2 marks*)

(iii) From what you know of strategies for memory improvement, how could Holtodo's memory for 500 cards be explained? (*3 marks*)

(b) The team designed a laboratory experiment to investigate the possible benefits to memory of drinking this special water. The results were recorded and placed in the table below:

MEMORY SCORE AFTER DRINKING DIFFERENT AMOUNTS OF WATER

Participant number	1 cup	2 cups	3 cups
1	10	13	12
2	13	15	25
3	9	9	30
4	12	15	17
5	4	8	12

(i) Identify the independent variable and the dependent variable in this experiment. (*1 mark*)

(ii) Identify the experimental design used here and give one limitation of this kind of design. (*3 marks*)

(iii) Identify one possible extraneous variable in this study. (*1 mark*)

(iv) Assuming that they used the mean as a measure of central tendency, what would be an appropriate 'measure of dispersion' for these data? (*1 mark*)

(v) What type of graph would you use to display these data? (*1 mark*)

(vi) Write a short summary of the findings of this experiment. (*3 marks*)

ETHICAL ISSUES

Researchers in the UK take care to adhere to the guidelines of the British Psychological Society (BPS).

ETHICAL ISSUE	EXPLANATION
INFORMED CONSENT	Participants must be told what they will be doing and why they are doing it so they can provide 'informed' consent.
DECEPTION	Participants should not be deceived unless absolutely necessary. If deception is required, great care and careful consideration must be given to the project.
DEBRIEFING	After the experiment is complete, participants must be 'debriefed' and informed of the motivations for the experiment. They must be given the chance to ask any questions they have.
RIGHT TO WITHDRAW	Participants should be free to leave the experiment at any time.
CONFIDENTIALITY	Any information and data provided by the participant must be confidential.
PROTECTION	The safety and well-being of the participant must be protected at all times.

If they do not adhere to these principles the researchers' licences may be revoked, or they may be expelled from the BPS, meaning that they can no longer carry out legitimate research, and their jobs and reputation will be at stake.

Apply Your Knowledge

Psychologists conducted a study into the quality of attachment relationship between children and their professional caregivers in a day care centre. The graph below shows their results.

(a) (i) What kind of correlation does this graph describe? (*1 mark*)
(ii) Identify the two variables measured in this study. (*1 + 1 mark*)
(iii) What conclusions might the psychologists draw from the findings of this study? (*2 marks*)
(iv) Within the context of this study, give one disadvantage of correlational research. (*2 marks*)

(b) From what you know of research into attachment, explain one difficulty that the psychologists might have encountered with assessing attachment type. (*2 marks*)

(c) Outline two ethical issues that arise in research involving children. (*2 + 2 marks*)

(d) As part of the study, the psychologists interviewed the professional caregivers about their attitude towards centre day care.
(i) Give one advantage of conducting interviews as part of this research. (*2 marks*)
(ii) Identify one potential problem with these interviews and suggest how this might be overcome. (*3 marks*)

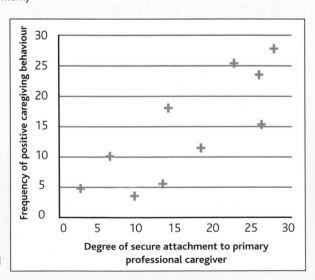

METHODS AND TECHNIQUES

THE LABORATORY EXPERIMENT

- Run in carefully *controlled* conditions (variables are carefully controlled).
- Uses a *standardised procedure* (everyone proceeds in exactly the same way).

Example: 'The more chocolate you eat the better you can remember things.'
Independent variable: number of chunks of chocolate eaten (one or two chunks).
Dependent variable: performance on a memory task.

Three possible experimental designs:

REPEATED MEASURES

Each participant takes part in both conditions of the experiment.

Each participant eats one and two chunks and does the task after each.

Advantages
The same people in each group, so no need to control for individual differences like age etc. Because of this you don't have to use so many participants (faster and cheaper to run!).

Weaknesses
Order effects. People may get better or worse because of practice or fatigue (possible confounding variables). Solution is to counterbalance the order in which they do the task. Some people eat two chunks first and do the task then one chunk, and other people eat one then two.

INDEPENDENT GROUPS

Two independent groups of participants.

One group eats two chunks and does the task, the other group eats one chunk and does the task.

Advantages
Eliminates order effects.

Weaknesses
Individual differences are a potential confounding variable. What if you had the world memory champion in one group and the world chocolate-eating champion in another! Solution: use very large groups. If you had 1,000 people in each group, just by chance, the groups might contain broadly similar people.

MATCHED PAIRS

Like an independent group design, but you carefully match members of each group, i.e. if you have a 23-year-old rugby player in one group, you need one in the other group and so on.

Advantages
Matching is a control for individual differences. Also there are no order effects.

Weaknesses
Matching is extremely difficult. Even if you use identical twins they may still have different abilities, and may have had different experiences. If you don't use twins (more likely) you can never be sure to match everything about the pairs of people you use.

THE QUASI-EXPERIMENT

This is an experiment that does not allow random allocation of participants to either experimental condition, e.g. investigating whether girls or boys are better at maths, the independent variable is 'gender' and is beyond your control. It may look like a lab experiment but it's not.

A GOOD LAB EXPERIMENT IS ONE THAT IS ...

Generalisable: findings refer to people *outside* the sample you tested.
Replicable: other researchers can *repeat* the experiment.
Reliable: if the experiment were repeated, the same or similar results would be found.
Valid: it measures what it says it measures.

Advantages

1 In a lab experiment, with careful control we can say confidently that the independent variable caused a change in the dependent variable.

2 They are replicable.

3 Variables are easier to control than they are outside the lab.

Weaknesses

1 In a lab experiment, the more you control, the less natural it is. They can be said to lack ecological validity as they are not like real life.

2 Sometimes it's impossible to use a lab experiment.

3 Demand characteristics and experimenter effects may reduce confidence in the results.

You could be asked to 'use your knowledge of research methods' to explain any number of things in the exam. Knowing the advantages and weaknesses of all the methods, not just the experiment, is a really useful way of showing understanding and applying your knowledge.

THE FIELD EXPERIMENT

Variables are manipulated in a natural environment like a town centre, or in an office, depending on your investigation.

Advantages
High ecological validity and demand characteristics are low or eliminated as people do not know they are being investigated.

Weaknesses
Time consuming and often expensive, with a lack of control of extraneous variables.

THE NATURAL EXPERIMENT

A naturally occurring independent variable is utilised (i.e. towns with more students are 'friendlier' than towns with less).

Advantages
High ecological validity where real-life problems can be investigated. Few or no demand characteristics.

Disadvantages
No control at all so you can't conclude that one thing caused another and the chance of confounding variables is extremely high. It is also almost impossible to replicate.

Apply Your Knowledge

It has been suggested that one important factor influencing the development of secure and insecure attachments is maternal sensitivity. To investigate this, a group of child psychologists conducted an observational study of maternal behaviour in a local mother-and-baby group.

(a) Suggest two behavioural categories that the researchers might have used in their observation. (*2 marks*)

(b) This study is a naturalistic observation.
 (i) Outline one advantage of naturalistic observations in the context of studies like this. (2 marks)
 (ii) It is important in such studies that participants remain unaware that they are being observed. Suggest two things that the researchers could have done to ensure that this was the case. (*2 marks*)

(c) How could the researchers have checked the reliability of the observations? (*2 marks*)

(d) Describe one method used by psychologists studying children to assess attachment type. (*3 marks*)

(e) Outline one ethical issue that should have been considered by the psychologists. (*2 marks*)

THE OBSERVATIONAL METHOD

The technique of observing can be used to gather data for a range of methods. The method of observing is a distinct category of research method in its own right. The observational method involves the careful watching and recording of events and behaviours occurring naturally.

● *Participant observation* – the researcher is directly involved, perhaps as part of the group being investigated.

● *Non-participant observation* – perhaps watching behaviour from behind a one-way mirror.

AWARENESS OF THE OBSERVER

If the participant is aware of the observer then behaviour will not be natural. There are ethical issues here. It is not necessarily ethically valid to observe or film without consent. A partial solution might be only to observe in places where people can naturally expect to be observed.

BEHAVIOURAL CATEGORIES

What is being recorded has to be decided upon. These categories of behaviour then appear on observational checklists, which are used to record events.

BIAS

The researcher must remain objective or the results will be biased. Can be overcome by having multiple observers or raters and comparing the results for inter-rater reliability.

SAMPLING OF OBSERVATIONS

Time sampling – recording behaviours for short time intervals.
Event sampling – all occurrences of the behaviour are recorded.

Advantages
● Natural settings, so natural behaviours are observed.

● Allows otherwise impossible or hard-to-examine behaviours (e.g. aggression in children) to be investigated.

● Few demand characteristics because the observed are not put into a false situation and may not know they are being observed at all.

Weaknesses
● Observer bias if researchers don't remain objective.

● Confounding variables may interfere, making it hard to determine the cause for something happening.

● Small groups are usually observed, making the results hard to generalise.

CONTENT ANALYSIS

A type of observation used in the analysis of the content of text or other media like film, or even a conversation. Behavioural categories, checklists for recording and issues of reliability apply here too.

Observation as a technique is not the same as observation as a method. Make sure you know the difference! For example, some experiments involve the technique of recording observations of behaviour, but they are different from observational methods, where there is no manipulation of variables.

SELF-REPORT TECHNIQUES

Here, participants report their own opinions or attitudes in interviews or questionnaires.

QUESTIONNAIRES

A list of pre-written questions. Open questions are those where free responses are allowed. Closed questions are those where alternative responses are offered. A rank-order question where you are asked to rank something is one type of closed question.

Advantages

Can be cheap and efficient ways of gathering large amounts of data where participant anonymity is retained.

Weaknesses

Data is descriptive so causal relationships are dependent on the quality of the questions. Selecting a sample is hard. Many refuse to help once 'randomly' selected. Also, the 'truthfulness' of the answers given can be questioned. There may be social desirability issues or participants may even lie.

INTERVIEWS

Like a questionnaire but questions are presented aurally. They can be structured, semi-structured or unstructured, each offering a different level of organisation and control.

Advantages

Can provide very rich, detailed, spontaneous and realistic data, and structured interviews in particular can be simple to do. If a large enough sample is obtained then findings can be generalisable. If administered carefully, they can be very insightful about often very complicated things.

Weaknesses

The right sample may be hard to find as the procedure can be lengthy so people may refuse to participate. Sometimes a person's responses to the same interview can be very different, which affects reliability. As with questionnaires, the truthfulness of responses may be doubtful.

Questionnaire

Male ☐ or Female ☐?

Do you think that time management is important?

Yes ☐   No ☐   Don't know ☐

Please indicate on the scale below, by circling a number, the extent to which you think you manage your time effectively:

Very   Not at all

1   2   3   4   5

If you are given two weeks to do homework do you:

☐ do it straight away

☐ complete it within the first week

☐ complete it in the second week

☐ complete it the night before it is due

☐ miss the deadline

CORRELATIONAL ANALYSIS

● A technique that shows whether or not two variables are associated.

● It is a method in its own right, but correlational analysis can be used with data from other techniques.

● The strength of a correlation is given as a statistic called a 'coefficient', which ranges between -1 and +1.

● Scattergrams are used to present correlations graphically.

Example: a correlational analysis of maths and science ability.

NEGATIVE (LESS THAN 0)
A 'downward slope' is seen.

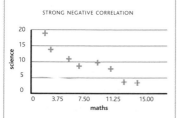

The more perfect the line, the closer to -1 the correlation is. A strong negative correlation is one close to a perfectly straight downward-sloping line.

'As maths ability increases, science ability decreases. The two are negatively correlated.'

ZERO CORRELATION
No slope is seen.

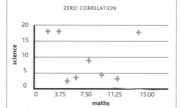

There seems to be no pattern here.

'Maths ability and science ability do not appear to be related.'

POSITIVE (MORE THAN 0)
An 'upward slope' is seen.

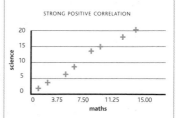

The more perfect the line, the closer to +1 the correlation is. A strong positive correlation is one close to a perfectly straight upward-sloping line.

'As maths ability increases, science ability also increases. The two are positively correlated.'

CORRELATIONS TELL YOU NOTHING ABOUT CAUSE!
Just because things are highly correlated does NOT mean that one causes the other! It just means that the two things happen to be related in some way! You cannot infer cause from correlations. It might be a causal relationship, but it might be chance, or it might be something else causing the relationship.

Advantages
Relationships between naturally occurring variables are possible, which can indicate trends for investigation in future research.

Weaknesses
Cause and effect cannot be inferred, and extraneous variables are practically impossible to control. Sometimes analysis suggests no relationship but the variables have a more complex relationship that the correlation analysis is not sensitive to.

CASE STUDIES

A case study is a systematic and detailed investigation of a single individual. An example is Freud's case of Anna O.

Advantages
Lots of detail produced, and pooling data from similar cases can be really informative. It's the only way to deal with very rare instances of behaviour.

Weaknesses
Generalisability is low as only one person is investigated. Also, information from the past is gathered, and people may forget things.

QUALITATIVE VS. QUANTITATIVE RESEARCH

Quantitative	Qualitative
To do with QUANTITY	To do with QUALITY
Focus on collecting numbers (not opinions)	Focus on collecting opinions (not numbers)
Is very controlled	Is less controlled
Analysis is objective (limited interpretation)	Analysis can be subjective (lots of interpretation)

The use of each depends on the type of research being done. Sometimes both are used in the same project, e.g. investigating the relationship between emotion and memory might involve quantitative measurements (scores on a memory task) and qualitative measures (how a participant feels).

Apply Your Knowledge

Maxi-cog is advertised as a scientifically proven way to promote mental alertness and performance naturally. Just two capsules a day will apparently lead to enhanced memory. Having failed to find this scientific proof, a team of psychologists set out to test the claims of Maxi-cog. They gave their participants the maximum daily dose of Maxi-cog and, for a period of two weeks, recorded their daily performance on a memory test. The results can be seen in the table below.

Participant number	No. of days on Maxi-cog	% Test score
1	0	20
2	0	12
3	2	24
4	4	39
5	5	46
6	5	40
7	8	50
8	6	56
9	12	34
10	14	76
11	15	45
12	13	76

(a) What does the data appear to show? (*2 marks*)

(b) What type of graph would you use to present these data? (*1 mark*)

(c) Suggest one way in which memory might have been tested in this study. (*2 marks*)

(d) Write a suitable hypothesis for this study. (*2 marks*)

(e) Is this hypothesis directional or non-directional? (*1 mark*)

(f) Identify one potential investigator effect in this study and suggest how it might be eliminated. (*3 marks*)

(g) Identify one sampling method that might have been used in this study and explain how this could have been used to select participants for this study. (*3 marks*)

PRESENTING DATA

Descriptive statistics are used to summarise data clearly so that it can quickly and easily be understood. The most simple descriptive statistics come in the form of measures of central tendency and dispersion, and graphs.

MEASURES OF CENTRAL TENDENCY

These are values that summarise the average value in a data set. There are three of them to know.

Data: 6 5 4 6 8 9 3 0 2 7

MEASURE OF CENTRAL TENDENCY	EXAMPLE	PROS AND CONS
Mean: add up the numbers and divide by how many numbers there were.	(6+5+4+6+8+9+3+0+2+7) all divided by 10 mean = 5	✓ Uses all the data. ✗ One rogue number can badly distort it.
Median: put the values in numerical order. Median in central number.	0 2 3 4 5 6 6 7 8 9 'even' number of values, so median is 5+6 divided by 2 median = 5.5 (with an 'odd' number of values there would be only one central number)	✓ Not badly affected by rogue scores. ✗ Not good for using with small data sets, i.e. median of data set 1, 2, 1000, 1001 is 501. Not really very informative of the data set!
Mode: the most common (or frequent) data value.	'6' occurs twice. All the other values occur once. mode = 6 (If two values occur 'most frequently' the data are bimodal – two modes)	✓ Great if you want to know how often something happens. ✗ Sometimes a data set doesn't have a most frequent value!

MEASURES OF DISPERSION

These are numbers that tell us how spread out the values in the data set are.

MEASURE	WHEN USED	PROS AND CONS
Range: the distance between the highest and lowest values in the data.	With a mode or median	✓ Easy to calculate and takes in extreme scores. ✗ Ignores most of the data, and may not reflect the true distribution of the data.
Semi-interquartile range: remove top and bottom quarter of data then calculate a range.	With a median	✓ Gives a better idea of distribution of most of the data around the mean. Not distorted by extreme scores. ✗ 50% of the numbers are ignored and it is laborious to calculate.
Standard deviation: a calculation that tells us the average 'distance from the mean' of the data points.	With a mean	✓ Uses every data point and is therefore representative of the data. ✗ Tricky to calculate by hand.

TABLES

Raw data are the numbers collected in the research before you have done anything to them. Summary statistics are ways of summarising the raw data.

The rule with tables is to be as clear as you possibly can.

In the exam you could be asked to show your understanding of tables by interpreting one, e.g. reading information from one and drawing a conclusion. You have to be able to know what each figure in the table means, and what it refers to. The best way to remember this, as with other things, is to become familiar with tables – reading them and creating them.

Table showing scores in control (no stress) and experimental (stress) conditions

Participant number	Control condition (no stress)	Experimental condition (stress)
1	6	5
2	5	5
3	7	4
4	9	3
5	8	8
6	5	4
7	6	5
8	7	6
9	8	5
10	6	7

Summary table showing concentration scores in control (no stress) and experimental (stress) conditions. (standard deviation rounded up to 2 decimal places)

	Control condition	Experimental condition
mean	6.7	5.2
mode	6.5	5.0
median	6	5
standard deviation	1.34	1.48

Apply Your Knowledge

People often have difficulty carrying out more than one task at a time, especially when they are quite similar tasks. To investigate this, researchers presented groups of participants with telephone numbers to remember and recall. There were three people in each group.

Group 1 had to remember the number 01267976432 and they were presented with it in silence.

Group 2 had to remember the number 0756382496 and they had to listen to the experimenter talk whilst trying to remember the number.

(a) The hypothesis tested was: 'Fewer numbers will be recalled in the right order when the person listens to a conversation whilst trying to remember.'
   (i) Is this a directional or non-directional hypothesis? (*1 mark*)
   (ii) What is the operationalised independent variable? (*1 mark*)

(b) Which type of experimental design is used in this experiment? (*1 mark*)

(c) Identify a flaw in this experiment and explain how the investigator might have avoided it. (*3 marks*)

(d) The data are presented in the graph.
   (i) What type of graph is this? (*1 mark*)
   (ii) What is the main finding indicated by the graph? (*1 mark*)

(e) Use what you have learned about the working memory model to explain these findings. (*3 marks*)

(f) This was a laboratory experiment. Using your knowledge of research methods, explain the value of such studies when investigating things that relate to 'real-life' experiences. (*4 marks*)

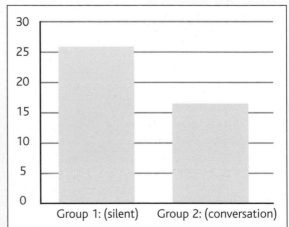

GRAPHS

The whole point of a graph is to convey information clearly, so it is important to use the right graph for the job.

GRAPH

Bar chart: numbers of things in different categories, i.e. number of petrol or diesel cars sold in a year, or number of students doing psychology or English at A level.

Histogram: like a bar-chart, but the x-axis measures a constantly changing scale, like mass or height.

Frequency polygon: like a histogram, but instead of bars a line is drawn joining the middle points of the top of each bar.

Scattergraph: values for the same individual for two different variables, each plotted on one axis (see also 'correlations' earlier). The example here shows a 'curvilinear' relationship.

EXAMPLE

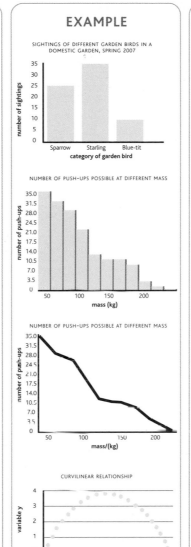

SIGHTINGS OF DIFFERENT GARDEN BIRDS IN A DOMESTIC GARDEN, SPRING 2007

NUMBER OF PUSH-UPS POSSIBLE AT DIFFERENT MASS

NUMBER OF PUSH-UPS POSSIBLE AT DIFFERENT MASS

CURVILINEAR RELATIONSHIP

CHARACTERISTICS

- Gaps between category bars.
- Categories on x-axis referring to discrete categories.
- Frequency (number) on y-axis.

- A continuous variable on the x-axis.
- No gaps between bars.

- A continuous variable on the x-axis.
- No bars, just a line.

- Used to depict correlation.
- Can show positive, negative or zero correlations or curvilinear relationships like this one.

Graphs appear everywhere in psychology and you really need to know something about them. Knowing the differences between types of graph will really help your understanding. Different graphs have particular applications, so be sure to choose the right one. The most common confusion is between histograms and bar charts – they really are different graphs! Remember that with the bar chart every bar stands for something different whereas with the histogram the bars all measure the same thing.

PRESENTING QUALITATIVE DATA

Qualitative data is concerned largely with opinion. To present it you need to organise your qualitative data into categories of response. This can then be put into tables and graphs. You might use a table like this which shows the time spent making positive comments is more than the time spent making negative comments.

Content analysis of discussions with young mothers

Category	Time spent	Examples
Positive comments about experiences	26 minutes 40 seconds	'He's just wonderful. I can't ever imagine being without him now' 'He really makes me smile. I look forward to playing with him all the time!' 'He's so beautiful, everyone says so' 'He's such a good boy. I love him so very much'
Negative comments about experiences	16 minutes 9 seconds	'I really miss my friends. I hardly see them at all these days' 'I would really have liked to go to university, but that will be hard now that I have a baby' 'I get so tired, I wish I had some more help' 'I had no idea it would be such hard work. If I'm honest I would have preferred to have been married when I had him'

Alternatively, you might prefer to choose the information to be presented and draw it as a bar chart, like this, which shows that more positive comments were made than negative comments.

Number of positive and negative comments made

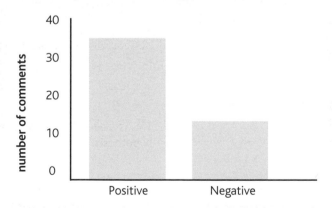

HOW SCIENCE WORKS

MATHS AND POOL PLAYING

Rob: Go on, I'll give you a game of pool.

Nigel: Not a chance. You'll hammer me!

Rob: How do you know? I've never played you at pool before.

Nigel: Well, you're superb at maths, right?

Rob: Well, I don't like to brag about it, but it has been said I am a mathematical genius …

Nigel: Well, everyone knows that pool is all about working out angles and velocities. So, good at maths, good at pool. I'm rubbish at maths, and so I'll be rubbish at pool. Simple.

Rob: You, Holt, are having a laugh!

What Nigel feels certain of is that there is a positive correlation between pool-playing ability and ability at mathematics. To investigate whether this really is the case, we'd better get some research done.

9 STEPS TO SUCCESS!

1 Identify the AIM of your research.

2 Turn the AIM into a hypothesis.

3 Identify your variables.

4 Decide on a design for your research.

5 Operationalise your variables.

6 Organise yourself for recording your data.

7 Try a pilot, then carry out the research.

8 Summarise your data and draw a graph.

9 What did you find out?

1. WHAT'S THE AIM OF YOUR RESEARCH?

Here you need to identify the reason for doing your research. What's the point?

'The AIM of the research is to see whether there is a relationship ....'

2. WHAT'S THE HYPOTHESIS?

Make a bold statement here. What will you show?

'There is a .... relationship between .... and ....'

This is a directional/non-directional hypothesis.

3. WHAT ARE YOUR VARIABLES?

The *task* is being varied by you, so your independent variables are one that measures pool playing and one that measures maths ability.

Your dependent variables are ....

....

Possible extraneous variables include ....

....

4. WHAT DESIGN WILL YOU CHOOSE?

We are looking at the relationship between two things here. You are not controlling anything in an attempt to alter something else, so we have a correlational design.

5. HOW WILL YOU OPERATIONALISE YOUR VARIABLES?

What TASKS will you use?

How do you measure pool-playing ability?

....

....

How do you measure maths ability?

....

....

6. GET ORGANISED!

You need some participants and some equipment. Note them down here.

I'll need ....

....

....

7. PILOT IT AND RUN IT!

Try a brief pilot procedure and then get some data. Remember, you need to collect as much as possible. Be aware of any ethical issues and make sure you are careful in your organisation and data recording.

8. SUMMARISE THE DATA AND DRAW A GRAPH

What type of things will you record here? All you can do with correlational analysis is draw yourself a graph. What type of graph will you choose?

Histogram   Frequency polygon

Scattergram   Bar chart

9. WHAT DID YOU FIND OUT?

'The results showed that ....'

'From this we can conclude that

....,

'However, there were some problems with the procedure, including ....

....,

ASK AN EXAMINER

This is a correlational design. Alarm bells should be ringing! What can you conclude? Does maths ability cause pool playing ability, or the other way around? Of course, you can't conclude either; only that they are positively related.

See page 196 for answers.

THE PILOT

We tried it out on two people and found the following:

Participant 1: maths score 3, pool score 8

Participant 2: maths score 3, pool score 3

That's not very conclusive at all. They both got 3 on the maths test, but one scored 8 at pool, the other 3. The relationship is pretty unclear from this tiny sample, but the tasks seem to work reasonably well, so we'll get on with the full research.

THE RESULTS

Maths ability and pool ability for each participant

To see what is really going on here, we'll need to draw ourselves a scattergraph.

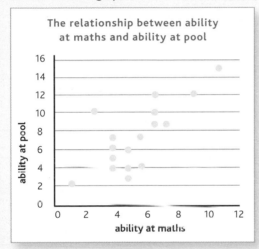

The relationship between ability at maths and ability at pool

Participant number	Maths	Pool
1	3	10
2	5	6
3	6	7
4	9	12
5	5	4
6	6	3
7	1	6
8	8	10
9	7	12
10	8	10
11	4	7
12	1	2
13	4	4
14	4	5
15	7	9
16	7	10
17	6	7
18	5	3
19	6	3
20	10	15

WHAT DOES THIS SHOW?

Looking at the scattergraph, we seem to have an 'upward-sloping' trend of plots. It is by no means perfect, but it is clear that, in general, maths and pool-playing scores are positively correlated. This means that a low score on one means a low score on the other, and a high score on one means a high score on the other. So Nigel was right, odd as it sounds; maths ability and pool-playing ability do seem to be positively correlated!

However, let's take a closer look. We only measured 20 participants, and these we found hanging about in the common room. They may not be a good sample. Perhaps we need people who are less familiar with maths or pool to try out these ideas.

Is the 'number of sums possible in an hour' really the best way to measure maths ability do you think? And pool-playing is much more than just the ability to pot balls. It can also involve strategy, careful planning and physical coordination, which our task was unable to measure.

TRY IT OUT FOR YOURSELF

How about these for alternatives? Think about the relationships between these things:

● Ability at maths and number of hours of TV watched.

● Number of hours of TV watched in a week and number of books read in a year.

● Miles cycled in a year and resting heart rate.

● Amount of chips a person can eat in five seconds and ability at darts.

HOW SCIENCE WORKS

'SHHHHHHHHH! I'M TRYING TO WORK!'

Jody: Oi! Turn that back on, I was watching that!

Ryan: You were not, you were reading that psychology book. Anyway, haven't you got an exam next week?

Jody: Well, I was listening to it... yes, but it makes no difference. I can revise and listen to things.

Ryan: No way! That's impossible! That's why libraries are all quiet and spooky.

Jody: I think you can. I'm sure I read something about that in here somewhere...

Sounds familiar? Jody and her brother are arguing about the TV. What she's on about here is the working memory model and the idea that if things use the same part of it then they will interfere with one another. Have a go at designing a quick project to see whether Jody or Ryan are correct. If Jody is correct then trying to remember things when listening to people talking on the TV is just as good as remembering things in silence. If Ryan is correct remembering things in silence is better.

9 STEPS TO SUCCESS!

1 Identify the AIM of your research.

2 Turn the AIM into a hypothesis.

3 Decide on a design for your research.

4 Identify your variables.

5 Operationalise your variables.

6 Organise yourself for recording your data.

7 Try a pilot, then carry out the research.

8 Summarise your data and draw a graph.

9 What did you find out?

1. WHAT'S THE AIM OF YOUR RESEARCH?

Here you need to identify the reason for doing your research. What's the point?

'The AIM of the research is to see whether
....
....'

2. WHAT'S THE HYPOTHESIS?

Make a bold statement here. What will you show?

'When listening to sounds people are..........at remembering than when............................'

This is a directional/non-directional hypothesis.

3. WHAT DESIGN WILL YOU CHOOSE?

You have three choices. Repeated measures, independent samples or matched samples. Which will you use? Remember there are pros and cons to each! Circle your choice

Repeated measures   Independent samples

Matched samples

4. WHAT ARE YOUR VARIABLES?

Independent variable is..
(the one you control!)

Dependent variable is ....
(the one you measure)

Extraneous variables might include

....

(Things other than the IV that are beyond your control that may influence the result!)

5. HOW WILL YOU OPERATIONALISE YOUR VARIABLES?

What TASKS will you use?

How are you going to measure your dependent variable?...

....

6. GET ORGANISED!

You'll need a way of recording the performance on the memory test, and a way of playing sounds. Write down what you'll need here. Remember, you also need participants! Where will you get your sample from?

I'll need ....

....

....

7. PILOT IT AND RUN IT!

Try it out with a pilot procedure. The result of this may make you reconsider your hypothesis! If so, return to Step 2.

Go ahead and collect your data! Remember to be careful and write down your values clearly and immediately. Don't try to remember what happened. More research has failed that way.

8. SUMMARISE THE DATA AND DRAW A GRAPH

What summary statistics will you use? You need a measure of central tendency remember ...

Mean   or   Median   or   Mode

You also need a measure of dispersion ...

Range   or   Standard Deviation

You also need a graph. What will you draw?

Bar chart   Histogram

9. WHAT DID YOU FIND OUT?

'The results showed that ....'

'From this we can conclude that ....

....,

'However, there were some problems with the procedure, including ....

....,

See page 197 for answers.

THE PILOT

Two participants (my mates!) tried it out, and I found these results.

Number of words remembered in silence – 8 out of 10

Number of words remembered listening to speech – 4 out of 10

The results are certainly suggesting that the hypothesis, that memory is better in silence than while listening to speech, seems to be supported. I now have a reason to go ahead with the full project.

THE RESULTS

Table showing the number of words remembered in silence and while listening to speech.

Participant number	Words remembered – speech	Words remembered – silence
1	9	10
2	8	8
3	4	10
4	4	9
5	5	9
6	5	8
7	6	6
8	3	7
9	7	9
10	7	9

Summary statistics

	Mean
Silence	8.5
Speech	5.8

The most appropriate measure of dispersion here is a standard deviation.

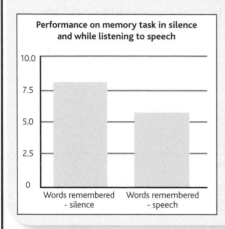

Performance on memory task in silence and while listening to speech

Experiments are a very important research method in psychology, and you can learn most things you need to know about research methods from a careful study of them. There's nothing better than experience though, so try running short experiments yourself. Don't be over-ambitious – follow the model presented here and you will really benefit.

WHAT DOES THIS SHOW?

The results show silence is better for remembering than listening to speech. This is support for Baddeley's working memory model, that says that listening to speech uses the short-term memory and so does memory for things. When we do both at the same time they interfere with one another and so memory is affected.

However, if we take a closer look we can say that we only used ten participants and these were gained from a volunteer sample. It could be that these people knew something of memory research and were interested in it, and that's why they agreed to help. It could also be that the cup of tea and biscuit they were given for volunteering was the thing that influenced their memory!

We can only really say that memory for lists of words is 'influenced' by the sound we used here. We didn't try it with anything else, and it could be that the type of sound mattered. What if we tried it with a foreign language? We can't be sure whether it was speech, or whether it was a 'human voice' that influenced the memory.

TRY IT OUT FOR YOURSELF

There are many ways to do a project like this. Try some out on your friends. Be careful to be ethically correct though.

What about introducing a male/female twist to the research? Perhaps boys are more influenced by speech than girls or vice versa.

Does one voice influence memory more than two or three?

Does the type of thing you were trying to remember make a difference?

Check your knowledge

EXPERIMENTAL RESEARCH

State whether the following research studies are laboratory, field, or natural experiments.

(i) Whether children who spend more than 20 hours a week in day care were more likely to be insecurely attached than those who spend less than 20 hours.

(ii) Whether there is a sex difference in obedience to authority.

(iii) Whether increases in temperature lead to greater stress.

(iv) Whether rates of conformity depend on whether a culture is individualist or collectivist.

(v) Whether age affects the accuracy of recall of witnesses who had just experienced a mock bank robbery.

(vi) Whether higher than normal percentages of insecure attachments are found in premature infants.

EXPERIMENTAL DESIGNS

Identify the type of designs used in experiments with the following hypotheses:

(i) Females are less likely to administer an electric shock to a woman than to a man.

(ii) The greatest attachment problems are experienced by children fostered after 12 months.

(iii) Leading questions have a greater influence on children's recall of a story than an adults' recall.

(iv) Performance is better on memory tasks in those using this technique than those remembering by rote.

(v) Obedience increases according to the status of the authority figure

(vi) Witnesses of violent crimes recall more details than witnesses of less violent crimes.

OBSERVATION

Which of the following are examples of observation as a research method and which are examples of observation as a data gathering technique?

(i) Researchers observe attachment behaviours in children attending a mother and toddler group.

(ii) Nursery staff used an observational checklist to measure behaviour of children attending either low or high quality day care.

(iii) Researchers investigate whether the more time children spend in day care, the more likely they are to be aggressive during the early primary school years.

(iv) A psychologist observes the attachment behaviour of a child from behind a one-way mirror.

(v) Researchers use the Strange Situation to investigate cultural differences in attachments.

(vi) An observation to see whether mothers of premature babies behave differently towards their infants than mothers of full-term infants.

CORRELATION

The following are correlations. For each:

1. State the kind of correlation each represents (i.e. positive or negative).

2. Give an explanation for the correlations (i.e. causal, chance, or third factor).

3. Re-write the statement as the opposite correlation (e.g. if positive re-write as negative).

(i) The more time spent studying for an exam, the better the grade.

(ii) There is increased conflict and stress at home when workers are overloaded at work.

(iii) The more quality day care a child receives the greater the social competence.

(iv) People who are good at managing time do better in assessments.

(v) The less control someone feels at work, the more stress they experience.

(vi) Children attending high quality day care centres are more likely to interact positively with others.

VALIDITY

Explain why the following examples of research may lack validity:

(i) A laboratory study to see whether the quality of attachment depends mainly on the temperament of the child.

(ii) An experiment to see whether the recall of a word list is improved by giving participants the category of the words to be recalled.

(iii) An investigation to see whether secure attachments occur to the same extent in Puerto Rican and US children.

(iv) An experiment to see whether conformity is greater in groups of five than in groups of nine.

(v) Research looking at whether students respond better to problem-focused methods than emotion-focused methods of coping with stress.

(vi) A study looking at whether parents of autistic children who are 'hardy' suffer less with the negative effects of stress than those who are not 'hardy'.

CORRELATION COEFFICIENTS

(a) Show what the following coefficients would look like on a graph by roughly sketching appropriate scattergrams. Then (b) state the type of correlation each coefficient/scattergram represents.

(i) r = -0.35

(ii) r = +0.78

(iii) r = +0.51

(iv) r = -0.07

(v) r = +0.91

(vi) r = -0.42

HYPOTHESES

First (a) decide whether the following hypotheses are directional or non-directional and then (b) identify the IV and the DV.

(i) The more stress a person experiences the more risk there is of a heart attack.

(ii) Stressful unemployment can influence the functioning of the immune system.

(iii) The risk of coronary heart disease is affected by feelings of hostility.

(iv) Stress management techniques improve the functioning of the immune system.

(v) Stressful life events increase the likelihood of illness.

(vi) The more complex the question the more likely a child is to give an inaccurate response.

IDENTIFY THE RESEARCH METHOD

State what the following is most likely to be – an experiment, an observation or a correlation.

(i) Children who begin centre-based day care during the first year of life show greater levels of aggression than those who start later in life.

(ii) The attachment behaviour shown by infants depends on whether they are with the mother or the father.

(iii) The more life events experienced, the more likely it is that ill-health will occur.

(iv) Acronyms improve memory most when they form a visual image.

(v) Higher levels of conformity occur in situations where people are face to face.

(vi) The more day care a child receives the more aggressive they are as adolescents.

POPULATIONS AND SAMPLES

(a) Identify the target population in the following studies and (b) suggest an appropriate sampling technique for selecting participants.

(i) Whether there are gender differences in conformity amongst participants under 19 years of age.

(ii) Whether the cognitive interview is more effective in stimulating recall than a standard interview in elderly eye-witnesses.

(iii) Whether children brought up with nurses show weaker attachments to their mothers.

(iv) Whether cognitive behavioural therapy reduces exam stress.

(v) Whether children attending high quality day care centres are more socially skilled than children in low quality day care centres.

(vi) Whether the recall of witnessed events by younger children is less accurate than the recall of older children.

OPERATIONALISING

Re-write the following hypotheses in a way that makes it clear how the dependent variable will be measured.

 (i) Rehearsal improves duration in short-term memory.

(ii) Stress increases the likelihood of illness.

(iii) Day care is related to aggression in children.

(iv) Leading questions influence recall.

(v) Cognitive behavioural therapy is a more effective therapy than psychoanalysis.

(vi) Mnemonics improve memory.

ETHICAL ISSUES

For each study identify one ethical issue, explain why it is an ethical issue and suggest a way of dealing with it.

(i) An experiment to investigate whether the memories of 3 to 4 year olds are more susceptible, and thus more vulnerable to reconstruction, than adults.

(ii) A study to investigate whether people are more likely to conform when it is the easiest thing to do.

(iii) An experiment to see whether child-rearing style affects attachment type.

(iv) An experiment to investigate whether the accuracy of recall is influenced by anxiety.

(v) A study to see whether workplace stress increases the likelihood of heart attacks.

(vi) A study which investigates whether long-term emotional and social stability depends on an infant forming an attachment with the mother within a critical period.

DEMAND CHARACTERISTICS AND INVESTIGATOR EFFECTS

Identify one potential demand characteristic and one potential investigator effect in each of the following pieces of research.

(i) A study investigating whether attachment is related to a mother's sensitivity to the needs of the child.

(ii) A study looking at whether managers at work with supportive supervisors experience an increased feeling of control and therefore greater job satisfaction and reduced stress.

(iii) A study to see whether reactance is more likely if the majority view is perceived to infringe on personal freedoms.

(iv) A study into day care to see whether it affects a child's ability to regulate behaviour.

(v) A study investigating whether secure attachments in early life are related to the security adults feel in their relationships.

(vi) A study investigating whether the cognitive interview is more effective than the standard police interview.

Example answers to these questions can be found at www.askanexaminer.com

USEFUL WEBSITES

http://psychology.about.com/od/researchmethods/ss/expdesintro.htm
A general research methods site with useful definitions.

http://www.onlinepsychresearch.co.uk/
Try it out! Here researchers are using the web to help them gather data for their research.
Taking part in research is a useful way to help you learn about it.

http://www.socialresearchmethods.net/tutorial/Colosi/lcolosi2.htm
Reliability and validity explained, a lot.

http://www.bps.org.uk/
The British Psychological Society. The website of the governing body that provides us with
useful information about ethical considerations, amongst many other things.

http://www.psyonline.org.uk/ASStudentLinks.php?module=6
Some good pointers here that will help your understanding.

http://www.socialresearchmethods.net/tutorial/Mensah/default.htm
An awful lot here. A chance to really stretch yourself. Remember, you don't need to know
everything here. We've included it for those who want a little more.

http://nces.ed.gov/nceskids/CreateAGraph/
A brilliant interactive site about graph drawing.

http://www.beaconlearningcenter.com/WebLessons/KindsOfGraphs/default.htm
Another website about graphs. Remember, the definitions of each type of graph in your
textbook are the right ones to use and know about for the exam!

http://argyll.epsb.ca/jreed/math7/strand4/4104.htm
Measures of central tendency with examples. Fill in values into the interactive windows here to
see your values calculated for you.

http://writing.colostate.edu/guides/research/content/
Explanations and examples of content analysis. Notice how wide ranging and flexible it is. For
instance, you can use it to investigate the prominence of different types of people (men,
women, etc.) in novels. This can tell us something useful about how attitudes might have
changed over the years.

Section 2

Cognitive Psychology
– Memory

WHAT YOU NEED TO KNOW

Cognitive Psychology is in Unit 1 of the specification. As you learn, you are expected to develop your knowledge and understanding of Cognitive Psychology, including concepts, theories and studies. This also includes a knowledge and understanding of research methods and ethical issues as they relate to this area of psychology. You also need to develop the skills of analysis, evaluation and application. Rather than just recall and reproduce information, you are expected to be able to apply your knowledge and understanding. The subject content is split into two parts:

Models of memory

- The multi-store model, including the concepts of encoding, capacity and duration
- The strengths and weaknesses of the multi-store model
- The working memory model
- The strengths and weaknesses of the working memory model

Memory in everyday life

- Eyewitness testimony, including the effects of anxiety and age on eyewitness accuracy
- Misleading information and the use of the cognitive interview
- Memory improvement strategies

THE MULTI-STORE MODEL OF MEMORY

The multi-store model (MSM) was designed by Atkinson and Shiffrin (1968). It says that memory involves a number of different processes and that there is actually more than one kind of memory.

The multi-store model has three parts: sensory memory, short-term memory (STM) and long-term memory (LTM).

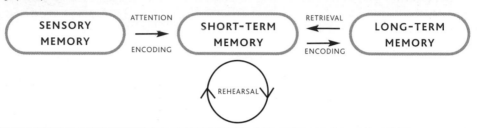

SENSORY MEMORY

Receives and stores information about the world from our senses. Information lasts just long enough for it to be transferred to STM.

ICONIC STORE
The visual part of sensory memory. Lasts for about half a second before information decays and is lost.

ECHOIC STORE
The auditory part of sensory memory. Can take several seconds for information to decay and be lost.

An attention mechanism, which works without our conscious awareness, selects information for transfer to STM. What is not selected decays and is lost.

SHORT-TERM MEMORY (STM)

ENCODING
Encoding is the process of changing information to a suitable form.

Sound is the preferred method of encoding.

Evidence
Conrad (1964) – people were asked to remember letter strings like 'AKJBSL'. People made errors by mixing up letters that *sounded* similar, like B and V, showing that they were encoding by sound.

CAPACITY
Capacity refers to the amount of information that can be held in memory.

According to Miller (1956), the capacity of STM is 5 to 9 (or 7+/- 2) items.

Chunking into 'items' can increase capacity, e.g. it is easier to remember 254739164826 as 254   739   164   826. We can remember 7 +/-2 of these 'chunks'.

Evidence
Jacobs (1890). Measured memory for strings of letters or numbers (serial digit or letter span). Average digit span was 9. Average letter span was 7. He showed that we get better with age. This shows that the capacity of STM is limited.

DURATION
Duration refers to the amount of time information lasts in memory.

Information lasts for a matter of seconds in STM. We can make it last longer by *rehearsing* it (repeating it over and over).

Information in STM is vulnerable to *interference*, and rehearsal can be disrupted.

Evidence
Peterson and Peterson's (1959) three letter study, which showed that STMs fade after about 18 seconds.

LONG-TERM MEMORY (LTM)

LTM is where we hold information for a longer period of time

ENCODING

Encoded is by 'meaning' (semantic encoding).

As shown by the kind of semantic errors we make – sometimes mixing up meaningfully similar things like barn, shed or hut but never confusing barn and born (a 'sound'-based error).

CAPACITY

The size of LTM seems to be unlimited.

People often manage to recall much more than they think they are able to.

DURATION

The duration of LTM is potentially a lifetime. This is why some call it a 'permanent' store.

Bahrick et al (1975) – suggest that information LTMs can be very long-term memories.

Apply Your Knowledge

'The number you require is 04963532146, thank you for calling.' When you call directory enquiries to request a telephone number you often forget to have a pen and paper handy.

Using what you have learned about the multi-store model of memory, how might you improve your chances of remembering the number correctly? (*3 marks*)

The three letter study – Peterson and Peterson (1959)

They wanted to know how long information could be held in STM.

How did they do it? They used the Brown–Peterson technique. Participants had to remember 'trigrams' (strings of three letters, such as 'ZPS') for different 'retention' intervals. While holding the trigram in memory they had to count backwards in threes to stop them from 'rehearsing'.

What did they find? The longer they had to hold the trigram for, the worse their memory was. Without rehearsal, memory lasted for a maximum of 18 seconds. This shows that the capacity of STM is limited to 18 seconds.

Take a closer look: ● The study might lack ecological validity – do the findings apply outside the experimental situation?

● There might be sample bias – only students were used and they might not be typical in the way they use their memory.

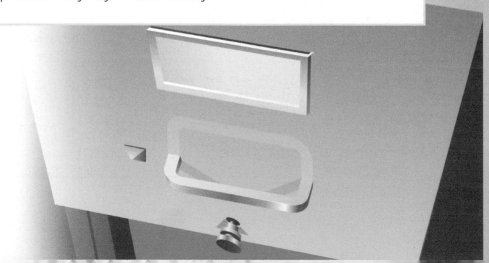

STUDY IN FOCUS

How long is long-term memory?
Bahrick et al (1975)

What were they doing and why? Bahrick et al were interested in the duration of long-term memories. They used participants from the US because of a tradition there of producing a 'yearbook' with pictures of and a statement about all those students who left school in the same year. Many previous studies had shown that much of what we need to store is rather unmemorable and therefore difficult to retrieve. By using meaningful information from their participants' past, they hoped to avoid this problem and tap into what they called very long-term memory (VLTM).

How did they do it? The experiment contained three main tasks. **First**, participants had to remember as many names of their ex-classmates as they could (free recall). **Second**, some pictures were taken from their yearbook and mixed with others that the participant would not previously have seen. This set of photos was then given to the participants to identify those which they recognised (visual recognition). **Third**, participants were asked to recognise names of people from school (verbal recognition).

What did they find? The findings were interesting. In all cases free recall was not great, with those having left school within 15 years being only 60% accurate and only 30% accurate for those having left 48 years previously. They found that verbal and visual recognition was highest (about 90% accurate!) in those who had left school less than 15 years previously. 48 years after leaving school, accuracy had dropped off to 70% verbal (names) and 80% visual (faces). We can conclude from this that long-term memories can last a VERY long time. It also shows however that long-term memories are not permanent since, with the passage of time, they get worse. The study also illustrates something which is already familiar to us all – that we remember something better by recognition than recall. Recognition involves being given some kind of clue which aids the search for information in LTM. Recall is more difficult because it doesn't have this advantage.

HOW SCIENCE WORKS

(a) What kind of experimental design is used in the Bahrick et al study?

(b) What might be the advantage of using such a design in this study?

(c) (i) Identify the IV and the DV in this study.

   (ii) Explain how these were operationalised in this study.

(d) Identify one extraneous variable that Bahrick et al did not control for.

(e) What did Bahrick et al do to increase the validity of their research?

(f) Identify one ethical issue arising from this research and consider how they could have dealt with this.

(g) Write a suitable non-directional hypothesis for this study.

(h) How might the researchers have controlled for investigator effects?

STRENGTHS AND WEAKNESSES OF THE MULTI-STORE MODEL OF MEMORY

STRENGTHS

● There does seem to be a difference between the STM and LTM. The case study of KF by Shallice and Warrington (1974) showed that he had STM problems but his LTM was intact.

● This STM/LTM difference is also seen in sufferers of Korsakoff's syndrome.

● The MSM can explain primacy and recency effects – the first items in a list are rehearsed and sent to LTM, the last are still in the STM, therefore we best remember items at the start and end of a list.

● The yearbook study and the trigram study support different features of the model.

WEAKNESSES

● There is more than one STM store. Shallice and Warrington (1974) showed that patient KF only had verbal STM problems. Non-verbal sounds (like doorbells etc.) were remembered normally.

● There is more than one LTM store. It does not distinguish between *procedural memory* (how to do things like make a cup of tea), *semantic memory* (memory for facts such as Paris is the capital of France), or *episodic memory* (memory for events you have experienced, such as whether bananas were on your shopping list).

● Rehearsal is not as essential for LTM encoding as the MSM suggests. Shallice and Warrington (1970) showed that brain-damaged people with no STM have long-term memories of events after the damage, so STM was not needed for these memories to reach LTM.

ASK AN EXAMINER

This is a good table to learn! Not only does it tell you about the three concepts (and yes, you have to know about all three), but it is also an excellent way to learn about STM and LTM and the differences between them.

	STM	LTM
ENCODING	Mainly based on sound (acoustic)	Mainly based on meaning (semantic)
CAPACITY	Limited (7+/-2 pieces or chunks of information)	Unlimited
DURATION	Short (less than 30 seconds without rehearsal)	Long (potentially a lifetime)

THE WORKING MEMORY MODEL

Originally designed by Baddeley and Hitch (1974), the working memory model (WMM) is an alternative to the MSM, which they saw as underestimating the complexity of the STM.

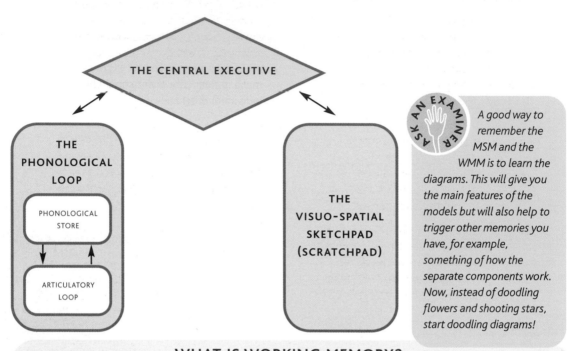

ASK AN EXAMINER

A good way to remember the MSM and the WMM is to learn the diagrams. This will give you the main features of the models but will also help to trigger other memories you have, for example, something of how the separate components work. Now, instead of doodling flowers and shooting stars, start doodling diagrams!

WHAT IS WORKING MEMORY?

It is a more complex and dynamic STM. All the information you are currently thinking about is held in the working memory, i.e. it is what you are *working on*.

It has several separate but connected parts, unlike the single STM store of the MSM.

It is an *active* system. It allows us to work things through, like mental arithmetic.

The capacity is limited, e.g. complex mental arithmetic of more than a few numbers is generally very difficult to do 'in your head'.

THE CENTRAL EXECUTIVE

It 'manages' the system – the other modules are 'slaves' to this one.

It decides what needs to be done and when. It integrates the activities of the other modules.

THE PHONOLOGICAL LOOP

An auditory store, rehearsing information to prevent loss and decay. It has two parts:

Phonological store: the 'inner ear'. Deals with the perception of all sounds and, in particular, speech.

Articulatory loop: the 'inner voice'. Baddeley (1986) says it rehearses sounds for up to two seconds. We can hold as much information here as we can rehearse in two seconds.

THE VISUO-SPATIAL SKETCHPAD

The 'inner eye'. Organises information visually, as you would by sketching them out on paper. It is the 'mental rough-paper' you might use when doing mental arithmetic.

STRENGTHS AND WEAKNESSES OF THE WORKING MEMORY MODEL

STRENGTHS

● Farah et al (1988) – some brain-damaged patients are good at spatial but not visual tasks, evidence that we have a visual and spatial system.

● Brain scans show that different parts of the brain become active when different types of tasks are presented to people. For instance, those requiring language or visual processing activate different areas. This is evidence for the different components detailed in the WMM.

● Short words are recalled better than long words (the word-length effect). This is evidence for the limited capacity of the phonological loop, since more short words can fit in it than long words.

● Baddeley and Hitch (1976) showed that if we do two tasks at the same time that both need the same part of the system, then performance on the tasks will suffer. This is in line with what WMM predicts.

WEAKNESSES

● There is little evidence for the role of the central executive as most research is done on the other components.

● Engle (1994) points out that there are individual differences in skills like reading, spelling and writing which are thought to be related to working memory function. The WMM does not make it clear why there should be individual differences.

● The relationship between working memory and long-term memory is not clear. It is not explained how working memory communicates with, draws information from and sends information to the LTM.

Apply Your Knowledge

Kelly talks all the time. In fact, her friend Sophie wonders if she ever stops! Whenever they sit together in class Sophie has trouble following what the teacher is saying, or concentrating on her written work.

Use what you have learned about the working memory model to explain Sophie's problem. (3 marks)

ASK AN EXAMINER

Whilst it is important to be able to describe the MSM and WMM, it is just as important that you know something of their strengths and weaknesses too. This is where studies are really useful – used in the right kind of way, they are great for evaluation. And what do we mean by that? Use 'trigger' words to tell the examiner that you are being evaluative. For example, 'support for the long duration of LTM comes from Bahrick et al...' sounds much more evaluative than 'Bahrick et al found that...'. Remember this – it is a very useful tip for questions that require extended written responses, and it is advice we offer elsewhere in this book.

Apply Your Knowledge

Sally struggles to cope with mental arithmetic of more than a few steps and digits. No matter how hard she tries she gets lost and has to start again.

Use ideas you have learned from the working memory model to explain Sally's problems with mental arithmetic. (4 marks)

ASK AN EXAMINER

You need to be able to do more than describe and evaluate the MSM and the WMM. You have to be able to apply them to everyday experience. Once you really understand them, this becomes much easier to do. Don't wait for revision and the exam to start applying the models – start now and increase your understanding of how your memory works. Look around you, be aware of some of the quirks of memory that we experience every day, try to explain them with what you know of the models. Practice makes perfect!

EYEWITNESS TESTIMONY

Rather than record things like a film, we tend to be selective about what aspects of events we commit to memory. This can cause us a problem in situations where accurate recall is vital, such as in eyewitness testimony (EWT). Research suggests that EWT may not always be accurate, and can be influenced by lots of things, including leading questions, anxiety, and age.

THE RECONSTRUCTIVE NATURE OF MEMORY

We tend to encode only the 'bare bones' of an event. When we then recall information, we unconsciously 'flesh out' these bare bones using common sense, logic, inference and expectation. Our memory then is a *reconstruction* of an event rather than an exact recall.

Loftus (2003) – 'memories are the sum of what (people) have thought, what they have been told, what they believe'.

ASK AN EXAMINER

The crashing cars study is such a useful one to know well! It might be tempting to just learn the simple details of this study, but that would be a mistake. This study tells us a great deal about the effects of misleading information on EWT, for example the effects of leading questions, and the nature of reconstructive memory. It is also a very good example of how psychologists investigate EWT and the problems psychologists encounter with this kind of research. Make sure that you learn what this study means for the reliability of EWT, and also how it works as an example of methods used in EWT research.

THE INFLUENCE OF ANXIETY ON EWT

Witnessing a crime may make us anxious. Giving evidence as an eyewitness may make us anxious. High levels of anxiety have been found impair our ability to store and retrieve memories.

Evidence
Peters (1988) – those receiving inoculations in a clinic (an anxiety generating event) had difficulty accurately identifying a picture of the nurse who gave the injection one week later.

Loftus et al (1987) – participants who saw a film of a robbery tended to focus their gaze on the gun used – this is called the 'weapons-focus' – making them less able to recognise the criminal.

Loftus and Burns (1982) – the details of less violent crimes were recalled better than very violent crimes. Violence increases anxiety, which then influences recall.

● All of the above studies were artificial experimental situations and therefore lack validity. More naturalistic studies have provided contradictory evidence.

● Yuille and Cutshall (1986) – interviewed 13 witnesses to a real-life crime. They found that the witnesses were resistant to the influence of leading questions. The accuracy of recall did not appear to be influenced by the anxiety caused by the event.

Apply Your Knowledge

It seemed like any other day for Kevin, working at the petrol station. That is, until a customer pulled out a shotgun and robbed his till. As Kevin told the police officer, he was terrified and thought he was going to die.

What has research told us about the effect that Kevin's anxiety during the robbery might have on his reliability as an eyewitness? (5 marks)

AGE AND EWT

Memory is not a constant thing – memories and the way that we use them change as we age.

A number of things have been found to influence *child* testimony:

SUGGESTIBILITY

Children appear more sensitive to leading questions than adults.

Evidence
Ceci et al (2000) – the memories of 3 to 4 year olds were most susceptible, and thus vulnerable to reconstruction.

Warren et al (2005) – leading questions influenced children's recall of a story more than adults' recall.

LANGUAGE ABILITY

Ability to understand the question can influence recall.

Evidence
Goodman and Schaff (1997) – the more complex the question the more likely a child was to give an inaccurate response.

Questions to young children need to avoid complex language or long sentences.

MEMORY PROCESSES

Young children tend to recall less complex memories than older children and adults do. Because of this, testimonies can appear incomplete or unconvincing.

Evidence
Goodman and Reed (1986) – showed that the recall of younger children was less detailed but no less accurate than the recall of older children.

Saywitz (1987) – showed that younger children tended to embellish their recall.

ASK AN EXAMINER

You won't have an exam question asking you specifically about eyewitness testimony in children or the elderly – the question will just ask you about age. If the question requires a short answer (e.g. 3 or 4 marks) then you can use one or the other in your answer. If, however, an extended written response is required, writing about both can be a good idea. Not only will you remember more by categorising your learning in this way, but you will have much more information available to answer the question. Learning the absolute minimum is not always a good idea!

Apply Your Knowledge

76-year-old Irena was walking through town with her 7-year-old granddaughter when they heard a loud 'smash!' A car had driven through a shop window, and they watched as two men loaded up their vehicle with electrical goods and drove off.

(a) What has research told us about the reliability of the testimony of these eyewitnesses? (*5 marks*)

(b) What technique might police officers use to ensure that the testimony of Irena is as accurate as possible? (*1 mark*)

STUDY IN FOCUS

Reconstruction of automobile destruction: An example of the interaction between language and memory Loftus and Palmer (1974)

What were they doing and why? Loftus and Palmer wanted to find out whether memory could be influenced by the type of questions people were asked, so they ran two experiments to see if this would happen.

What did they do in Experiment 1? In their first experiment Loftus and Palmer showed a series of car crash videos to 45 students. They asked each student to fill in a questionnaire after they had seen a video. The questionnaire had lots of questions. One of them was important. It asked:

● **'How fast were the cars travelling when they .... into each other?'**

The blank space was filled with one of:

● **'Smashed, Collided, Bumped, Hit, Contacted'.**

The participants were split into five groups. Each group received a sentence with a different verb.

What did they find? The results were very interesting indeed. As you can see from Figure 1, the word placed at the end of the sentence made a huge difference to the estimated speed of the cars. The sentence 'How fast was the car going when they smashed into each other?' drew the fastest estimate of all.

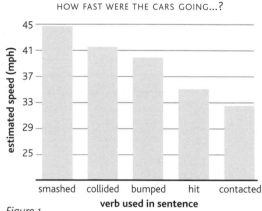

Figure 1

Averages of estimated speed
'Smashed' - 40.8 mph
'Collided' - 39.3 mph
'Bumped' - 38.1 mph
'Hit' - 34.0 mph
'Contacted' - 31.8 mph

It is clear that information presented after an event can significantly influence our perception of that event. Here, the word used in the question influenced people's perception of speed. Loftus and Palmer concluded that this alteration may be one of two things. It could be *distortion* (where memory is changed) or it could be a *response-bias* (where the word influenced a judgement, perhaps because they were not sure of the speed, so the word 'suggested' a speed of some kind).

What did they do in Experiment 2? In a similar experiment, 150 students were shown videos of cars crashing and then they were presented with the questionnaire. This time the question hidden in the questionnaire only used the verbs 'hit' and 'smashed' (so there were only two experimental groups). A third group was not asked about the speed at all. In addition to this, participants were asked another question a week after the experiment. That question was:

● Did you see ANY broken glass?

There was no broken glass in the film used.

STUDY IN FOCUS

What did they find? Average estimates of speed depended on the verb used in the sentence, just as in Experiment 1. The estimate of speed with 'smashed' was higher than that for 'hit'.

The result of the 'broken glass' question can be seen in Figure 2.

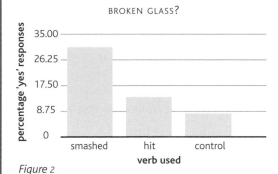

Figure 2

Percentage of those indicating they had seen broken glass
'Smashed' group - 32%
'Hit' group - 14%
'Control' Group - 12%

It is very clear that questions following an event can influence our memories, so much so that those who were asked about the speed of the cars using the word 'smashed' felt that there was indeed smashed glass. Those not asked about the speed, and those in the group where the word 'hit' was used, were much less likely to remember seeing glass. Using the word 'smashed' builds the concept of 'broken glass' in memory and, as a result, people really felt that they had seen broken glass in the film they had watched the previous week.

This supports a **reconstructive memory hypothesis** where information retained at the time of an event can be altered or influenced in some way by information presented after the event. Once all this information is linked together, separating it becomes at worst impossible, and at best extremely difficult indeed.

HOW SCIENCE WORKS

(**a**) The researchers used questionnaires to gather quantitative data.

    (i) What quantitative data is gathered in Experiments 1 and 2?

    (ii) Write one question that they might have used to generate qualitative data.

(**b**) What kind of experiment is the Loftus and Palmer study?

(**c**) What kind of design is used in Experiment 1?

(**d**) Suggest a suitable directional hypothesis for Experiment 1.

(**e**) What kind of graph is Figure 1?

(**f**) Why might Loftus and Palmer have conducted a pilot study?

(**g**) How is the IV operationalised in Experiment 2?

(**h**) How is the DV operationalised in Experiment 2?

(**i**) (i) What is meant by the term *validity*?

    (ii) Suggest one way in which the validity of this study could be questioned.

(**j**) Explain two extraneous variables that would have been controlled in Experiment 1. Hint: think of participants and stimuli.

THE COGNITIVE INTERVIEW (CI)

Eyewitnesses are usually considered the most important source of leads in a criminal investigation. It is important therefore that testimonies are not influenced by leading questions. One way to help people remember accurately is to use a cognitive interview. According to Waddington and Bull (2007), it is based on two principles:

Principle 1: Organisation

The way that memory is organised means that memories can be accessed in various ways.

A series of actions can help – first you did this, then you did that and so on until you reach your memory.

Alternatively, thinking about things related to the item you are trying to recall can help. If it is what a person was wearing, then thinking about fashion and shops might help.

Principle 2: Context-dependency

Memories are context-dependent, meaning they are linked to the situation in which they were encoded. Retrieval will be easier if the cues present at encoding are present at recall. This means that the interviewer has to carefully reinstate the context in which the memory was encoded.

THE CI USES FOUR TECHNIQUES:

1 Reinstate the context: help the interviewees go back in their mind to the context in which they encoded the memory, e.g. what they were feeling at the time, what they were doing just before the event.

2 Change sequence: changing the order in which events are recalled can be very beneficial as it ensures details are not skipped and gaps can be filled, e.g. the witnesses might be asked to repeat their account in reverse order.

3 Change perspective: interviewees are encouraged to recall events from the perspective of an observer. This helps the interviewer identify what the interviewees actually know, not what they are 'filling in'.

4 Report everything: every detail is reported regardless of how irrelevant something may seem. It could stimulate a memory that could be important or relevant.

Apply Your Knowledge

During the interview of a witness to a serious crime, the police officer encourages the witness to report everything that comes to mind regarding the experience. She also encourages the witness to imagine and explain how the events might have appeared to another observer.

(a) Outline **two** other techniques that the police officer should use to ensure that she is doing the cognitive interview correctly. (2+2 marks)

(b) Give **one** limitation or **one** strength of the cognitive interview. (2 marks)

Evaluation of the CI

Gieselman et al (1985) – the CI is more effective in stimulating recall than a standard interview or hypnosis.

Stein and Memon (2006) – even with little training in the technique, the CI can still be more effective than standard interviews.

Milne and Bull (1999) – the success of the CI depends on the skill of the interviewer, and this is a difficult thing to assess.

Eysenck and Keane (2005) – more information is indeed recalled, but much of it is irrelevant. Secondly, context is good for improving recall but not recognition, so identifying a culprit is not improved by the technique. Thirdly, the CI becomes less effective the further in time from the actual event it takes place.

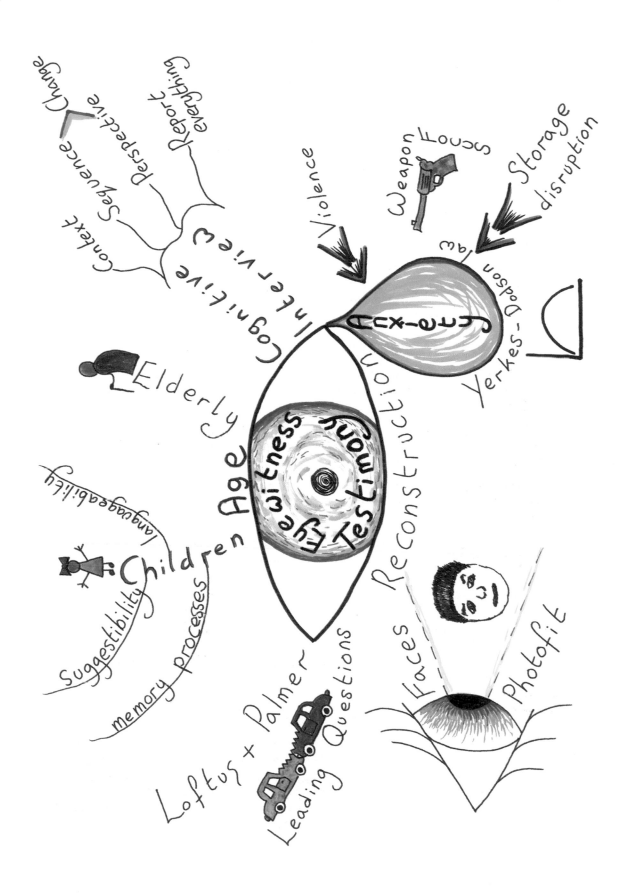

IMPROVING MEMORY

ORGANISATION OF MEMORY

Memory is organised, and the more organised it is the better it operates.

Evidence
DeGroot (1966) – organisation happens at storage. Expert and beginner chess players shown board positions. Experts better at reproducing the positions later because their existing memory helped them 'organise' their memories of the chess boards.

Memory will be improved by organisation but, even if badly organised, memory can still be improved by anything that makes retrieval more effective.

Two ways to improve retrieval:

Retrieval Cues

Knowing the rough location of a memory can help us find it because it narrows down the search. The location can be indicated by retrieval cues – when we commit something to memory we also encode other related information. These can act as cues to where to find the target memory. Memory can be improved by storing information efficiently, for example by categorising it.

Evidence
Tulving and Pearlstone (1966) – recall of a word list was improved by giving participants the category of the words to be recalled (i.e. colours, animals, etc).

State-dependency

Physical or emotional state at encoding can cue the recall of a memory, e.g. if you were sad or happy when memory is encoded, then returning to that state can help you recall the memory. Memory could be improved by returning to the same physical or mental state during which the memory was first stored.

This is an example of *encoding specificity*, i.e. there must be a match between cues at encoding and at retrieval.

Evidence
Bower et al (1981) – recall of sad parts of a story was better than happy parts if the person was in a sad mood when reading it, and vice versa.

In an exam, you could take a general approach and use organisation to explain how memory could be improved, with retrieval cues and state dependency as examples. On the other hand, you could be more direct and use specific mnemonics. This latter approach could be very useful, especially when you are applying your knowledge to a scenario because it means that your answer will really look as though it is directly addressing the question. Examiners like this – it shows you know your stuff and are answering the question effectively. Let's not forget the other big bonus of course – you use the mnemonics successfully in your own learning!

Apply Your Knowledge

The twins each had 12 items from the shopping list to buy and each decided to use a different method of remembering the items.

(a) Identify two different strategies for improving memory that the twins might have used. (*2 marks*)

(b) Explain how one of the techniques identified in part (a) would be used to remember the shopping list. (*3 marks*)

Mnemonics – don't just learn about them, use them! How about this for an example –
KLEAN your memory.
K – *keyword*
L – *loci*
E – *elaborate*
A – *acronyms*
N – *narrative chaining*

STRATEGIES FOR IMPROVING MEMORY

1. METHOD OF LOCI

In your imagination, leave items you want to remember in 'locations' around a familiar place like your home, or a route you regularly walk. To recall, imagine walking through your home, or on your route identifying the items as you go.

Good for learning ideas and the connections between them; especially good for 'visual learners'.

Evidence
Crovitz (1971) – better performance on memory task in those using this technique than those remembering by rote.

Yesavage and Rose (1994) – the richer the mental image used in loci, the better the memory.

2. NARRATIVE CHAINING

Make up and remember a short story encompassing the things you have to remember. The 'narrative' provides an organisation, which 'links' the information to be remembered into a 'chain'.

Good for learning lists of items; especially good for 'verbal learners'.

Evidence
Bower and Clarke (1969) – those remembering a list as a narrative performed at 94%. Those not using a narrative performed at 14%.

Bower (1970) – it is more effective when items are meaningfully related using visual images.

3. ACRONYMS

Form a word or phrase from the first letters of a list of items to be remembered. For instance **ROY.G.BIV**, or **Richard Of York Gave Battle In Vain** are acronyms for the colours of the rainbow.

Good for learning items that have to be recalled in the right order.

Evidence
Bower (1972) – some acronyms are more useful than others. If they form a visual image they are more useful. For instance, imagining Richard of York Battling in Vain can be a vivid and easy-to-recall image.

4. ELABORATION

Elaborative rehearsal is more effective than *maintenance rehearsal* because the information is made meaningful and therefore encoded in a way that suits long-term memory.

Evidence
Craik and Tulving (1975) – more elaborate encoding helps us recall it later because it involves deep processing.

Morris et al (1981) – elaboration depends on existing knowledge, e.g. football fans better at recall of football scores than non-fans.

5. KEYWORD TECHNIQUE

A three-stage technique:

1 *Acoustic stage* – the word is pronounced. The 'sound' is linked to the sound of a familiar (English) word (i.e. *bouteille* in French contains the sound 'boot').
2 *Visual image stage* – make an image out of the 'item' and the English word (i.e. a bottle in a boot).
3 *Rehearsal stage* – rehearse the image and commit it to memory.

Particularly good for learning foreign vocabulary.

Evidence
Roberts (1985) – memory for words using the technique a week after encoding was much better than memory by rote.

May be more useful in some languages than others. Zhang (2005) – good for Chinese students of English but Atkinson and Raugh (1975) say not for American students of Russian.

Waugh and Tomas (1995) – works best when learners make up their own images.

Check your knowledge

1 Correctly complete the following diagram to give three differences between short-term memory (STM) and long-term memory (LTM) in the multi-store model of memory:

	STM	LTM
Encoding		
Capacity		
Duration		

2 Outline the main features of the multi-store model of memory. (*6 marks*)

3 Give **two** strengths of the multi-store model of memory. (*2 + 2 marks*)

4 Give **two** weaknesses of the multi-store model of memory. (*2 + 2 marks*)

5 Outline the main features of the working memory model of memory. (*6 marks*)

6 Give **two** strengths of the working memory model of memory. (*2 + 2 marks*)

7 Give **two** weaknesses of the working memory model of memory. (*2 + 2 marks*)

8 According to the multi-store model of memory, STM and LTM are separate stores. Outline evidence to support this. (*4 marks*)

9 Explain how psychologists have investigated the effects of misleading information on eyewitness testimony. (*5 marks*)

10 Explain **one** criticism of the cognitive interview. (*3 marks*)

11 (a) Identify **two** main techniques used in the cognitive interview. (*2 marks*)

   (b) Outline the features of **one** of the techniques identified in (a). (*3 marks*)

12 Outline **one** study into the use of the cognitive interview. (*4 marks*)

13 Outline **one** study into the effects of age on eyewitness testimony. (*4 marks*)

14 Describe the effects of age on eyewitness testimony. (*6 marks*)

15 Outline **one** study into the effects of anxiety on eyewitness testimony. (*4 marks*)

16 Describe the effects of anxiety on eyewitness testimony. (*6 marks*)

17 (a) Outline **two** strategies for improving memory. (*3 + 3 marks*)

   (b) Evaluate the effectiveness of **one** of the strategies identified in (a). (*3 marks*)

HOW SCIENCE WORKS

Think about the multi-store model of memory

We can demonstrate chunking in STM with a simple experiment.

● Design a memory test, for example participants digit strings that can be given to 'unchunked' or chunked.

● This string of numbers should be beyond the capacity of STM. For example, 129214552122 contains 12 items but can be chunked into four 'dates'.

● Choose an experimental design, decide on a procedure and pilot your study

● Once you have run the study for real, calculate the average number of chunked and unchunked digits recalled and plot these figures on a graph.

Things to consider

● What do the results show about the nature of STM?

● Were adjustments made to the study following the pilot?

● What were the IV and DV?

● What extraneous variables needed controlling in this study?

● Which experimental design did you choose and what were the advantages of it in this context?

HOW SCIENCE WORKS

Think about the working memory model

We can demonstrate chunking in STM with a simple experiment.

● We can investigate the importance of the articulatory loop with a simple experiment.

● Write a directional hypothesis, not forgetting that it should be operationalised and should clearly indicate both the IV and DV.

● Design a memory test that uses the phonological store, for example a list of ten words which have to be read and immediately recalled.

● There are two experimental conditions – one where the word list is read and recalled, the other where the same happens except that participants repeat out loud 'the the the' as they read the list.

● Calculate a measure of central tendency and dispersion for both sets of data you have gathered and draw a summary table.

Things to consider

● Explain your findings in the context of the working memory model. For example, why was there a lower rate of recall of words in the 'the the the' condition?

● What does your table of scores say about your hypothesis – have you supported it or must you reject it?

● Explain your choice of experimental design. Would the experiment work as well with an alternative design?

● Comment on the validity and reliability of this study.

The extended written response

Outline and evaluate research into the effects of age on the accuracy of eyewitness testimony. (12 marks)

Research has consistently shown that age is an important factor when considering the accuracy of an eyewitness's testimony. The recall of children, for example, has been found to be influenced by a number of factors.

This is giving the answer a context – it is indicating that the answer is going to focus on the testimony of young children in particular. It isn't a 'filler' however – it is also gaining marks because it is saying something about eyewitness testimony.

Ceci et al argued that the memories of younger children are weaker and fade faster, and that this makes them more uncertain about the details of events. They found that, as a result, 3 to 4- year-old children were more sensitive to leading questions than older children.

Remember, the question requires an *outline* of research. This is the first piece of relevant research.

This is supported by Warren et al who questioned adults and children on a story they had earlier been given to read. They found that children were more likely to be influenced by those questions that were leading.

Notice that this is research again, but this time it is used as evaluation – it clearly states that it is supporting the findings of Ceci et al. What make it evaluative are the opening three words – 'This is supported...'. Without these it would be just another study outline.

Research has also shown that the kind of language used in the questions might affect children's recall. For example, Goodman and Schaaf found that children were more likely to give an inaccurate answer when the question was too complex to understand properly. This suggests that the accuracy of child testimony could be improved by matching the language used in the questions with the child's developmental level.

This is a clever paragraph. It starts out by being descriptive – another factor is identified and another piece of research is outlined. However, it turns evaluative with the last sentence – examiners call this kind of thing *informed commentary*. This is not just being descriptive; the information is being used to make a point.

Research suggests that young children tend to recall less complex memories than do older children and adults. For example, Goodman and Reed found that, compared to 6-year-olds, 3-year-olds remembered less detail of a game played several days earlier.

The final descriptive point is being made here, and once again it is outlining research just as the question requires.

However, whilst they recall less detail, their memories are still accurate. Where they really differ is in the type of error children make. This is supported by Saywitz, who suggests that children's testimony is more likely to contain embellishments and exaggerations.

The answer ends with some more evaluation. Enough of the right kind of words are used to inform the examiner that you are sustaining an evaluative point through a few sentences – i.e. 'however' and 'supported'.

COMMENTS

This answers the question in a very straightforward, simple way. It asked for an outline of research – three appropriate pieces of research are outlined. The question required evaluation of research – and this was done systematically. Every time some research was outlined, it was followed by a bit of evaluation. This ensured that it struck the right balance between the knowledge/recall and analysis/evaluation skills that are needed in these pieces of extended writing. Note that the research was presented very briefly – basic findings, maybe with a bit of procedure. There really isn't the space available to go into great detail. Here, a judgement was made that three pieces of research would provide better coverage of the issue than one, or maybe two, in more detail.

A decision was made to focus only on the eyewitness testimony of children in this essay. This was allowed by the question. Of course, you could discuss research into eyewitness testimony in the elderly instead. Indeed, with careful planning you could use both children and the elderly in the same essay. Be careful though – you do not want to run out of time and space because you have set yourself too ambitious a task.

In The News

Research suggests that children's memory may be more reliable than adults' in court cases

The U.S. legal system has long assumed that all testimony is not equally credible, that some witnesses are more reliable than others. In tough cases with child witnesses, it assumes adult witnesses to be more reliable. But what if the legal system had it wrong?

Researchers Valerie Reyna, human development professor, and Chuck Brainerd, human development and law school professor – both from Cornell University – argue that like the two-headed Roman god Janus, memory is of two minds – that is, memories are captured and recorded separately and differently in two distinct parts of the mind.

They say children depend more heavily on a part of the mind that records, "what actually happened," while adults depend more on another part of the mind that records, "the meaning of what happened." As a result, they say, adults are more susceptible to false memories, which can be extremely problematic in court cases.

Reyna's and Brainerd's research, funded by the National Science Foundation (NSF), sparked more than 30 follow-up memory studies (many also funded by NSF), which the researchers review in an upcoming issue of Psychological Bulletin.

This research shows that meaning-based memories are largely responsible for false memories, especially in adult witnesses. Because the ability to extract meaning from experience develops slowly, children are less likely to produce these false memories than adults, and are more likely to give accurate testimony when properly questioned.

The finding is counterintuitive; it doesn't square with current legal tenets, and may have important implications for legal proceedings.

"Because children have fewer meaning-based experience records, they are less likely to form false memories," says Reyna. "But the law assumes children are more susceptible to false memories than adults."

The court's reliance on adult testimony has a long history. Before the early 1970s, children younger than eight years old rarely testified, because they failed the court's competency requirements. Then in the 1970s, when statistics showed an increase in the number of child abuse cases, courts were forced to allow the testimony of young victims, only to reemphasize adult testimony in the 1990s, when some children's testimony was proven to be unreliable.

"Courts give witness instructions to tell the truth and nothing but the truth," says Brainerd. "This assumes witnesses will either be truthful or lie, but there is a third possibility now being recognized – false memories."

According to Brainerd, "Things are about to change radically."

Fuzzy Trace Theory

Traditional theories of memory assume a person's memories are based on event reconstruction, especially after delays of a few days, weeks, or months. However, Reyna and Brainerd's Fuzzy Trace Theory hypothesizes that people store two types of experience records or memories: verbatim traces and gist traces.

Verbatim traces are memories of what actually happened. Gist traces are based on a person's understanding of what happened, or what the event meant to him or her. Gist traces stimulate false memories because they store impressions of what an event meant, which can be inconsistent with what actually happened. False memories can be identified when witnesses accurately describe what they remember but those memories are proven false based on other unimpeachable facts.

"When gist traces are especially strong, they can produce phantom recollections – that is, illusory, vivid recollections of things that did not happen, such as remembering a robber brandished a weapon and made threatening statements," says Reyna.

Brainerd argues that because witness testimony is the primary evidence in criminal prosecutions, false memories are a dominant reason for convictions of innocent people.

Recently, in Cook County, Ill., more than 200 murder confessions were identified as being based on adults' false memory reports because they conflicted with unimpeachable facts. For example, a person may have falsely remembered being in

one location, but a sales receipt showed that he was in another location at the same time a crime was committed.

In child abuse cases where the law gives the benefit of the doubt to adult testimony, the results can be even more disconcerting. "Failure to recognize differences in how adults and children produce memory unfairly tilts the U.S. legal system against child witnesses," says Reyna. "Children do not have the same fullness of emotional and intellectual experience as do adults when it comes to deriving meaning from situations," says Reyna. "So, meaning-based memory is less likely to influence a child's testimony."

The researchers say their transformative "two-mind" memory approach can reduce the number of false memories in court cases and give more validity to children's testimony.

Memory Science
Reyna and Brainerd developed several mathematical models associated with Fuzzy Trace

Theory that can be used to predict memory outcomes in both adults and children. The models, which test memory, have been used to determine ways in which attorneys, investigators, law enforcement officials and others can ask questions to help people access verbatim memories while suppressing false memories. The researchers say using neutral prompts to cue witnesses can help them remember what actually happened.

Reyna and Brainerd also say returning a witness to the scene of an event in a highly neutral way can cue verbatim memories and help the legal process.

The models provide the most accurate information to date on the causes of false memories. Using them, researchers can determine with surprising accuracy when a person accesses both verbatim and gist memory.

Reyna and Brainerd's findings are summarized in a new book, *The Science of False Memory,* published by Oxford University Press.

States News Service
March 6, 2008 Thursday
ARLINGTON, Va.

Stretch and Challenge

1 Why is it important that testimony from eyewitnesses is accurate?

2 How does the article explain why adults might be more susceptible to false memories than children?

3 According to Fuzzy Trace Theory, there are two types of memory, verbatim and gist. State which produces the most accurate recall, and explain why.

4 'Traditional theories of memory assume a person's memories are based on event reconstruction...'

(a) What is meant by the term 'reconstruction'?

(b) How does research into the effects of misleading information, e.g. Loftus and Palmer, relate to Fuzzy Trace Theory?

5 One of the most important aspects of research into eyewitness testimony is that it can be used to improve the recall of eyewitnesses.

(a) What two suggestions do Reyna and Brainerd make for applying Fuzzy Trace Theory when interviewing eyewitnesses?

(b) How do these suggestions compare with the cognitive interview technique?

6 Under what conditions might a child's eyewitness testimony be more reliable than an adult's?

7 Witnessing a traumatic event will have caused a child anxiety. From your knowledge of research, consider how this might impact on the accuracy of the child's recall.

THE EXTENDED WRITTEN RESPONSE – ADDITIONAL QUESTIONS

1 Describe and evaluate the multi-store model of memory. (*12 marks*)

2 Discuss the effects of misleading information on eyewitness testimony. (*12 marks*)

3 'Whilst many police officers consider eyewitnesses to be the most important source of leads in a criminal investigation, they often don't get as much information from them as they would want.'

Discuss the use of the cognitive interview in eyewitness testimony. (*12 marks*)

Example answers to these questions can be found at www.askanexaminer.com

USEFUL WEBSITES

http://changingminds.org/explanations/memory/multi-store_model.htm
A fast, clear explanation of the multi-store model, with useful links and definitions of each part.

http://users.ipfw.edu/abbott/120/AtkinsonShifrin.html

More on Atkinson and Shiffrin than you would ever need, but it's clearly laid out and great for helping you revise in a hurry.

http://faculty.washington.edu/eloftus/

You'll find links here to the pages of Elizabeth Loftus with some really interesting articles she has written about, among other things, eyewitness testimony.

http://www.pbs.org/wgbh/pages/frontline/shows/dna/interviews/loftus.html

Here's an interview with Elizabeth Loftus where she talks about traumatic experiences and memory, amongst many other things.

http://www.totse.com/en/law/justice_for_all/coginte.html

There's a useful description of the cognitive interview technique here.

http://www.helpguide.org/life/improving_memory.htm

This is a useful site for memory in general, but towards the end of this page you'll find a list of mnemonics and a definition of each that you may find useful.

http://www.web-us.com/memory/mnemonic_techniques.htm

How useful is this for revision? More tips on developing your memory.

http://www.youtube.com/watch?v=WNfx0FO4hzs

A bit of fun. Tom Lehrer shows us how a song (and a lot of practice!) can help you remember the elements of the periodic table, maybe.

http://www.memoryarena.com/resources/podcasts.asp

A podcast with Alan Baddeley, he of the working memory model.

http://www.mppl.org/research/online_memory_games.html

You'll find a number of memory tasks and games here. Don't just play them, have a think about the kind of questions they are asking you and their relevance to what you know about memory.

Section 3

Developmental Psychology – Early Social Development

WHAT YOU NEED TO KNOW

Developmental Psychology is in Unit 1 of the specification. You are expected to develop your knowledge and understanding of Developmental Psychology, including concepts, theories and studies. This includes a knowledge and understanding of research methods and ethical issues as they relate to this area of psychology. You also need to develop the skills of analysis, evaluation and application. Rather than just recall and reproduce information, you are expected to be able to apply your knowledge and understanding. The subject content is split into two parts:

Attachment

- Explanations of attachment, including learning and evolution
- Types of attachment, including secure and insecure attachment
- Attachment and culture
- The disruption of attachments, including privation and institutionalisation

Attachment in everyday life

- The impact of day care on social development
- Implications of research for childcare practices

EXPLANATIONS OF ATTACHMENT

Attachment is the desire for closeness and frequent interaction a child and caregiver share.

THE EVOLUTIONARY EXPLANATION

Evolution: behaviour and physical characteristics change and evolve with each generation. Darwin describes natural selection as a way in which this happens. Many young are produced, not all can survive. The young with the best chance of survival will be those with characteristics that help them cope with the demands of the environment. This is the principle of survival of the fittest. The survivors will pass on these characteristics to their offspring, and so on.

RESEARCH WITH ANIMALS

Konrad Lorenz (1935) – the theory of *imprinting* says that animals have an innate ability to recognise their caregiver. This provides protection and allows them to learn important behaviours. *Imprinting* must occur within a certain time called a *critical period* (e.g. within 36 hours for geese) or it will not happen.

Evaluation

Sluckin (1965) – imprinting can occur outside the critical period.

Kendrick et al (2001) – imprinting is not necessarily permanent. Sheep raised with goats could revert to a preference for their own species after they had imprinted on the goats and vice-versa after one or two years.

Harry Harlow (1962) – monkeys reared in isolation show a preference for a cloth-covered surrogate 'mother' rather than a bare wire one providing food. This experience affected the monkeys emotionally, e.g. females showed a lack of nurturing, caring behaviour. This was an effect of *maternal deprivation*. Monkeys need physical contact with a living caring mother to develop normal social skills.

Evaluation

Klaus and Kennel (1976) – a need for physical comfort is also shown in human babies, e.g. babies given extra time with their mothers early in life showed stronger attachments later.

Fox (1977) – Israeli children brought up with nurses still showed stronger attachments with their mothers. It is the *type* of attachment that matters not the *quantity*.

ASK AN EXAMINER

Look at the exam question carefully to see where it is directing you – for example, is it a general question of the evolutionary perspective? Is it a scenario describing an example of human attachment? If an exam question does not specify human attachment then you can answer it using the research of Lorenz and Harlow. Even if it requires a human focus, animal research can still be relevant, for example as evaluation.

Apply Your Knowledge

Mary has noticed that her young baby does things to attract her attention, such as babbling, smiling and crying.

How does the evolutionary perspective on attachment explain these behaviours? (*4 marks*)

RESEARCH WITH HUMANS

BOWLBY'S THEORY OF ATTACHMENT IN HUMANS

● Bowlby uses the word *attachment* instead of *imprinting*.

● Human infants form an attachment to one primary caregiver, usually the biological mother (*monotropy*).

● The bond is a reciprocal one between the primary caregiver and child.

● *Social releasers* are signals from the child identifying the need for food, protection and closeness and trigger attachment behaviours in carers.

● The relationship with the caregiver creates an *internal working model* for future relationships.

● The critical period for attachment formation is about three years.

● The *continuity hypothesis* states that consistent, responsive and sensitive care early on will show themselves later in life.

● The *secure-base hypothesis* states that if children feel sufficiently comforted by the presence of a caregiver then they are likely to explore their environment, encouraging development.

Attachment develops in a fixed sequence:

1. Non-focused orienting and signalling – signals like crying are not directed at anyone in particular, but there is a preference for the company of people. → **2. Focus on one or more figures** – by 3 months of age infants recognise the usual caregivers and will direct signals towards them rather than strangers. → **3. Secure base behaviour** – by about 6 months signalling is focused primarily on the main caregiver. Begin to show *separation anxiety* and *stranger anxiety*.

Evaluation

● Shaffer and Emerson (1964) – have cast doubt on the *monotropy* concept. Some infants have no preference for an attachment to a single person and seem to show *multiple attachments*.

● Bowlby may have over-emphasised the role of the mother and under-emphasised the role of the father in the attachment process.

● *Separation anxiety* could be described as a lack of *object permanence*, which is an understanding that when things are out of sight they still exist.

● The theory is very influential and has stimulated a great deal of research, e.g. into the experience of children in care.

ASK AN EXAMINER

Bowlby's theory of attachment is really important! Make sure you have a good understanding of it – it is the theory that underpins most of this section on early social development, and a good grasp of what Bowlby was getting at will help you to understand types of attachment, culture and attachment, disruption of attachments and day care. Not forgetting of course that you could get a question on Bowlby's theory in the exam!

Apply Your Knowledge

You have been invited to give a talk to the local mother-and-baby group. Using ideas from Bowlby's theory of attachment, what advice might you give the mothers about how they could form a strong mother–child bond? (*4 marks*)

THE LEARNING THEORY EXPLANATION

Attachments are *learned* through a satisfaction of *drives*, e.g. hunger, thirst.
They are learned through classical conditioning, operant conditioning and social learning.

CLASSICAL CONDITIONING

Babies learn to associate their primary caregiver with providing food, satisfying hunger, and other physical comforts.

How it happens:
Actions of caregiver (unconditioned stimulus – UCS) generate contentment in infant (unconditioned response – UCR).

If the UCS is presented over and over, it becomes associated with contentment.

Contentment eventually becomes a CR (conditioned response), and caring behaviour the CS (conditioned stimulus).

SOCIAL LEARNING

Learning happens through *observation* of those around us. We *imitate* behaviours of a *model*, in this case our primary caregiver. Infants watch the loving and caring behaviour of parents (models) and imitate. Parents who value this caring behaviour reinforce it when they see it.

OPERANT CONDITIONING

Once the primary caregiver has become associated with the reduction of drives, the infant will engage in behaviours that encourage the presence of the mother.

How it happens:
The presence of the caregiver is *reinforcing* for the infant (i.e. the infant gets pleasure from it and therefore engages in behaviour that encourages it, such as smiling).

The behaviour of the infant is *reinforcing* for the caregiver (i.e. the caregiver gets pleasure from it and therefore engages in behaviour that encourages it, such as providing care).

The reinforcement process is therefore reciprocal (i.e. the infant and caregiver reinforce each other's behaviour thereby strengthening the bond).

ASK AN EXAMINER

It makes more sense to have a grasp of how the three types of learning – classical, operant and social – explain attachment than it is to try to know about just one. This makes it much easier to get full marks when there are 6 on offer for describing this explanation.

EVALUATION OF LEARNING THEORY

PREDICTION	EVALUATION
Punishment reduces likelihood of behaviour occurring.	Not necessarily. Children still show attachment behaviours to punishing or even cruel parents.
Without reinforcement, learned behaviours will fade.	Not necessarily. Even when separated from parents (therefore not receiving reinforcement), children continue to have very strong attachments.
Strongest attachments will be shown to the person providing food, comfort, etc.	Emerson (1964) showed that this was not necessarily the case. Harlow showed that with monkeys other factors, such as social contact, were important.
Feeding activity is crucial for attachment, and the infant is a passive participant in this, i.e. learning 'just happens'.	Harlow contradicts this. Infant monkeys seek attachment with the comforting mother rather than with the one providing food.

Apply Your Knowledge

Marion provides most of the care for her son, Joseph – feeding, comforting and playing with him. She has noticed that, whilst he is happy to spend time with his dad, Joseph seems most content when he is with her.

Use your knowledge of the learning theory of attachment to explain Josephs' behaviour. (*4 marks*)

TYPES OF ATTACHMENT

The type of attachment formed varies from one infant to another.

ATTACHMENT TYPE B (SECURE)
- Explores
- Distressed on separation
- Greets mother warmly
- When mother present is friendly with strangers

ATTACHMENT TYPE A (INSECURE – ANXIOUS/AVOIDANT)
- Little interest in exploring
- Little distress on separation
- Avoids contact when mother returns
- Not nervous around strangers

ATTACHMENT TYPE C (INSECURE – ANXIOUS/RESISTANT)
- Appears anxious
- Very distressed on separation
- Ambivalent when mother returns
- Child nervous of strangers when mother present

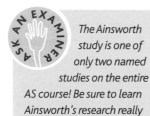

The Ainsworth study is one of only two named studies on the entire AS course! Be sure to learn Ainsworth's research really well – it might come up as an exam question!

EVALUATION OF THE STRANGE SITUATION

- Standardised procedure makes it easy to carry out and replicate.
- The situation is unfamiliar therefore behaviour in the procedure may not be natural.
- Subjective evaluation is required in observing the behaviour – there may be observer bias.
- If it is a *reliable* classification method, attachment should be rated the same on different occasions, but they are not.
- Lamb (1977) – it only assesses attachment with the person the child is with at the time (mother). The rating of attachment may well be different with someone else. This is a *validity* problem.
- It's highly artificial and stressful for both the child and the separated mother.

Make sure that you are able to describe and recognise both secure and insecure attachments. For example, what kind of behaviours would be typical of a securely attached child? How would you recognise the behaviour of a child as an insecure attachment?

ATTACHMENT TYPE D
Main and Solomon (1990) – A mixture of Types A and C. When the mother returns, the child is confused whether to approach her or not; 5-10% of children show this type of attachment.

Apply Your Knowledge

Andrea has noticed that her two sons are quite different. When she gets home from work the first thing Sam does is run to her and give her a great big hug, whilst she has to go to find Rob to make sure he is okay. When a plumber came to the house the other day Sam was fine with him, but Rob wouldn't stop crying and appeared scared.

(a) Identify:
   (i) The type of attachment shown by Rob. (*1 mark*)
   (ii) The type of attachment shown by Sam. (*1 mark*)

(b) Explain how the type of attachment shown by each child could be assessed. (*4 marks*)

STUDY IN FOCUS

The Strange Situation – Ainsworth and Bell (1970)

What were they doing and why? The researchers wanted to see how a child behaved towards strangers and their caregiver under controlled conditions of stress, in which the infant might seek comfort, and also conditions of 'novelty' where the infant might be encouraged to explore their surroundings. The researchers would then use 'exploration behaviour' and 'comfort-seeking behaviour' as indicators of type of attachment.

How did they do it? 100 middle class American mothers and their children took part. The researchers employed a *controlled observational* technique, which means that the researchers controlled the activities in which the mother and child took part.

The following procedure was used, and is made up of eight episodes. Each episode, apart from the first one, lasts about three minutes, the whole procedure lasting not more than half an hour.

1 Mother and child enter the room.
2 Mother responds to the child if the child seeks attention.
3 Stranger enters the room, speaks to mother and slowly approaches the child, mother leaves room.
4 Stranger lets child play, encouraging play with toys if child shows inattention. If child becomes distressed the procedure ends.
5 Mother enters room. Stranger leaves. Child settles again. Mother leaves child alone in the room.
6 If the child is distressed, procedure ends.
7 Stranger enters, and repeats procedure outlined in step 3.
8 Mother returns. Stranger leaves.

During the procedure, the researchers noted down how much the following behaviours were exhibited.

• The infant's unease when the mother left the room – '**separation anxiety**'
• The infant's willingness to explore
• The way the infant greeted the mother on her return – '**reunion behaviour**'
• The infant's response to a stranger – '**stranger anxiety**'

What did they find? The results led the researchers to conclude that there were three main attachment types that they described as Type B (secure) and Types A (insecure-avoidant) and Type C (insecure-resistant). In this study the researchers concluded that the type of attachment formed by the child depends upon the responsiveness and sensitivity of the caregiver.

HOW SCIENCE WORKS

(a) Ainsworth and Bell used observation in their study of attachment types.
   (i) Did they use an observational technique or observational method?
   (ii) What is the difference between these two kinds of observation?

(b) There are several IVs (independent variables) and DVs (dependent variables) in this study. Identify one IV and one DV and explain how these were operationalised.

(c) (i) What was the target population of the Ainsworth and Bell study?
   (ii) Suggest one technique that Ainsworth and Bell might have employed to select their participants.

(d) The Strange Situation has been accused of lacking validity. Explain what this means in the context of this study.

(e) How could you assess the reliability of the Strange Situation?

(f) Identify one ethical issue arising from this research.

STABILITY OF ATTACHMENTS TYPES

Waters (1978) – a secure attachment in infancy remains at 12–18 months for those in stable caring relationships.

Vaughn et al (1979) – infants experiencing change (i.e. stressful experiences) may change from secure to insecure attachments.

Waters et al (2000) – adults received the same attachment type on an adult attachment test as they did when 12 months old in the Strange Situation.

Lewis et al (2000) – in a longitudinal study, 1 year olds were followed up at 18 years old and found that changes could occur in attachment patterns, especially in those who experienced negative life events.

WHAT INFLUENCES THE DEVELOPMENT OF SECURE AND INSECURE ATTACHMENTS?

MATERNAL SENSITIVITY

Responding to the needs of the child, says Bowlby, is very important in developing attachments. More secure attachments form with more sensitive caregivers.

Ainsworth et al (1978) – attachment is closely related to mothers' sensitivity to the needs of the child (the *sensitivity hypothesis*).

Other studies recognise that it is not just maternal sensitivity that matters, other factors play a role, e.g. positive parental attitude.

INFANT TEMPERAMENT

Thomas and Chess (1977) claim babies can be categorised according to their temperaments:

1 Easy babies.

2 Difficult babies.

3 Slow-to-warm-up babies.

Difficult and slow-to-warm-up babies are harder to cope with and this affects the emotional bond between them.

Kagan (1984) – His t*emperament hypothesis* states that the quality of attachment depends mainly on the temperament of the child.

This is supported by Hsu et al (2006) who found that type of attachment is associated with the temperament of the child.

Vaughn and Bost (1999) – a meta analysis showed only small and inconsistent links between temperament and attachment. Temperament does not directly cause differences in attachment but may cause stress in the carer, which may itself influence attachment.

EMOTIONAL AVAILABILITY

This is the quality of emotional interaction between mother and child; it is an *exchange* of interactions. The parent needs to *understand* the emotional experience of the child and respond accordingly.

Beringen et al (2005) – children in emotionally available relationships were more likely to form secure attachments and also have better peer relationships.

ASK AN EXAMINER

This material on this page expands your understanding and knowledge of attachment. Remember, a good understanding of psychology is needed in order to get top marks in the exam. Really knowing your stuff gives you an appreciation and comprehension of the material, which allows you to write and speak with confidence. Do yourself a favour and do more than simply learn and regurgitate facts and figures. It might not be the easiest option, but it is the best one.

HOW SCIENCE WORKS

Think about the importance of quality in day care.

We can investigate this with the observational technique of content analysis.

● Research what is meant by quality in day care and operationalise it by drawing up a checklist of behavioural categories.

● Search the internet for websites advertising day care centres (choose at least five).

● Use your checklist to analyse and record the content of each website.

● Present the data gathered from the websites in the form of a bar chart.

Things to consider

● From your bar chart, what aspects of quality are most frequently used in day care centre adverts? What aspect of quality on your checklist appears least? Does your data suggest that day care centres are recognising the importance of quality?

● How could you check the reliability of this research?

● How could your selection of websites have introduced bias into this research? What would you do in future research to avoid this?

HOW SCIENCE WORKS

Think about types of attachment.

Imagine that you are a researcher conducting a study into types of attachment.

You have decided to conduct a naturalistic observation of toddlers being left at nursery for the first time by their primary caregiver.

You will need to observe their behaviour: 1) on being left by their caregiver, 2) for the duration of their stay, and 3) on being collected by the caregiver.

● The variable you are measuring is attachment behaviour – how are you going to operationalise this variable? Carefully operationalising this variable will create behavioural categories.

● Use the behavioural categories to draw an example of the data collection sheet you would use at each phase of the observation.

● For this research you are going to employ both event sampling and time sampling. Explain why and when you will use each method.

● Explain how observer bias could occur in this research.

● Identify ethical issues with this research and suggest ways of dealing with them.

● Describe how you would ensure observer reliability.

CULTURE AND ATTACHMENT

Do attachments vary by culture? Bowlby says that they are universal (they do not vary), but different cultures may achieve attachments in different ways. We can think of cultural differences in broad terms: an individualist culture is one where importance is placed on individual achievement, whilst a collectivist culture is where importance is placed on the social group. Some aspects of culture may well influence attachments.

CULTURAL DIFFERENCES IN ...

... LONG-TERM GOALS OF CHILD REARING

Collectivist cultures emphasise social cooperation, compliance, etc. as a goal of child-rearing. Individualist cultures, on the other hand, emphasise individual achievement and independence.

Caroson and Harwood (2003) – Puerto Rican families (collectivist) have a strong sense of community. Lots of physical control seen in child-rearing of securely attached children; in contrast to Ainsworth who saw this as indicating an insecure attachment.

... THE WAYS THAT PARENTS RESPOND TO CHILDREN'S NEEDS

Child-rearing practices are passed down through generations and satisfy cultural needs.

True et al (2001) – the Dogon (from Mali) keep their children very close at all times, explaining why there is very little insecure attachment, but lots of insecure disorganised attachment. The high infant mortality rate creates a fear of separation in mothers, and this affects the type of attachment seen in infants.

... HOW CHILDREN AND CAREGIVERS ARE VALUED

The relationship between child and specific caregiver is valued in some cultures more than others.

Tronick et al (1992) – children of the Efe people of Zambia spend up to 60% of their time with women other than their mothers. The bonds they form with multiple caregivers are as strong as those formed in Western cultures with children and single carers.

ASK AN EXAMINER

Using specific examples of how cultures vary in attachment can add a lot to an exam answer. It shows that you not only understand that cultures do vary but also how they vary and even why.

Apply Your Knowledge

A psychologist intends to conduct cross-cultural research into attachment and has moved with her family from Britain to Japan. She is having problems finding a nursery place for her 8-month-old baby.

(a) Use what you know of culture and attachment to explain the problem of finding a nursery place. (*2 marks*)

(b) Explain the difficulty that the psychologist might have using the Strange Situation in her research. (*4 marks*)

The amae study – Rothenbaun et al (2007)

The researchers wanted to investigate the difference between Japanese and US perceptions of secure attachment with reference to amae – a special kind of bond unique to Japanese parents and infants.

How did they do it? A semi-structured interview was constructed in Japanese and English in the two different cultures.

What did they find? Cultural similarities:

● Children with 'desirable' characteristics perceived as securely attached in both cultures, with the most desirable children being those with responsive mothers.

Cultural differences:

● Japanese mothers focused on social roles as being desirable, American mothers on individual achievement.
● In the Strange Situation, Japanese mothers less likely to see exploration as desirable.
● A child's demanding behaviour regarded as indicating interdependence by Japanese mothers (reflecting the desire for amae), and attention seeking by Americans.

Take a closer look: ● There were sampling problems. The size of the sample was relatively small. Families were approached to take part (not at random). Families from different cultures were not matched.

● Interviews were used, providing self-report data, asking how they or their children might respond in different situations. This may have been misleading and observing them may have been better.

CULTURAL BIAS – A JAPANESE PERSPECTIVE

Rothenbaum et al (2000) argue that the concepts of attachment are rooted in a Western perspective. It is a Western idea and reflects Western cultures, ideals and norms. Three aspects of attachment theory show particular bias.

THE SENSITIVITY HYPOTHESIS

Western: attachment patterns arise because of sensitive and responsive caring to develop independence and autonomy.

Japanese: responsiveness and sensitivity are used to encourage closer dependency on the mother and to control infant emotions.

THE SECURE BASE HYPOTHESIS

Western: a healthy attachment is one where the child has a secure base, encouraging exploration and eventual *individuation*.

Japanese: *dependency* is more desirable. *Amae* encourages closeness and interdependence, both classed in the West as undesirable anxious-resistant characteristics.

THE COMPETENCE HYPOTHESIS

Western: *social competence* results from a secure attachment, with children showing self-expression, autonomy and emotional openness.

Japanese: *social competence* is viewed not as individual achievement but as group accomplishment and reliance. Individual behaviour and emotional openness would be frowned upon.

CULTURAL DIFFERENCES IN THE STRANGE SITUATION

Van IJzendoorn and Kroonenberg (1988) – a meta-analysis of 32 studies from eight countries found that Type B (secure attachment) was most common, with Type C least common (the standard pattern).

Type C was most common and Type A least common in Israel and Japan. Highest Type A attachment was found in Germany.

They found a greater variation in attachment patterns within cultures than between cultures.

The high rate of Type A attachment in Germany may be due to the high value placed on independence and self-reliance in that culture.

The high rate of Type C attachment found in Japan may be due to a child-rearing practice where mother and child are rarely apart for the first 12 months.

Evaluation

● It used limited studies (32) and 18 of them were from the US. Only one was from China. Care should be taken when generalising these results.

● Using the Strange Situation in different cultures is not necessarily appropriate. It was designed in the US and reflects the customs of the US, not other cultures.

● All 32 studies took part in countries exposed to Western media and child-rearing practices.

	No of studies	Secure (Type B)	Avoidant (Type A)	Resistant (Type C)
UK	1	75	22	3
USA	18	65	21	14
NETHERLANDS	4	67	26	7
WEST GERMANY	3	57	35	8
ISRAEL	2	64	7	29
SWEDEN	1	74	22	4
JAPAN	2	68	5	27
CHINA	1	50	25	25
Average		65	21	14

ASK AN EXAMINER

The Van IJzendoorn and Kroonenberg study is a very well-known one in psychology and it is well worthwhile putting effort into understanding it. Two key things to get from this study are: 1) Cultures differ from each other in terms of attachment types and 2) even within cultures there are differences in attachments.

Apply Your Knowledge

'Would the mother of Maddy please come to the customer services desk where she will find her lovely little girl.' A 2-year-old girl has got lost in a supermarket.

(a) What type of attachment is Maddy most likely to have? (*1 mark*)

(b) Outline the attachment behaviour you might expect from Maddy if she had the type of attachment you identified in (a). (*3 marks*)

DISRUPTION OF ATTACHMENTS

Attachments can sometimes be disrupted and these children find themselves growing up outside the traditional family environment. Not forming attachments can also have serious consequences for the development of the child.

DISRUPTION

Bowlby (1951) – long-term emotional and social stability depends on an infant forming an attachment with the mother within a *critical period*. Failure to do so is described as *maternal deprivation*.

Bowlby (1944) – 44 Thieves Study showed that, of children referred to a behavioural clinic because they were thieves, 85% were *maternally deprived*, and showed signs of *affectionless psychopathy*.

Freud and Dann (1951) – children who grew up in a Nazi concentration camp without adult care showed no signs of affectionless psychopathy. They appeared to benefit from attachments to each other.

FOSTER CARE

Periods in often-temporary foster care may have implications for emotional development. Forming attachment to temporary carers may be difficult because:

1 Previous experiences may have caused resistant, avoidant or disorganised attachments to develop, which will influence any new relationships.

2 When fostered, there are disruptions of the primary attachment. This can lead to problems like, among other things, withdrawal, all influencing the formation of new attachments.

Tyrell and Dozier (1998) – timing of separation is important. The greatest problems were with children fostered after 12 months.

Dozier et al (2001) – the carer's state of mind is important. Those who can process their *own* attachment experiences properly (*autonomous carers*) are more likely to foster securely attached children.

PREMATURE BIRTH

Premature babies are likely to be smaller, more fragile, cry weakly and are less responsive than full-term babies. They are harder to comfort and the social releasers encouraging closeness with the caregiver are often weak or absent. They may also have more medical problems and procedures, regularly interrupting contact with the caregiver.

DiVitto and Goldberg (1995) – mothers behave differently towards premature babies; for instance they are over-attentive.

Plunkett et al (1988) – higher than normal percentage of insecure attachments are found in premature infants.

Minde (1999) – stability of attachments in preterm infants is not strong. At 12 months they may be Type B (secure) but at 4 years they may be Type D.

Goldberg (2000) – the over-attentiveness of mothers to preterm children only happens on 'reunion' after separation and it disappears by 12–18 months, where the relationship becomes similar to that of full-term babies.

Apply Your Knowledge

'Operation Pied Piper' involved children being evacuated from six British cities deemed vulnerable to German bombing. In September 1939, 1.9 million children gathered at rail stations not knowing where they were going or if they would be split from brothers and sisters gathered with them.

From what you have learned about attachment, assess the possible effects of this experience on the children involved. (*4 marks*)

FAILURE TO FORM ATTACHMENTS

Rutter distinguishes between *deprivation* (where there has been an attachment but it has been disrupted) and *privation* (where no attachment has formed). Privation is more serious than deprivation.

Privation is unusual but can sometimes be seen in children raised in *institutionalised care*.

Gunnar et al (2000) – levels of privation in institutions:

1 Lack of attention to basic needs, e.g. nutrition, hygiene and medical care.

2 Lack of environmental stimulation, including social stimulation.

3 Lack of opportunity to form relationships and develop an attachment with a consistent caregiver.

EFFECTS OF INSTITUTIONALISATION

Group day care or 'institutionalised care' may cause problems for emotional development, particularly if the institutions are inadequate (e.g. Gunnar et al). There may, for example, be a need to change staff regularly (in the evenings and at weekends), so consistent caregivers are few and far between.

Early research
Goldfarb (1943) – their research found that children who were immediately fostered at birth were much more socially skilled than those who had experienced three years of institutionalised care first.

Tizard and Hodges (1978) – investigated the long-term effects of institutionalised care. Those adopted from care scored better on cognitive, behavioural and social development tests than those remaining in care. However, problems persisted in the institutionalised children's social relationships, such as inability to form close relationships, indiscriminate friendliness, attention-seeking and poor peer relationships.

Rutter et al (2007) found that the effects of early institutionalisation persisted later in life. Those who stayed in care longest had the most problems, even though they had been adopted for seven years by this stage.

ASK AN EXAMINER

Be very sure to recognise the difference between disruption of attachment *and* failure to form attachment, *as both could appear in the exam and require quite different responses from you. Get them mixed up and it will cost you. You have been warned!*

Apply Your Knowledge

Russian institutions are bursting with children abandoned at birth. They now total more than 600,000 children and are defined by the state as being 'without parental care'.

What might be the long-term effects of this kind of early experience? (*4 marks*)

General evaluation institutionalised care research
● We don't know whether adopted groups and institutionalised groups differed in any other ways, so interpretation of the results is difficult. Prematurity, birth weight and parental alcohol exposure, for instance, may have had effects.

● The extent of privation experienced before adoption is hard to assess.

● The tests used may not have been sensitive enough to reveal subtle problems of cognitive processing. Because language is used differently after institutionalisation (not really used much for emotional expression), any tests that use language may not have sufficient sensitivity, or the results may be misleading.

STUDY IN FOCUS

Early global privation and cognitive competence
O'Connor et al (2000)

What were they doing and why? The English and Romanian Adoptees (ERA) study follows the development of 165 Romanian children adopted between February 1990 and September 1992. All had experienced severe privation whilst in institutional care before their adoption. This study was a follow-up to a previous study which investigated the effects of early experience on cognitive development at age 4.

How did they do it? This was a natural experiment. That is, different groups of participants are chosen – some that have been exposed to privation and some that have not.

The sample was as follows.

WHEN WERE THEY ADOPTED?	NUMBER OF CHILDREN	WHERE WERE THEY FROM?
Between 0 and 6 months	58	Romania
Between 7 and 24 months	59	Romania
Between 24 and 42 months	48	Romania
Between 0 and 6 months	52	UK

Most of the children were originally from **Romania** and had experienced privation in their early development. The group of children from the **UK** was a comparison group. The children in this group had differing backgrounds but none had experienced privation.

Assessment at age 4
A semi-structured interview was carried out, with the adoptive parents, about attachment signs and behavioural problems and children themselves were assessed for intellectual functioning.

Assessment at age 6
The interviews with adoptive parents were repeated and the children given further tests for intellectual functioning.

What did they find? Cognitive performance at 4 and 6 years was related to the amount of time the children had spent in institutions before their adoption.

Children adopted before 6 months scored similarly to UK adoptees.

Children aged between 6 and 24 months at adoption had slightly below average scores.

Children aged over 24 months at adoption showed the greatest impairment.

● There was also a strong relationship at both 4 and 6 years between the **duration of institutional care** and **attachment quality**. It seems that the later the adoption (or in other words the longer the institutional care) the greater was the risk of insecure attachment and attachment disorder.

● Romanian children aged less than 24 months at adoption had 'caught up' with the UK comparison group in terms of cognitive ability by the age of 4 years but showed little evidence of further gain between 4 and 6 years. Where there was catch-up this was most evident in children who were particularly impaired at 4 years of age.

STUDY IN FOCUS cntd

● Recovery in physical development was very strong and nearly complete in most of the Romanian children, with a few persistent problems. There was no clear evidence that physical deprivation was related to cognitive performance.

● Many of the Romanian children demonstrated an inattention/overactivity behavioural disorder.

HOW SCIENCE WORKS

(a) Suggest an appropriate aim for this study.

(b) Why was it necessary for O'Connor et al to conduct a natural experiment?

(c) In the context of this study, identify one weakness with natural experiments.

(d) One technique for gathering information used by O'Connor et al was a semi-structured interview.
  (i) What is a semi-structured interview?
  (ii) State one advantage for O'Connor et al in conducting an interview.
  (iii) What kind of data would an interview generate?
  (iv) Why do you think they conducted an interview rather than give out a questionnaire?

(e) The O'Connor et al study found a strong relationship between duration of institutionalised care and attachment quality. This kind of relationship is indicated by the graph below.

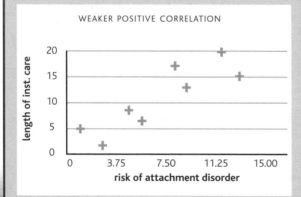

(i) What is the name given to this kind of graph?

(ii) What kind of research technique seeks to find relationships between two or more variables?

(iii) What kind of relationship is this graph showing?

(f) Why did O'Connor et al use a comparison group of UK-born children?

(g) Identify one ethical issue arising from this research.

DAY CARE

Many parents work and leave their children in the care of nurseries, childminders, relatives, etc. Childcare experiences are likely to influence social behaviours, from being shy or insecure to being self-confident and assertive, socially skilful or aggressive.

THE IMPACT OF DAY CARE ON SOCIAL DEVELOPMENT

Research indicates that an important factor determining children's social development and hence their *peer relations* is the quality of their environment.

Clarke-Stewart et al (1994) compared the experiences of children in home care (e.g. looked after by a parent or childminder) with those in centre care (e.g. nursery or pre-school group). They found that social competence was related to both quality and quantity of day care.

Being around a variety of children in day care results in more positive interactions with friends outside of day care, such as playing, cooperating, showing affection and reduced aggression. They also gain from having some home care.

CENTRE CARE – QUALITY
Children given some independence, e.g. had less direct contact and guidance during play from caregiver. Such children interacted more with peers, thus developing social skills.

HOME CARE – QUALITY
Children given more attention by caregiver, e.g. playing, direct contact and talking. The caregiver was the main source of interaction, developing the social skills of the child.

CENTRE CARE – QUANTITY
The children spending most time in centre care (hours a week and number of months) showed poorest development of social competence.

HOME CARE – QUANTITY
The more home care, the better the development of social competence.

FURTHER EVIDENCE OF THE IMPORTANCE OF QUALITY IN DAY CARE FOR SOCIAL DEVELOPMENT

Phillips et al (1987) – children attending high-quality day care centres were rated as more cooperative, sociable and confident, less dependent and engaged in less negative play.

Anderson (1989) – the more quality day care a child receives, the greater the social competence.

Field (1991) – day care is most beneficial when there is a combination of quantity and quality. High-quality day care results in better social relationships during teens. They are rated as more attractive, popular, having higher self-esteem, greater leadership and assertiveness, and less aggressive.

Some research suggests that day care can have negative effects on social development, for example it might lead to increased *aggression*.

Vlietstra (1981)	**Belsky et al (2001)**	**Haskins (1985)**
2½ and 4½-year-old children attending full-day pre-school care were less sociable and more aggressive with peers than those attending half-day pre-school day care.	Found that the more time children spent in day care, the more likely they were to be aggressive during the early primary school years.	Found that children who began centre-based day care during the first year of life showed greater levels of aggression than those who started later in life.

Belsky et al (2007) suggest the effects of day care might emerge later in life in the form of negative behaviour. Long hours spent in day care are related to problem behaviour in the early teens.

Kopp (1982) suggests that day care disrupts cognitive development so that a child's ability to regulate behaviour is reduced.

Children who experience high-quantity and low-quality day care are less able than others either to control aggressive behaviour or initiate alternative responses.

Not everyone agrees with the link between day care and aggressive behaviour.

According to Borge et al (2004), childcare effects are different for different social groups. Increases in aggression are not due to day care but related to family circumstances.

According to Bradley and Vandell (2007), 'childcare experiences interact with experiences at home and the child's own characteristics'.

Arsenio (2004) – there is conflicting evidence regarding whether or not day care is responsible for aggressive behaviour because the various studies operationalise aggression in different ways. For example, Clarke-Stewart (1989) says that a benefit of day care (e.g. greater independence and assertiveness) might sometimes be interpreted as a cost (e.g. aggression).

ASK AN EXAMINER

The specification says that you need to know about the impact of different forms of day care on social development. A question might be quite broad therefore and ask you about social development, in which case you can talk about either aggression or peer relations or both. However, a question might focus specifically on either of these two, in which case you have to be quite focused in your response. Aggression and peer relations are related factors of course – for example, aggression can be one aspect of peer relations. Whilst this might appear confusing at first, it really isn't. Only those who have not been careful and thorough in their preparation need be concerned!

Apply Your Knowledge

Having taken a short career break, Sinita has to return to work. She needs to put her 1-year-old son into a day care centre.

(a) What should Sinita be looking for in a good-quality day care centre? (*3 marks*)

(b) What benefits could there be for the child's social development? (*3 marks*)

STUDY IN FOCUS

Experiences of day care – A longitudinal study
Vandell et al (1988)

What were they doing and why? The researchers were interested in the long-term impact of day care experiences of varying quality. Are the effects of poor quality day care short lived, or does this kind of early experience have any long-term impact in the child's development?

How did they do it? This was **longitudinal** research. An **observational** method was used with 4-year-olds at day care centres and again when the same children were 8 years old during play sessions. The data gathered for behaviour at 4 years of age were part of a previous (1983) study by Vandell and Powers.

● *Observations at 4 years of age (from Vandell and Powers, 1983)*

A total of 20 children (ten boys and ten girls) were observed in a random order during a free play period at their day care centres at 20 second intervals for 16 minutes. The behavioural categories used in the observation were as follows:

– positive/negative interaction with peers
– positive/negative interaction with adults
– solitary play and unoccupied behaviour

● *Observations at 8 years (new observations)*

Children were videotaped through one-way glass for 45 minutes whilst engaged in prearranged triadic (i.e. three-child) play. The play was designed by the researchers to encourage social behaviour. Whilst the children were playing, the mothers completed a questionnaire about family circumstances and the child's day care history.

A behavioural checklist was completed for each child using the following behavioural categories:

● **Friendly** interactions (positive or neutral exchanges between two or more children)

● **Unfriendly** interactions (negative behaviours including sarcasm, negative actions, etc.)

● **Solitary** play (child plays alone with objects without communicating with peers, and not doing what another child is doing at the same time)

The child play observations were coded separately to the videotapes: A single-blind technique for controlling investigator effects was adopted, so that different observers and videotape coders were used and neither was aware of the children's day care history.

The reliability of the observations and behavioural checklist were checked by having different observers code a random selection of 35% of the children.

What did they find?
Correlational analysis of the data showed that:

Compared to children from poorer quality day care, children from better quality day care had **more friendly interactions** and **fewer unfriendly interactions** with peers, and were rated as more socially competent and happier.

There was a relationship between the 4-year-olds' behaviours in the day care centres and the children's functioning at 8 years:

● There was a positive correlation between positive interactions of 4-year-olds with adults and ratings of empathy, social competence and peer acceptance at 8 years.

STUDY IN FOCUS cntd

● There was a negative correlation between unoccupied (i.e. aimless) behaviour at 4 years and ratings of empathy, conflict resolution and social competence at 8 years.

HOW SCIENCE WORKS

(a) One finding from Vandell et al's study of day care appears in the graph below.

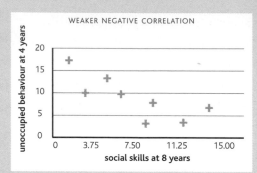

WEAKER NEGATIVE CORRELATION

unoccupied behaviour at 4 years

social skills at 8 years

(i) What kind of correlation does this scattergram show?

(ii) What conclusions can be drawn about day care from this scattergram?

(iii) In the context of this study, state one limitation of using correlational analysis.

(b) Identify the target population and suggest a suitable sampling technique for this study.

(c) (i) Suggest a suitable hypothesis for this study.

  (ii) Justify your choice of hypothesis as either directional or non-directional.

(d) Why did Vandell et al have different people analyse the child play observations and the play videotapes?

(e) Why might the researchers have conducted a pilot study?

(f) A single-blind technique was used to control investigator effects.

  (i) What is a single-blind control?

  (ii) What is meant by the term 'investigator effect'?

  (iii) Identify one investigator effect that the researchers were trying to control.

(g) Identify one possible ethical issue arising from this research.

(h) In the context of this study, explain the difference between reliability and validity.

(i) Identify one extraneous variable that was not controlled and explain how it might have influenced the results.

ASK AN EXAMINER

There is more than one way to answer questions that go something like 'explain how psychologists might research...' (watch out for variations in the wording!). One way is to outline the procedures of a study you have learned that has done what the question suggests. Another way is to take a more methodological approach and use your knowledge of a relevant research method to suggest a research design. Prepare well, be able to take either approach, and be guided by the question as to which is the best to take at the time.

Apply Your Knowledge

An educational psychologist is conducting research using primary school children. He has noticed that one child, Lucas, is particularly disruptive. School records show that Lucas attended a day care centre.

(a) What might the psychologist assume about Lucas's experience of day care? (*3 marks*)

(b) Explain how the psychologist might research the effects of day care on children. (*4 marks*)

IMPLICATIONS OF RESEARCH INTO ATTACHMENT FOR CHILDCARE PRACTICES

Beksky and Rovine (1988) – found that children who spent more than 20 hours a week in day care were more likely to be insecurely attached.

NICHD (2003) – study found that quality, quantity, age of entry, and type of day care had no significant effects on attachment quality.

Howes (1999) – the attachment relationship is a complex one.

● The primary attachment to the mother influences all other experiences. Any kind of non-parental care is always going to be less important than that of the primary caregiver.

● The child might be able to develop multiple attachments of equal importance, in which case good-quality childcare could serve a very important purpose in compensating for poor-quality home care.

Evidence
Programmes such as Headstart indicate that disadvantaged children can benefit from compensatory childcare.

NICHD (1997) – study found that the quality of parental care is more important than the quality of non-parental care, so although compensatory programmes can benefit disadvantaged children, they do not undo harms caused by poor-quality home care.

IMPLICATIONS OF RESEARCH INTO DAY CARE FOR CHILDCARE PRACTICES

The importance of quality of care a child receives has been highlighted by research.

Vandell and Powers (1983) – children attending high-quality day care centres are more likely to interact positively with others.

Features of GOOD-QUALITY centres

Well-trained teachers

Spacious accommodation

Lower enrolments

Lower adult–child ratios

Plentiful materials

GOOD

POOR

Features of POOR-QUALITY centres

Carers receive less training

Cramped and crowded accommodation

Higher enrolments

Higher adult–child ratios

Fewer materials

According to Clarke-Stewart (1989), whether or not childcare is provided in the home or in day care, *quality* is crucial.

FACTORS INDICATING GOOD QUALITY CHILDCARE

IN HOME CARE, MORE SOCIALLY COMPETENT CHILDREN...	IN DAY CARE, MORE SOCIALLY COMPETENT CHILDREN WERE FOUND IN CENTRES WHERE...
...were in more child-orientated physical settings (e.g. fewer hazards and less mess, more toys and less adult decoration)	...there were lower adult–child ratios
...were with fewer younger children	...they interacted with fewer peers who were older
...were offered more school-like activities and individual attention	...they spent more time watching and listening to older children
...had caregivers who were less controlling and demanding	...they spent more time in group activities with older children
...spent less time interacting with other children in the home setting	...they received more individual attention and discipline from the caregiver

Belsky et al (2007)

● The issue is whether children should receive non-parental care at all, not the quantity or quality of such care.

● Whilst high-quality childcare can have benefits, e.g. improved language skills, non-parental childcare of any sort can result in problem behaviours later in life.

● They found that the more time children spent in non-parental care from birth to pre-school, the more problem behaviours were observed in early adolescence, such as arguing, disobedience and aggression.

Apply Your Knowledge

A child psychologist has been asked to give advice to a company that wants to set up a good-quality day care centre.

(a) From what you know of the implications of research into attachment for childcare practices, what advice might she offer? (*3 marks*)

(b) From what you know of the implications of research into day care for childcare practices, what advice might she offer? (*3 marks*)

Check your knowledge

1 Identify **three** behaviours typical of a securely attached child. (*3 marks*)

2 What is meant by the term 'insecure attachment'? (*2 marks*)

3 Identify **four** behaviours typical of a securely attached child. (*4 marks*)

4 Define the term 'attachment'. (*2 marks*)

5 What is meant by the term 'privation'. (*2 marks*)

6 How does privation differ from a disrupted attachment? (*2 marks*)

7 What would you conclude from Ainsworth's study of attachment? (*3 marks*)

8 Explain how psychologists have investigated types of attachment. (*4 marks*)

9 How does learning theory explain attachment? (*5 marks*)

10 Describe Bowlby's theory of attachment. (*5 marks*)

11 (a) Outline the main features of the evolutionary perspective of attachment. (*5 marks*)

(b) Give **one** strength and **one** limitation of this theory. (*2 + 2 marks*)

12 State **two** ways in which attachments can vary across cultures. (*2 marks*)

13 Outline what **one** study has shown about cultural variations in attachment. (*4 marks*)

14 Explain how psychologists have investigated cultural variations in attachment. (*4 marks*)

15 Outline what research has shown about the effects of institutionalisation. (*5 marks*)

16 Give **two** examples of ways in which attachments might be disrupted. (*2 + 2 marks*)

17 State the findings of **one** study into the effects of day care on social development. (*4 marks*)

18 (a) What is 'day care'? (*2 marks*)

(b) State **two** forms of day care. (*2 marks*)

19 What has research told us about the effects of day care on:

(a) Aggression (*4 marks*)

(b) Peer relations (*4 marks*)

20 Outline **two** implications of research into day care for childcare practices. (*3 + 3 marks*)

The extended written response

Describe and evaluate evolutionary explanations of attachment. *(12 marks)*

The evolutionary perspective assumes that attachment evolved because it improves the chances of survival. An attachment ensures that a young animal has a regular source of food and receives protection. Because it is more likely to survive, there is an increased chance that it will grow to pass on its genes to the next generation. This perspective considers humans to be complex animals so therefore the same evolutionary principles apply to humans.

> The question asks for a description of the evolutionary perspective, and here it is! There is a lot more that could be said, of course, but always remember the limited space available. The key points must be communicated as accurately and succinctly as possible.

According to Lorenz, the young of precocial species have an instinct to recognise and follow a caregiver very soon after birth. This bonding helps them survive what is a very vulnerable time in life. He claimed that there was a critical period during which this bonding (which he called 'imprinting') occurs and that animals that do not properly imprint were unlikely to survive very long.

> This is continuing to describe the evolutionary perspective but now it is a bit more focused, giving a brief summary of a particular evolutionary explanation of attachment. The two paragraphs add up to about the limit of what could be expected for a six mark description of the evolutionary perspective.

The idea that early bonding experience is important is supported by Harlow. He removed infant monkeys from their mothers soon after birth and raised them with surrogate wire or cloth covered 'mothers'. He found that this early experience had long-term consequences. For example, whilst their physical health was unaffected, they had problems with emotional development. As adults they had poor social and parenting skills. Harlow said that the monkeys had experienced maternal deprivation.

> This paragraph is giving research support for the evolutionary perspective. Harlow is used here – rather than endlessly described it is used as evaluation. Notice that the word 'supported' is used to make this material evaluative. This is a good example of how something can be used as description or evaluation – how information is used determines how it is credited. You must think about how you want something marked, not just about what to write.

The research of Lorenz and Harlow was supported by Bowlby, who applied their ideas to the human infant–caregiver relationship. Bowlby argued that infants have an instinct to form an attachment to one caregiver (this is called monotropy) and that the quality of this relationship is important for healthy psychological development. Care is encouraged by the infant through signalling behaviours, e.g. smiling and crying.

There might be a big temptation to write lots about something just because it has been learned, and this is a good example of that. There is lots that could be written about Bowlby, but his theory is only being used as evaluation here so this temptation must be resisted. Just enough has been written here to show how Bowlby has applied the evolutionary perspective to humans.

Bowlby's evolutionary perspective has been very influential and has stimulated a great deal of research. However, it has been questioned whether or not the findings of research into lower animals could or should be applied directly to humans. Humans are far more complex than other animals in their feelings and emotions. Some of Bowlby's core concepts have also been questioned, for example he over-emphasised the importance of attachment to one person since research shows that children are capable of multiple attachments.

The end of the available space is very near here, just enough room to add a couple of sentences to grab as many of those evaluation marks as possible. You have some extra lines on the exam paper – if you have the time and something to say, use them!

COMMENTS

This is about as simply organised as an answer could be. The question asked for a description and evaluation and that is exactly what was given – the first half of the essay described the evolutionary perspective, the second half offered some evaluation. Having used the planning space to really plan the essay, appropriate material was selected at the right kind of depth of detail for the top mark band. Because the response was logical, focused and organised, the material looks as though it is used effectively. Fairly 'open' questions like this might trigger a 'big' response from some people. After all, evolution theory is a pretty big topic! The trick here is to be selective – pick three or four things to include in the answer that can be described. This will give the answer a sense of breadth and depth which is needed for the top mark band.

The question doesn't ask for Bowlby's theory. In fact, it allows a fairly broad description of the evolutionary perspective and much more detail of the research by Lorenz and Harlow could be included. However, even though the question doesn't explicitly refer to research with humans, the use of the word 'attachment' in the question does imply it. (This kind of behaviour is usually referred to as bonding or imprinting when it is applied to animals.) It is probably a good idea to always refer to human attachment in an essay, even if the focus of research is animal. In this essay, Bowlby's theory was used to do this.

A similar alternative question might actually ask for Bowlby's evolutionary explanation, in which case his theory would be the focus of the description and evaluation, and anything else would be used as evaluation.

In The News

Day care is bad for babies - Biddulph: PARENT TRAP

IT'S A tough call and one that no working parent will want to hear: childcare used "too much, too early, too long" damages babies' brain chemistry and affects their social and emotional development.

But when the warning is delivered by a parenting guru and psychologist with 30 years' experience – and 4 million book sales under his belt – ignoring the message may not be an option. Previously an advocate of quality childcare, author Steve Biddulph has spent the past five years examining and distilling the results of national and international studies of infants in long day care.

In a new book, Raising Babies – Should under 3s go to Nursery?, he argues that this growing international body of work combined with neurobiological research clearly suggests that at least during the first two years of life, brain development unfolds at its optimum with one-to-one care. This care could be from mother, father, a loving relative or, if necessary, a single, attentive paid carer.

Significant among the reams of research are the so-called cortisol studies which measured the presence of stress hormones in young babies and consistently found these levels to be higher in children in long day care. These have been linked with greater aggression and anxiety found in older children in long day care but are also known to affect the development of a range of neurotransmitters, whose pathways in the brain are still being built. These permanent brain changes are now thought by scientists and psychiatrists to affect the way the child will react to stress, anxiety and negative feelings in later life.

"This book presents much objective evidence, but it also carries a strong professional opinion for which I don't apologise," writes Biddulph. "It is likely that some people will feel angry after reading this book and it will be unsettling for those who feel trapped by economic circumstances into placing their babies and toddlers into nurseries when they would rather not. But my responsibility as a psychologist and educator is to be honest, and convey current findings and knowledge without gloss or deception."

In his author's foreword, Biddulph writes he was initially "afraid to release this book … its message was so confrontational, so against the tide".

But when his own and fellow psychologists' disquiet began to be matched by research and this was coupled with the burgeoning trend towards corporatisation of childcare and the imposition of profit over quality, he decided it was time to speak up: "I had started out as a believer in the ideal of quality nursery care and the role it played in allowing women to broaden their lives … but the more I saw of the reality of day-care centres and nurseries and the more conversations I had with parents and carers, it became clear to me that the reality never matched the fantasy.

"The best nurseries struggle to meet the needs of very young children in a group setting. The worst were negligent, frightening and bleak: a nightmare of bewildered loneliness that was heartbreaking to watch.

"Children at this age – under three – want one thing only: the individual care of their own special person. Even the best run nurseries cannot offer this." Biddulph says the invention of childcare has been necessary, thanks to the harried nature of modern life. Whether motivated by idealism or corporate greed, it aimed to "slot messy and needy young children into the new economic system, while at the same time reassuring us that it is good for them, socially and educationally".

childcare is now so well marketed, he writes, that even parents at home have begun to feel that they might not be as good for their babies as the "professionals".

"The critical, rarely mentioned core of nursery care is that our children will be looked after in bulk — on a 1:5 or 1:8 ratio, compared to 1:1 at home. Like

McDonald's fast food, we can enjoy the convenience of drive-through, ready-made, fast-parenting; through the miracle of mass production."

Biddulph believes the rapid adoption of childcare in the early years has been a huge social experiment, a gamble by parents that "everything will be OK". But the results of that experiment are now emerging and the worldwide epidemic of teenage depression, anxiety and substance abuse suggests all may not be well.

"Society has become

more materialist and fatally neglected the place of caring ... governments have failed to protect families from corporate pressures and many people can no longer afford to care for their own children," Biddulph writes.

"Quality care appropriate to very young children does not exist. It is a fantasy of the glossy magazines. If your heart has been uneasy about these things, it is probably right. [But] you can find a better way."

Paola Totaro
Sydney Morning Herald
March 18, 2006 Saturday
First Edition

CARE OPTIONS IN ORDER OF PREFERENCE:

1 Engage a close relative or friend who you trust and who loves your child.

2 Employ a trustworthy family day carer you know personally.

3 Find a quality day care centre with stable staff you can get to know and about whom you feel comfortable.

WHAT'S BEST BY AGE:

0–1 No childcare at all. Keep baby with parent, relative (or trusted babysitter for short breaks).

1–2 One short day with a trusted carer. Ideally a one-on-one carer-to-child ratio; one-to-three at most.

2–3 Two short days a week with a trusted carer. Building up to short days in a quality centre but only if the child settles well.

3–4 Up to three short days or half days in quality care.

4–5 Up to four short days or half days in quality care.

Stretch and Challenge

1 What does Biddulph suggest about the optimum time for brain development?

2 Why do you think that Biddulph believes some people might feel angry after reading his book?

3 The arguments around the effects of day care are complex. For example, the age at which a child starts day care seems to be an important factor.

(a) Identify four other factors that impact upon a child's experience of day care.

(b) Explain the impact of two of these factors.

Stretch and Challenge cntd

4 One conclusion that Biddulph comes to is that long-term separation from the primary caregiver, especially during the first year of life, can be damaging for a child.

(a) Name the theory of attachment being referred to by Biddulph.

(b) What elements of this theory can you identify in the article?

THE EXTENDED WRITTEN RESPONSE – ADDITIONAL QUESTIONS

1 Discuss research into the effects of institutionalisation. (*12 marks*)

2 Outline and evaluate **two or more** explanations of attachment (*12 marks*)

3 Discuss the implications of research into day care for childcare practices. (*12 marks*)

4 'Bowlby developed his theory of attachment on the basis that the features of attachment are universal – that is, they apply to all human beings in all cultures.'

Discuss cultural variations in attachment. (*12 marks*)

Example answers to these questions can be found at www.askanexaminer.com

USEFUL WEBSITES

http://psychology.about.com/od/loveandattraction/ss/attachmentstyle_2.htm
Ainsworth's Strange Situation has been used in researching attachment for many years. Here you'll find a useful description of it.

http://nobelprize.org/nobel_prizes/medicine/laureates/1973/lorenz-autobio.html
The life of Konrad Lorenz, whose work on imprinting is extremely important in the area of attachment.

http://darwin-online.org.uk/
Sometimes the internet reveals itself as a priceless and wonderful resource. This is one of those times. These are the original writings of Charles Darwin. Some are a little tricky to get your head around, but take some time. The illustrations are particularly interesting.

http://psychclassics.yorku.ca/Harlow/love.htm

Harry Harlow's thinking on the psychology of love. This paper contains his original thinking and some images from his research.

www.psychology.sunysb.edu/attachment/online/inge_origins.pdf

This paper draws together a lot of thinking on human attachment. In particular, the work of John Bowlby and Mary Ainsworth are discussed.

http://nobelprize.org/educational_games/medicine/pavlov/readmore.html

Read about Ivan Pavlov and then see if you can make his dog dribble on demand! This isn't just for fun; it's really about classical conditioning, part of learning theory and one way to think about human attachment.

http://www.youtube.com/watch?v=I_ctJqjlrHA

Watch as B. F. Skinner and his team describe how pigeons in the famous 'skinner box' can be trained to respond to stimuli. This is operant conditioning, another way to think about how attachment behaviours are learned.

http://www.attachmentacrosscultures.org/research/index.html

Here you'll find a summary of a great deal of work on how attachment varies across cultures.

http://www.relieffundforromania.co.uk/romanian_orphans.html

A description of the psychological problems experienced by a large number of children from Romanian orphanages can be found here, along with an informative perspective of their situation.

http://socialbaby.blogspot.com/2007/04/richard-bowlby-stress-in-daycare.html

This comes from Sir Richard Bowlby, son of the great John Bowlby. As you can see, Sir Richard has an interest in his father's work too.

Section 4

Biological
Psychology – Stress

WHAT YOU NEED TO KNOW

Biological Psychology is in Unit 2 of the specification. You are expected to develop your knowledge and understanding of Biological Psychology, including concepts, theories and studies. This includes a knowledge and understanding of research methods and ethical issues as they relate to this area of psychology. You also need to develop the skills of analysis, evaluation and application. Rather than just recall and reproduce information, you are expected to be able to apply your knowledge and understanding. The subject content is split into two parts:

Stress as a bodily response

- The body's response to stress, including the pituitary-adrenal system and the sympathomedullar pathway
- Stress-related illness and the immune system

Stress in everyday life

- Life changes and daily hassles
- Stress and work
- Stress and personality, including Type A behaviour
- Emotion-focused and problem-focused approaches to coping with stress
- Stress management, including psychological methods (cognitive behavioural therapy) and physiological methods (drugs)

THE BODY'S RESPONSE TO STRESS

When we are stressed, our bodies respond by preparing us for fight or flight. Our heart beats faster, our legs begin to shake a little as adrenaline is released, our stomach feels tight, our mouth dry and our palms may feel a little clammy.

The stress response involves the action of two major systems in the body: the nervous system and the endocrine system.

THE NERVOUS SYSTEM

- Divided into central and peripheral nervous systems (CNS and PNS).

- CNS – neurons in spinal cord and brain (responsible for thoughts and behaviours).

- PNS – neurons outside spinal cord and brain (carry information to and from the body).

- Autonomic nervous system (ANS) – part of the PNS. It operates automatically and controls involuntary aspects of behaviour.

- The ANS has two parts: *the sympathetic branch* is involved in arousing the body; *the parasympathetic branch* is involved in returning the body to a normal relaxed state.

THE ENDOCRINE SYSTEM

- System of glands that release hormones into the bloodstream.

- These hormones control many biological functions and behaviours, including stress.

- The pituitary gland is the master gland and influences all parts of this system.

- The adrenal gland releases important stress hormones such as corticosteroids, adrenaline and noradrenaline.

THE PITUITARY-ADRENAL SYSTEM

This is also known as the hypothalamic pituitary adrenal (or HPA) system. It is a chemical (i.e. hormone) based system and whilst fast is not as fast as the sympathomedullary pathway. It can be thought of as the mechanism that prolongs the stress response.

How it works
- A stressor is sensed and the hypothalamus (in the brain) readies the body for action (the fight or flight response).

- The hypothalamus signals the pituitary gland to release adrenocorticotrophic hormone (ACTH).

- The adrenal cortex detects ACTH and releases more hormones called corticosteroids.

- These have a range of effects on the body, including helping blood to clot, and influencing the sugar and salt levels in the blood.

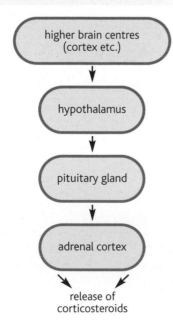

higher brain centres (cortex etc.)

↓

hypothalamus

↓

pituitary gland

↓

adrenal cortex

release of corticosteroids

THE SYMPATHOMEDULLARY PATHWAY

This system uses electricity (i.e. communication along nerve fibres) and is very fast indeed, faster than the chemical-based pituitary-adrenal system.

How it works

● Hypothalamus activates sympathetic branch of the ANS.

● The sympathetic branch sends a signal to the adrenal medulla.

● In response, the adrenal medulla releases adrenaline and noradrenaline.

● These contribute to the stress response e.g. increasing blood pressure and heart rate.

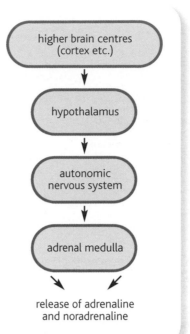

higher brain centres (cortex etc.)
↓
hypothalamus
↓
autonomic nervous system
↓
adrenal medulla
↓ ↓
release of adrenaline and noradrenaline

ASK AN EXAMINER

It is essential that you have a good knowledge not only of how the stress response starts, but also how it stops. Remember, the sympathetic branch arouses you, and the parasympathetic branch relaxes you. The arousal is explained by the pituitary-adrenal system and the sympathomedullary pathway – learn the various processes involved in each (a diagram is really helpful!).

Apply Your Knowledge

The athletes at the start of the race take their marks and prepare for the sound of the starter's pistol. 'BANG!' they're off!

(a) Identify one physical feeling that tells the athletes that they are feeling stressed. (*1 mark*)

(b) Explain how the physical feeling you identified in part (a) was generated by the body's response to stress. (*4 marks*)

STRESS-RELATED ILLNESS AND THE GAS

Hans Selye developed the General Adaptation Syndrome (GAS) to describe how our physical reactions to stress can lead to illness.

STAGE 1 – ALARM
The systems that deal with the stressor (pituitary-adrenal system and sympathomedullary pathway) are activated. The body becomes prepared to fight or run away. Heart rate increases and we become alert as our breathing and energy levels increase.

STAGE 2 – RESISTANCE
The body changes and adapts to any persistent stressor, arriving at a stable, long-term level of arousal. Longer-term use of hormones means that we begin to run out of them as the stressor persists or more stressors arrive.

STAGE 3 – EXHAUSTION
If the stress continues for an extended period of time our body's resources deplete and we become less able to deal with the stress. Our immune system becomes less efficient, we show signs of chronic stress and we can become ill.

STRESS-RELATED ILLNESS AND HEART DISEASE

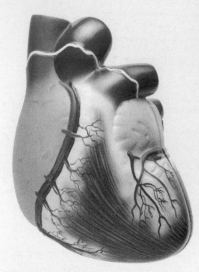

● Long-term stress and heart disease (cardiovascular disease) are related.

● Hypertension, or increased blood pressure, is part of the stress response, provided by the sympathomedullary pathway.

● Hormones that regulate salt and water in the blood also put strain on the heart.

● Long-term stress can mean that the blood vessels in the heart become permanently constricted.

● Coronary Heart Disease (CHD) caused by coronary atherosclerosis means that blood vessels become blocked up.

● Some stress hormones increase fatty acids that make this clogging-up worse.

ASK AN EXAMINER

Although you won't be asked a question specifically on stress and heart disease, it is very useful to know about when answering a general question on stress and illness. It gives you much more to write about, which is especially useful in questions requiring extended written responses.

Rosengren et al (1991) – Men who said they were stressed at the start of the study were more likely to have a heart attack within 11.8 years, suggesting a link between stress and cardiovascular disease.

STRESS-RELATED ILLNESS AND THE IMMUNE SYSTEM

● The immune system fights off invaders that cause disease (antigens).

● The cells in the system are leukocytes (white blood cells) called phagocytes and lymphocytes.

● Phagocytes are the first line of defence, providing a general barrier against antigens.

● Leukocytes are more focused and are a second line of defence against specific antigens.

● T-lymphocytes (T-cells) attack anything carrying disease in the body.

● B-lymphocytes (B-cells) are tuned to a particular antigen, and produce antibodies to destroy them.

● Immunosuppression is a reduction in the effectiveness of the immune system and can be caused by stress.

Arnetz et al (1991) – Reduced lymphocyte activity in farm labourers was associated with periods of stressful unemployment.

Fawzey et al (1993) – Cancer patients who reduced their stress through stress-management during illness showed higher immune system functioning six months after treatment and less likelihood of a recurrence of cancer six years later.

Irwin et al (1987) – Immune system of recently widowed women functioned at a lower level than age-matched women who had not experienced a stressful event.

The stressed medical students study – Kiecolt Glaser et al (1984)

The researchers wanted to know whether the immune system was influenced by *external stressors* such as examinations. The more T-cells in the blood stream, the more efficient the immune system.

How did they do it? Medical students gave blood at *low stress time* (a month before exams) and also at a *high stress time* (during exams). The blood was tested for T-cell content.

What did they find? During the exams the blood had lower NK (Natural Killer) cells, meaning that at times of high stress the immune system was less efficient at fighting disease.

Take a closer look:
- The research is correlational. The study only says that stress and illness are related in some way.
- There may be a sampling bias – different people respond to stress in different ways.
- It is a natural experiment, so whilst it is high in ecological validity, there may be extraneous variables influencing the results.

ASK AN EXAMINER

Having a basic understanding of what the immune system is and how it works is vital. It is especially important that you remember that illness results because stress has reduced the efficiency of the immune system in fighting infection, and you are able to support this if necessary by describing the findings of research.

Apply Your Knowledge

Jason always seems to have a cold at exam time. Just his luck!

Why might Jason be prone to colds around exams? (*4 marks*)

HOW SCIENCE WORKS

Logan and Ganster (2005) found that stress at work was linked to a sense of personal control. Part of their study involved giving out a questionnaire to employees. Their results are shown in the graph below.

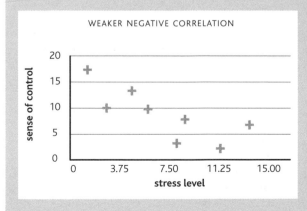

WEAKER NEGATIVE CORRELATION

sense of control (y-axis: 0, 5, 10, 15, 20)
stress level (x-axis: 0, 3.75, 7.50, 11.25, 15.00)

(a) (i) What kind of graph is this? (*1 mark*)

(ii) What does the graph tell us about the relationship between sense of control and stress? (*2 marks*)

(b) Give one weakness of using questionnaires in this type of research. (*2 marks*)

(c) What would you do to test the reliability of these findings? (*2 marks*)

(d) Describe one method psychologists have used to investigate the relationship between stress and the immune system. (*3 marks*)

PERSONALITY FACTORS

A 'type' of personality is one characterised by certain traits and patterns of behaviour. Research suggests that different personalities react to stressors in different ways.

PERSONALITY TYPES

Characteristics of two different personality types were described by Friedman and Rosenman (1975) and Rosenman et al (1975) in the Western Collaborative Group Study.

TYPE A	TYPE B
● excessive competitive drive ● impatient and hostile ● fast movements ● rapid speech ● very 'intense' ● more likely to suffer from coronary heart disease	● less competitive ● less hostile and more patient ● easygoing and tolerant ● slower speech ● slower movements ● less likely to suffer from coronary heart disease

Evaluation of the Type A personality concept

1 Assessing with certainty that someone is a TYPE A or TYPE B is very difficult. Questionnaires and scales designed to do it often give conflicting results.

2 Type A is a collection of characteristics (or traits), and some traits are better predictors of CHD problems than others.

> **Hecker et al (1988)** – The hostility trait is the best predictor of CHD, whilst other traits seem to have nothing to do with CHD at all.

> **Ironson et al (1992)** – Anger is the best way to make the heart beat faster. Control that and you might be able to help a Type A person reduce their risk of CHD.

3 According to **Ragland and Brand (1988)**, whilst Type B personalities are less likely to get heart problems, when they DO get them they are more likely to die from them than Type A personalities.

The heart disease study – Rosenman et al (1975)

The Western Collaborative Group Study (WCGS) wanted to see whether Type A men were more likely to suffer from CHD than Type B men, and why.

How did they do it? 3,154 Californian men were assessed to see whether they were Type A or Type B, and also Type X (a mixture of A and B). The men were studied for eight years.

What did they find? CHD was twice as likely in men with Type A personalities than Type B.

They concluded that if we help people change the Type A behaviour pattern we can reduce the likelihood of CHD.

Take a closer look:
● It is correlation research. Just because a man is Type A does not necessarily mean that he will suffer with CHD.

● The researchers could not possibly control all aspects of the behaviour of 3,154 men over eight years, so other factors might have contributed to the rates of CHD.

THE HARDY PERSONALITY – KOBASSA (1979)

Certain aspects of a personality can make us resistant to the effects of stress. Kobassa (1979) identified the hardy personality as having the 3-C's:

Commitment – Have a sense of purpose and tackle problems head on. Be organised!	**Control** – Be in charge of your life, don't expect people to help you, go out and solve your problems!	**Challenge** – Treat problems as a challenge and devote time and energy to solving them.

Evaluation of the hardy personality concept

1 Weiss (2002) tested parents on the Hardiness Scale. Some had children with autism and some had children without autism. Parents of autistic children suffered more with the negative effects of stress, but hardy parents with autistic children suffered less. Hardiness is a buffer that increases resistance to stress.

2 Hardiness training can improve resistance to stress, Maddi et al (1988), although this research was done with the business community, so it may be difficult to generalise the findings.

3 According to Funk (1992), the 3-C's are less important than negativity. A negative person is a hardy person and the effects of stress vary with negativity.

4 There is some dispute about whether or not hardiness is a personality characteristic that is stable over time.

STRESS REACTION STYLE

Just knowing what personality type someone is doesn't tell us how they will respond in a stressful situation. The stress reaction style is a possible alternative approach. Guenole et al (2008) argue that the stress reaction style questionnaire successfully assesses how people might respond to future stressful events.

Evaluation of the stress reaction style

1 It has real-world applications including:

Job selection Selecting people for stressful jobs	**Organisational stress management** Companies can train employees to actively help them cope with stressful events	**Self-awareness** If you know something will make you stressed you can plan for it with training or appropriate lifestyle and employment choices

2 Stress reaction style research is VERY new indeed and needs more research.

ASK AN EXAMINER

You could be asked questions in the exam specifically on Type A behaviour, so make sure that you are able to recognise and describe it. And don't forget the research! The heart disease study is quite easy to learn and is very useful as you can use it in a number of different ways. For example, you can use it to support the relationship between Type A behaviour and stress, and you can use it as an example of how psychologists have researched the link between the two.

Apply Your Knowledge

Two men meet every morning walking their dogs and exchange greetings. One day, one of the men does not turn up. His friend later finds out that the man has suffered a heart attack.

Using what you have learned from studying stress in everyday life, what might make one man less likely to suffer with coronary heart disease (CHD) than another? (*4 marks*)

WORKPLACE STRESS

Work can be a source of satisfaction and fulfilment or it can be stressful. You need to know three things about the workplace, and these are the work environment, work overload and control.

WORK ENVIRONMENT

The place in which we work can significantly affect our stress levels.

1 Noise – can affect concentration which leads to stress.

2 Temperature – the hotter the temperature, the more likely we are to be aggressive, leading to frustration and hence stress.

Halpern (1995) – Increases in temperature can lead to frustration and stress, and even aggression. This is possibly because of a lack of control and physical discomfort.

WORK OVERLOAD

The amount of work we are required to do can affect our stress levels. Work overload means having more work to do than the time given to do it.

1 Quantitative: Having more work to do than the time allowed to do it.

2 Qualitative: The work you have to do is too complex under the work-conditions.

Wallace (1999) – Lawyers reported increased conflict and stress at home when they were overloaded at work.

CONTROL

More stress is felt in situations where the person feels they have little or no control.

Logan and Ganster (2005) – Managers at work with supportive supervisors reported an increased feeling of control and therefore greater job satisfaction and reduced stress.

The sawmill study – Johansson et al (1978)

What were doing and why? Finishers in a *noisy* sawmill had little *control* over the pace of their work. The *quantity* of their work dictated everyone else's pay.

How did they do it? Stress-related hormones and stress-related absenteeism in finishers were measured and these were compared with other workers in the factory.

What did they find? There were higher levels of stress-related illness and more stress hormones in finishers than other workers.

This shows that a combination of *work environment*, *work overload* and *control* leads to greater stress.

Take a closer look:
● Individual differences (e.g. personality type) might have been a factor affecting the stress response of different workers.

● Because the study is not a laboratory experiment, there are uncontrolled variables. This means that a number of factors could be causing stress, e.g. lack of control, poor environment.

Apply Your Knowledge

Tom shares an office with John, a young new employee. John regularly listens to music, and talks on the telephone with his colleagues and friends constantly.

(a) Identify one workplace factor that might be affecting Tom. (*1 mark*)

(b) Explain why the factor you have identified in part (a) might lead to Tom experiencing stress. (*3 marks*)

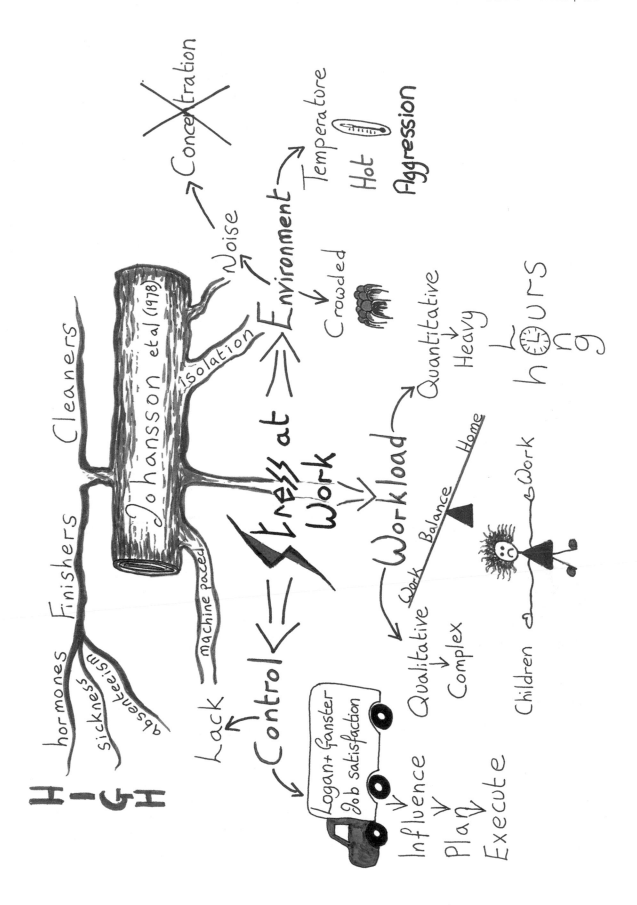

LIFE CHANGES AND DAILY HASSLES

Our lives change all the time and accommodating and adjusting to these changes, or life events, can be extremely stressful.

ASK AN EXAMINER

You could be asked to describe life change research, in which case you can use information about the SRRS and LES in your answer. If you are asked to include evaluation in the question, for example if it is an extended written response, then you can describe the SRRS and LES, use the criticisms of them, as well as the Navy study, as evaluation. If you wanted to you could even use the LES to evaluate the SRRS. In the section that follows we discuss daily hassles and they can also be used as evaluation of the SRRS. In fact, there are lots of ways to evaluate life change research!

SOCIAL READJUSTMENT RATING SCALE (SRRS)

Measuring the influence of life events was made possible by Holmes and Rahe (1967), when they developed the SRRS:

● 43 common life events listed (e.g. divorce, retirement, marriage).
● Each event was given 'score' of stressfulness called a Life Change Unit (LCU).
● Scores for each life event were added up for each person.
● Score of over 300 = 80% chance of a stress-related illness in the following year.

Evaluation of the SRRS

1 *Individual differences*: Impact of a life event is not the same for everyone.

2 *It's a correlation*: Life events are *correlated* with stress. This doesn't indicate *cause*.

3 *It's got positive and negative events*: There is no reason to assume that positive events are related to stress-related illness.

4 *It's a little out of date*: The more up to date version of Insel and Roth (1985) includes things like 'pregnancy' and ' number of missed classes'.

5 *It's easy to use*: It is a relatively simple and easy to use scale.

6 *It relies on accurate recall*. Inaccurate memory of events will influence the scale. People tend to over-report negative past events.

The life experiences survey (LES)

Sarason et al (1978) created an alternative to the SRRS because they did not believe that life changes necessarily had negative effects, as the SRRS assumed. What's important in the LES is how the life event is perceived.

● 57 item questionnaire. Life events rated in terms of positive and negative impact.
● Positive, negative and total LES scores are calculated.
● Negative scores correlate more highly with health problems than positive or total scores.

Evaluation of the LES

1 It takes individual differences into consideration.

2 Some people never experience the events identified in the LES scale (cross).

Apply Your Knowledge

Linda has had a lot to put up with lately. Not only did her close friend pass away, but she lost her job just before Christmas. Now she isn't looking forward to her forthcoming holiday very much.

What has research into the effects of life changes told us about the likely effects of these events on Linda's future health? (*5 marks*)

The Navy study – Rahe et al (1970)

The researchers wanted to know whether stress and illness were related to one another.

How did they do it? Male US Navy personnel completed the SRRS (providing a total LCU score) and were monitored for illnesses during a six month tour of duty.

What did they find? Higher total LCU scores correlated with higher rates of illness. This shows that life events are related to an increased risk of illness.

Take a closer look: ● The research is correlational, so there is the causality problem.

● The correlation was very weak – it is quite likely that if they replicated this study (i.e. did it again) they would not find a correlation.

● The sample was very limited (naval personnel) so it would be difficult to generalise the findings.

THE HASSLES AND UPLIFTS SCALE

● This was designed by DeLongis et al (1988).
● Each event is rated as an uplift (a positive event) and a hassle (negative event). Items include your physical appearance, the weather and the amount of free time you have.
● If the overall score is negative, more hassles have been indicated than uplifts and this is more likely to have health consequences than a more positive score.

Evaluation of Hassles and Uplifts scale
1 It's a correlation, so it is difficult to be sure about cause and effect.

2 A measure of daily hassles is a better predictor of day-to-day health than measures of life events.

3 Individual differences; people are likely to interpret hassles differently.

4 Like the rating of past events in the SRRS, this scale requires accurate recall.

Apply Your Knowledge

Some psychologists say that our experience of the annoyances and irritations of everyday life are better predictors of health and well-being than major life events.

(a) What name is given to these annoyances and irritations of everyday life? (*1 mark*)

(b) Outline the problems of using measures of these annoyances and irritations as predictors of health and well-being. (*4 marks*)

ASK AN EXAMINER

Life changes and daily hassles are different things on the specification, so be sure to treat them as such and learn them equally as well. This is not to say however that they are unrelated, because they are. For example, daily hassles can be used as a very effective evaluation of life events (and, though perhaps less convincingly, vice versa). Just don't confuse the two! You might be asked a question on either life changes or daily hassles or you might be asked to talk about both, so watch out for that!

COPING WITH STRESS

To experience some degree of stress is normal, and in moderate amounts is good for us. Life presents us with a range of stresses and we must cope with them as best we can. Sometimes, however, we may need extra support to help us manage our stress.

PROBLEM-FOCUSED METHODS OF COPING

Also known as 'approach' methods. Stress is treated as a problem to be solved. There are two techniques:

SEEKING SOCIAL SUPPORT
Talking through problems can help things make sense, or get a new perspective to help us cope. Discussing a problem can often help us make more sense of it.

ANTICIPATORY COPING
Anticipate the symptoms and feelings of stress and we can do something to avoid them. This is an example of controlling our environment. If we can work out what it is that triggers the stress we can 'train' ourselves to anticipate and deal with it. This might be by using a *psychological therapy*.

PSYCHOLOGICAL METHODS OF STRESS MANAGEMENT

Stress-Inoculation Training (SIT) is a form of cognitive behavioural therapy designed by Michenbaum. Just as we might be inoculated against a disease, we might be inoculated against stress. In **three phases**, people are helped to restructure the way they think about events, so that they are better prepared when they meet the stressor.

Phase 1: Conceptualisation: What about the event makes it stressful? How to cope?

Phase 2: Training and rehearsal: Taught coping skills that can be general or event-focused.

Phase 3: Application and follow through: Apply training to real world. If necessary, follow-up training sessions provided.

Evaluation of SIT
1 It's flexible and can be tailored to individuals and lots of different stressors.

2 It's expensive and slow and requires clients to be motivated and driven.

3 Benefits of SIT can be long-term (unlike drugs), and teaches general coping skills that can be applied to a variety of stressors in the future.

The exams study – Michenbaum (1975)

Meichenbaum wanted to find out how effective his SIT was.

How did he do it? An assessment of the effectiveness of SIT was made by comparing three groups of stressed pre-exam students. Group 1: eight weeks of SIT; Group 2: eight weeks of systematic desensitisation; Group 3: no therapy

What did they find? The SIT group gave most positive self-reports, and out-performed the other groups in their exams. They concluded therefore that SIT was the most successful therapy.

Evaluation
1 They used self-reports of success – these are not necessarily reliable.

2 It could be that the other treatment would have been successful had it been given longer – the study did not consider optimum treatment period.

EMOTION-FOCUSED METHODS OF COPING

These are also known as 'avoidant' methods and are used when a person feels there is nothing that can be done to change the problem. If the situation which causes the stress must be accepted, then methods are employed to regulate the emotional responses to the stressors. There are three emotion-focused techniques:

DEFENCE MECHANISMS
Psychological barriers are put up by the stressed person. One of these is *denial* (pretending it's not happening). Another is *intellectualisation* where they somehow explain away the stress to themselves.

REAPPRAISAL
They take another look at the stressful situation and may change the way they feel about it. If they care less about the event they will feel less stressed.

AROUSAL REDUCTION
The heightened reactions due to stress are reduced. The person is less aroused, and therefore feels less stressed. Meditation, exercise or drugs can help with this.

PHYSIOLOGICAL METHODS OF STRESS MANAGEMENT

Drugs can be used to combat stress by reducing or removing the symptoms of the stress. Anxiolytics (which reduce the symptoms of anxiety) include:

Benzodiazepines that lessen tension and nervousness and have a calming effect. They act by increasing the level of GABA, a neurotransmitter responsible for 'quietening' the activity of another neurotransmitter called serotonin.

Beta-blockers that reduce heart rate and blood pressure and block the influence of adrenaline, lowering the fight or flight response.

Evaluation of drug therapy

1 They are fast-acting and provide speedy relief. Once taken people can seek more permanent support.

2 Drug therapies treat the symptoms not the problem itself.

3 Some drugs may have side effects. Mental alertness can be slowed so normal activities are influenced.

4 Long-term use can result in tolerance and addiction.

Apply Your Knowledge

Julia has a brother serving overseas in the armed forces. She is very worried about his safety. In fact, she feels anxious all the time and is having difficulty concentrating on anything.

Outline emotion-focused methods of coping that Julia might use in dealing with her stress. (*5 marks*)

ASK AN EXAMINER

You could be asked questions in the exam specifically on cognitive behavioural therapy for stress, or you could be asked specifically about drug therapy. Be sure that you are able not only to describe these methods of stress management, but also to evaluate them.

WHICH IS BEST? EMOTION-FOCUSED OR PROBLEM-FOCUSED METHODS?

Both have strengths and weaknesses. Whatever method is chosen depends on the person, the stressful event, whether the person is male or female (females prefer emotion-focused methods according to Soderstrom et al (2000)) and how much money the person has!

● Problem-focused strategies aim to remove the problem. Emotion-focused strategies provide control of the symptoms.
● Problem-focused methods are slower and more expensive than emotion-focused methods.
● There may be side effects and long-term effects of emotion-focused methods such as drug use.

Check your knowledge

1 Outline the response of the pituitary-adrenal system to a stressor. (*4 marks*)

2 Outline the response of the sympathomedullary pathway to a stressor. (*4 marks*)

3 Outline the key features of the immune system. (*4 marks*)

4 Describe the relationship between stress and the immune system. (*6 marks*)

5 What is meant by the term Type A behaviour? (*2 marks*)

6 What has research shown us about the relationship between personality and stress? (*5 marks*)

7 Identify *two* factors associated with stress in the workplace. (*2 + 2 marks*)

8 Give the findings of *one* study into workplace stress. (*4 marks*)

9 State what is meant by the term 'life change' as it relates to stress. (*2 marks*)

    (a) What methods have psychologists used to investigate life changes as a source of stress? (*4 marks*)

    (b) Give *two* limitations of the method you have identified in (a).

10 What do psychologists mean by the term daily hassle? (*2 marks*)

11 Give *two* criticisms of research into daily hassles as a source of stress. (*3 + 3 marks*)

12 State *one* difference between a life event and a daily hassle. (*2 marks*)

13 Describe emotion-focused approaches to coping with stress. (*3 marks*)

14 Describe problem-focused approaches to coping with stress. (*3 marks*)

15 State *two* differences between emotion-focused and problem-focused approaches to coping with stress. (*2 + 2 marks*)

16 Describe physiological methods of stress management. (*5 marks*)

17 Describe *one* psychological method of stress management. (*5 marks*)

18 Give *two* limitations of psychological methods of stress management. (*3 + 3 marks*)

19 Give *two* criticisms of the use of drugs as a method of stress management. (*3 + 3 marks*)

HOW SCIENCE WORKS

Think about methods of coping with stress

We can investigate this by carefully designing a simple questionnaire.

● Design a questionnaire to gather information which tells you about emotion-focused and problem-focused methods of coping.

● Ask questions about how people deal with their stressors.

● Use closed questions to generate simple quantitative data.

● Include one question which would generate qualitative data.

● Consider ethical issues in the design of the questionnaire.

● Draw a bar chart of the findings.

Things to consider

● What does the bar chart show? What could you conclude about the effectiveness of these two methods of coping?

● Identify the problems with: (a) designing, (b) conducting and (c) analyzing the questionnaire.

● Why would it have been useful to conduct a pilot study?

● If you were to carry out the research again, what would you do differently and why?

HOW SCIENCE WORKS

Think about bodily responses to stress

We can investigate this by conducting an experiment.

● Devise a mild stressor, for example an unsolvable word search or dot-to-dot.

● Find a way to measure the stress response, for example pulse rate.

● Compare the stress response to the mild stressor with the stress response in a control condition, for example a solvable puzzle.

● Calculate the average stress response for the two conditions and draw a graph of these data.

Things to consider

● What can you conclude from the graph?

● What were the IV and DV and describe how you operationalised them.

● What kind of experimental design did you use? What were the advantages and disadvantages of this design for this particular study?

● How did you get participants for the study?

● Identify any extraneous variables which may have affected your results.

● If you were to carry out the research again, what would you do differently and why?

The extended written response

Discuss the relationship between stress and illness. (12 marks)

Selye was one of the first people to find a link between stress and illness. According to his General Adaptation Syndrome (GAS), the body responds in the same way to all stressors. At Stage 1 there is the 'fight or flight' response. At Stage 2 the body adapts to the stressor. With continued stress, the body enters Stage 3 where resources are depleted and there is a risk of stress-related illness.

This opening paragraph is describing the link between stress and illness. Using Selye's GAS is an effective way of doing this. Notice that GAS has NOT been described in great detail – this wouldn't be a sensible use of the space available. The key point about GAS and illness has been made here.

One type of illness related to stress is heart disease. Whilst the body's response to stress is normal and healthy, over a period of time the hormones released during stress can cause damage to the cardiovascular system because of high blood pressure, wear-and-tear and narrowing of blood vessels.

The next paragraph is giving an example of a stress-related illness, and briefly describing how this illness might come about as a result of stress.

Support for this link comes from research by Rosengren et al. They studied the health of several thousand men over a number of years and found that those who assessed themselves as having the highest levels of stress during this time were more likely to have myocardial infarction.

This is the first bit of evaluative material in the essay. It is using a piece of research to support the idea in the preceding paragraph. Note the phrasing – 'Support for this link...'. This is clearly indicating to the examiner that you are being evaluative.

Rosengren et al however didn't seem to take into account other important individual differences such as personality. For example, research has shown that people with Type A personalities are more prone to heart disease than other personality types.

This is a second bit of evaluation, but this time it is a criticism of the Rosengren et al study. This can be a good way of gaining evaluation marks, but it must be done effectively. That is, a comment like 'the sample was biased' is rather weak unless it is justified as an important criticism with further explanation. In this case, the generic 'individual differences' criticism is used, but to good effect. You know that personality is an important factor in stress, so use your knowledge here!

Another way that stress can lead to illness is by reducing the effectiveness of the immune system. The immune system is the body's defence against infection and if it is not functioning efficiently then the body becomes vulnerable to disease and illness.

This is a descriptive paragraph introducing another way in which stress is related to illness.

Support for the idea that the immune system is influenced by stress comes from Kiecolt-Glaser et al. They found that blood samples taken from medical students during examinations were much lower in NK cells than in samples taken a month earlier. This shows that the body had fewer natural defences during a stressful time.

Another opportunity has arisen to use research which you have learned. Notice the 'support' evaluation 'trigger' at the start and how in the final sentence the findings are clearly being linked to stress and illness. You haven't got the time or writing space to describe this study in detail in this particular essay.

However, the findings show a correlation between stress and NK activity. We can't be absolutely sure that stress caused the reduction in immune system functioning, only that the two events are related in some way.

This is an example of how you can use your knowledge of research methods to gain marks for evaluation. The Kiecolt-Glaser study is correlational research so feel free to use this to cast doubt on the idea that one event has caused the other to happen.

This finding is supported by Irwin et al, who found that the immune systems of women whose husbands had recently died were functioning at a much lower level than similar women who had not experienced such a stressful life event.

The essay ends with a final piece of evaluation. If there are two studies with related findings then the one study might be used to support the other. An opportunity arose in this case to do just that – easy marks!

COMMENTS

In summary then, a broad range of evidence is used to demonstrate knowledge and understanding of the relationship between stress and illness. Four appropriate pieces of research are presented here, described in reasonable detail, to illustrate two areas where stress might be related to illness. Research is used effectively as evaluation and is also evaluated. The way that the material is organised shows effective use of the material, with a fair balance between description and evaluation.

As always, there is more than one way in which this essay could be answered. You could, for example, have restricted your answer to stress and the immune system, or stress and cardiovascular disorders. You might have used your research in a different way – one obvious way is to give fewer pieces of research but in more detail, for example Kiecolt-Glaser et al. You should try not to restrict your answer to one piece of research, however – this might be interpreted by an examiner as poor selection of material or a restricted range of evidence.

In The News

Stress is no reason for Distress

The past few years have been difficult for Jean Harris. In addition to a long and messy divorce that ended in court, there was her adult daughter's treatment for a disfiguring eating disorder. Small wonder that she was feeling stressed.

But Harris, 55, is not the only one. Faced with a long-hours culture, fragmented family life and all sorts of fears, we are all feeling very, very stressed.

Popular theory has it that everyone falls victim to stress at some time. Certainly, there are reams of scientific material to support the theory. An estimated 80 per cent of all visits to GPs are believed to be due to stress or stress-related illness, which are said to cause depression and anxiety – leading to high blood pressure, nervous breakdowns, heart disease and strokes.

As a result, anywhere from 30 million to 130 million working days are thought to be lost every year.

But expert speakers at a conference, the first of its kind, in London on Monday, do not believe a word of it. They are seeking to debunk the stress myth and blow the whistle on the burgeoning industry that markets solutions.

Stress: A Change of Direction is the brainchild of Angela Patmore, whose report on the subject is one of the showcases of the day's agenda. She spent 18 months with scientists at the Centre for Environmental and Risk Management at the University of East Anglia, analysing more than 250 studies on stress.

"The research that spawned this hugely lucrative and influential industry is factually poor," says Patmore. "We found sloppy methodologies and a lack of definition that was quite horrifying. The same word, stress, was used to mean basically anything to fit the remit of the specific research project. This would not be tolerated in any other field of science."

According to Patmore, many of the flaws in stress research stem from a heavy reliance on animal models – which are not psychologically comparable with people – and confused logic between cause and effect.

The originator of the modern stress concept was Hans Selye, who experimented on rats in high-pressure situations. When the rats became ill and died, Selye concluded that, since this followed the induced stress, it must also be caused by it.

Patmore has a different interpretation. "Selye's rats reacted in three stages," she says. "First, they were shocked; second, they put up a struggle for their lives; and third, seeing no escape from the laboratory, they gave up." It was this final stage that suppressed the rats' immune systems and left them open to disease and death, not the stress itself, she explains.

Many of the offerings of the stress-management industry, such as relaxation techniques, prescription drugs and counselling, do not regard stress – the immediate response to a threat – as a survival mechanism which alerts people to problems, such as overwork or debt, that should be dealt with rather than run from, Patmore adds.

"It's better to face up to the problem and try to help yourself," she says. "When you run away from a monster, it doesn't go away; it tends to get bigger and come after you."

Jennifer Smith, of the International Stress Management Association, acknowledges that the fashionable definitions of stress are vague, but are necessarily so because stress varies depending on the individual and their situation.

"The term stress is a helpful starting point for people to describe the experiences — emotional, behavioural and physical — that they have when the pressure they face seems to be more than they can handle," she says.

But she believes that relaxation techniques are a small part of a helpful tool kit that might also include rational thinking exercises, lifestyle changes (such as diet, physical fitness, smoking and drinking), and managing your time better.

Nevertheless, rather than trying to manage stress, Patmore advocates challenge-based exercises that actually wind you up rather than calm you down.

Her suggestions include spectator sport, horror films and adventure games — anything that arouses high tension. These provide a rehearsal of the stress-response pattern that can prepare you for dealing more effectively with real-life

crises, she says.

Jean Harris, who attended a course run by Patmore two years ago, says: "What she (Patmore) claims makes a lot of sense, but I think you have to put your own interpretation on it." Harris now tackles her problems head-on while still making regular visits to a spiritualist healer for that extra bit of relaxation.

Terri Paddock
The Times, June 13, 1998

Stretch and Challenge

1 What problems with defining the term 'stress' are highlighted by the article?

2 A number of suggestions for coping with stress are mentioned in the article.
(a) Identify those that are problem-focused and those that are emotion-focused approaches.
(b) Compare the effectiveness of these two approaches.

3 The past few years have been difficult for Jean Harris.
(a) What do stress researchers call the kinds of events that Jean Harris is experiencing?
(b) What would these same researchers predict about the future health of Jean Harris?
(c) Not everyone will react to events in the same way as Jean Harris. Describe factors underlying such individual responses to stress.

4 Anywhere from 30 million to 130 million working days are thought to be lost due to stress every year. What factors in work have been found to contribute to stress?

5 The article appears to be critical of the conclusions drawn from Selye's research.
(a) Outline two criticisms that the article makes of Selye's research.
(b) Explain how stressful experiences can lead to illness.

6 Using your knowledge of stress and information in the article, assess the relationship between stress and illness.

THE EXTENDED WRITTEN RESPONSE – ADDITIONAL QUESTIONS

1 Describe and evaluate psychological methods of stress management. (*12 marks*)

2 'It is not just major life events that can be stressful. We often find ourselves concerned with more "everyday" worries. Both have been related to ill-health.'

Outline and evaluate research into the effects of stress caused by life changes and/or daily hassles. (*12 marks*)

3 Discuss the role played by personality in the experience of stress. (*12 marks*)

Example answers to these questions can be found at www.askanexaminer.com

USEFUL WEBSITES

http://www.vet.ed.ac.uk/animalpain/Pages/HPAsystem.htm
Looks like non-human animals have a pituitary-adrenal system too!

www.mmu.k12.vt.us/teachers/kefferm/humanbio/nervous/articles/1997%20mind-body%20interaction%20disease.pdf
The mind–body interaction in disease. One to really extend your knowledge and stretch yourself!

http://www.kidshealth.org/parent/general/body_basics/endocrine.html
This page gives a great overview of the endocrine system. Surf around here, you'll find more useful information. Use the search box and look for 'nervous system' and 'immune system', for instance.

http://pni.psychiatry.ohio-state.edu/jkg/
Kiecolt-Glaser's webpage. She of the stressed medical students study. Notice the other things she is studying – investigating stress in psychology is not all about disease.

http://psychcentral.com/lib/2006/the-impact-of-stress/
How does stress show itself? Some things to look out for here!

http://stress.about.com/od/understandingstress/a/type_a_person.htm
Different personality types show different reactions to stress. The Type A personality is defined here.

http://www.psych.uncc.edu/pagoolka/TypeA-B-intro.html
Ever wondered what type you are? Then wonder no more. Take an online test here that says it measures whether you are a Type A or Type B person.

http://encarta.msn.com/encyclopedia_761572052/stress_(psychology).html

Some useful links through this well-known web resource. There are all sorts of links to a wide variety of areas here.

http://www.eoslifework.co.uk/transprac.htm

An interesting perspective that takes what we have learned about life changes further. See how what you are learning about is really being applied in the real world.

http://psyclab1.psych.ubc.ca/~adlab/member.php?mID=13

The webpage of Anita DeLongis, who knows everything there is to know about life changes in relation to stress! You can read a lot of her research for free here!

HOW SCIENCE WORKS

Think about stress and daily hassles

We can investigate this by conducting research that looks at the correlation of two variables.

- Decide on a target population and think up a few everyday hassles which apply to them.

- Devise a simple scale where people have to rate these hassles between 1 and 5.

- Total the hassle score for each participant.

- Ask another question to measure how stressed the participants feel, e.g. 'On a scale of 1 to 10, how stressed do you feel today?'

- You now have two scores for each participant – draw a scattergraph of these data.

Things to consider

- What does the scattergraph show about the relationship between the two variables?

- Relationships can be explained in three ways – causal, chance or third factor. If you have found a relationship between the two variables, explain it.

- How could the design of the materials be improved?

- Would it have been better to use a different method? How could you have investigated the same thing using a different method?

Section 5

Social Psychology
– Social Influence

WHAT YOU NEED TO KNOW

Social Psychology is in Unit 2 of the specification. As you learn you are expected to develop your knowledge and understanding of Social Psychology, including concepts, theories and studies. This also includes a knowledge and understanding of research methods and ethical issues as they relate to this area of psychology. You also need to develop the skills of analysis, evaluation and application. Rather than just recall and reproduce information, you are expected to be able to apply your knowledge and understanding. The subject content is split into two parts:

Social influence

- Conformity, including internalisation and compliance
- Explanations for conformity, including informational and normative social influence
- Obedience
- Explanations for obedience

Social influence in everyday life

- Explanations for independent behaviour, including resistance to conformity and obedience
- Individual differences and independent behaviour, including locus of control
- Implications for social change of research into social influence

CONFORMITY

Conformity occurs when people alter their behaviour to match the behaviour of a majority of others.

TYPES OF CONFORMITY

According to Kelman (1958), there are three types of conformity:

Compliance – going along with a group without a change in personal opinion. It lasts only as long as the group pressure lasts, and we can go along with the group whilst still disagreeing with it.
Example from research: Asch's line study.

Identification – behaviour is changed because we want to be like the influencing group. It lasts as long as the group we want to be a part of remains attractive to us, therefore the change in behaviour can be temporary.
Example from research: Zimbardo's prison study.

Internalisation – group opinion and behaviour is accepted as part of who we are. It can occur without any particular conscious effort. Because the individual changes both their public and private view, it is the most permanent form of conformity.
Example from research: Moscovici's colour slide study.

> **ASK AN EXAMINER**
> *Compliance and internalisation are particularly important to learn.*

The line study – Asch (1951)

Asch investigated whether majority group pressure is strong enough to cause individuals to answer questions wrongly when the correct answer was obvious.

How did he do it? Participants had to say which of three lines was the same size as a 'test' line. Participants were sixth in line to answer in a group of seven – all other six 'participants' were accomplices of Asch, instructed to give the wrong answer.

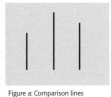

Figure a: Comparison lines   Figure b: Standard line

What did he find? 32% of participants conformed to the wrong (majority) decision.
74% of participants conformed at least once.
26% of participants never conformed.

The study shows the impact that a majority can have on an individual.

Take a closer look: ● *The social climate*: conformity was a stronger social norm in the 1950s.
● *The method used by Asch*: Crutchfield (1956) found lower levels of conformity using a different technique where people were not face to face.
● *Culture*: Smith and Bond (1996) suggest that variations might depend on whether the culture is individualist or collectivist.
● *Ethical issues*: Asch's participants were deceived and made to feel anxious.
● *Objective measure of conformity*: Unlike in Sherif's autokinetic study, there was a 'right' answer therefore conformity could be accurately measured.

Apply Your Knowledge

Zach really doesn't like horror films, but all his friends do. Whenever they go to the cinema together they always choose to watch a horror film.

(a) What type of conformity does Zach's behaviour demonstrate? (*1 mark*)
(b) Outline the findings of one study that demonstrates this type of conformity. (*4 marks*)

WHY PEOPLE CONFORM

It has been suggested that people conform for two reasons: to *be right* and to *be liked*:

INFORMATIONAL SOCIAL INFLUENCE

When there is no correct or obvious answer to a problem we often turn to others for information. The more uncertain people are, the more likely they are to conform.

Support
Sherif (1935) – showed with the autokinetic effect that people gather as much information as possible before making a decision because they want to be correct.

NORMATIVE SOCIAL INFLUENCE

Sometimes we want to be liked or accepted by a group, or want to avoid embarrassment. In this case we go along with the majority because we don't want to be *different*.

Support
Asch (1951) – people conformed to line judgements even though they knew the answer given by the rest of the group was wrong. They wanted to be liked and accepted by the group.

Other ways of explaining conformity:

THE POWER OF SOCIAL ROLES

We are expected to act in a certain way that is consistent with the social role we occupy.

The power of social roles is subtle, so that usually we do not know that our behaviour is being influenced.

Support
Zimbardo (1973) – in the Stanford Prison Study, participants soon conformed to their respective roles.

After a short while the prisoners became subdued and submissive, whilst the guards asserted their given power and some became very aggressive.

This shows the power that roles play in influencing behaviour.

SOCIAL IMPACT THEORY

The amount of influence a person has in a social situation depends on:

Number
Strength
Immediacy

Support
Asch (1951) – showed that increasing the *number* in a group can increase conformity.

Crutchfield (1956) – reducing *immediacy* by putting people in separate booths reduced conformity.

Mullen et al (1990) – showed that jaywalking could be reduced by having non-jaywalking people around of high status (*strength*).

Apply Your Knowledge

Everyone seems to think that Emma is funny – she makes people laugh with her jokes. Except Kate. Kate doesn't think that Emma is funny at all. She still laughs at her jokes though.

Use what you have learned about why people conform to explain Kate's behaviour. (*4 marks*)

ASK AN EXAMINER

*A word of warning! Students very often confuse types of conformity with explanations for conformity. This could easily happen in this exam if you are not careful because of the way that questions are sometime asked. Look at the previous two **Apply Your Knowledge** questions. Can you see the difference between the types and explanations questions, and will you be able to do this in the exam?*

OBEDIENCE

Obedience is when people react in direct response to an authority figure.

STUDY IN FOCUS

The electric shocks study – Milgram (1963)

What was he doing and why? Milgram wanted to know whether people would obey a legitimate authority figure even if they were asked to do something that was clearly morally wrong.

How did he do it: The procedure involved a 'teacher' (the participant) testing a 'learner' (an accomplice of the experimenter) on a memory task. The learner was seen to be strapped to a chair and electrodes fixed to the wrists to deliver an electric shock. From another room (so the teacher could hear the learner but not see him), the teacher delivered an electric shock each time there was a wrong response from the learner. The shocks increased in 15-volt increments from 15 to 450 volts. The experimenter encouraged the teacher to continue when there was dissent.

What did they find: All participants gave shocks up to 300 volts. 65% of participants went to the full 450 volts, even though this was enough to kill the learner. Even though teachers often complained about delivering the shocks, they still obeyed the experimenter.

This study appears to show that people will obey orders from someone in authority.

HOW SCIENCE WORKS

(**a**) (i) Identify one ethical issue arising from research into conformity. (*1 mark*)

    (ii) Explain how the issue identified in (i) could be dealt with. (*2 marks*)

(**b**) (i) What is the research method used by Milgram in his study of obedience? (*1 mark*)

    (ii) Give one advantage and one weakness of the method you have identified in (i). (*2 + 2 marks*)

(**c**) The validity of Milgram's study has been questioned.

    (i) What is meant by the term 'validity' in the context of this research? (*2 marks*)

    (ii) Explain why Milgram's study has been criticised for lacking validity. (*2 marks*)

(**d**) The following graph shows some results from Milgram's study.

    (i) What kind of graph is this? (*1 mark*)

    (ii) Use the information from the graph to summarise briefly Milgram's findings. (*3 marks*)

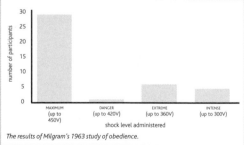

The results of Milgram's 1963 study of obedience.

Not only is Milgram's study really important in answering any general question on obedience you might get in an exam, but you could be asked a question just on this study! Milgram's research is famous in psychology, and let's be honest, is not that difficult to learn. You don't need every nuance and every detail of the many variations — just learn the basics of what he did, what he found out, and a few criticisms. Understand the study well enough to apply it to the question.

ETHICAL ISSUES

Psychological harm: Every effort should be made to prevent psychological and physical harm to participants.

Milgram's research – likely to cause stress, damage to self-esteem.

The right to withdraw: Participants should be free to leave the study at any time.

Milgram's research – the nature of the study (encouragement by the experimenter to continue) is at odds with the principle of allowing people to remove themselves from the study.

Deception: Participants should not be deceived – if it is necessary then great care must be taken to debrief.

Milgram's research – participants were not told exactly what was going to happen, e.g. they were told the study was on learning and memory, they were led to believe they were actually giving electric shocks. They were, however, debriefed.

Informed consent: Participants should be told what they are doing and why they are doing it.

Milgram's research – without being given the right information, participants were not in a position to give informed consent.

ASK AN EXAMINER

An understanding of ethical issues is important to every part of AS Psychology, so learn about them and be prepared to apply your knowledge of ethical issues wherever it is required. Milgram's research however raises so many ethical issues that it is a good place to start understanding and applying the issue of ethics in psychological research.

Apply Your Knowledge

At the start of the experiment the participant met a man called Mr Wallis, who was then hooked up to a shock generator. Mr Wallis was in fact a confederate. The participant sat in another room and tested Mr Wallis on word pairs. When he got one wrong, the participant was to give him an electric shock. These increased from 15 to 450 volts as more incorrect answers were given. There was no actual shock given. A pre-recorded sound played, indicating Mr Wallis in varying degrees of pain, until after 315 volts there was silence. Another confederate called 'Mr Williams', wearing a lab coat, encouraged the participant to continue.

(a) Identify one ethical issue that arises from this research. (*1 mark*)
(b) Suggest how you might deal with the ethical issue identified in (a). (*3 marks*)

WHY PEOPLE OBEY

There are a number of possible explanations for why people obey authority figures.

MILGRAM'S AGENCY THEORY

Individual social consciousness can operate in two ways:

The autonomous state: individuals assume responsibility for their own actions.

Because of this their values and beliefs are more likely to cause them to behave in pro-social ways.

The agentic state: individuals feel that they have diminished responsibility because they are the 'agents' of others.

When people obey an authority figure they are in an agentic state; they are not feeling responsible for their own actions because they are 'doing what they are told'. This is sometimes called 'agentic shift'.

PERSONAL RESPONSIBILITY

People are more likely to obey when they can relinquish personal responsibility for the consequences of their actions.

Some people are more liable to relinquish authority than others – this is probably due to individual difference in personality characteristics.

Support
Hamilton (1978) suggests that obedience levels drop dramatically when participants are told clearly that they are responsible for their own actions, not the person giving the orders.

LEGITIMATE AUTHORITY

People are most likely to obey an authority figure when he or she is considered credible and legitimate.

Support
Obedience levels reduced in Milgram's study when he conducted it in a run-down setting or when someone other than the experimenter gave the orders.

SOCIAL IMPACT THEORY

Immediacy – the experimenter was in the same small room as the participant.

When immediacy was reduced by instructions being given over the phone, obedience reduced substantially.

Strength – the experiment took place at a prestigious university, so therefore the experimenter had high status. When strength was reduced by running the experiment in a shabby office, obedience levels dropped.

Number – the participant was alone except for the experimenter so any dissent had less impact. When there was another 'teacher' present who dissented, obedience levels dropped.

ASK AN EXAMINER

Four explanations for obedient behaviour are provided here. These are not the only ones – if you do your own research you will find others. However, what you have here is more than enough to answer any exam question you might get, and the variety of explanations has been carefully selected to ensure that you will always have something to use to answer any Apply Your Knowledge type questions.

Apply Your Knowledge

A researcher used a confederate to ask passengers on a train to give up their seat, even when there were other seats available. This request was refused. However, when the confederate made the same request accompanied by a train guard, it was granted without argument.

Use what you have learned from your studies of obedience to explain the behaviour of the passengers. (*4 marks*)

INDEPENDENT BEHAVIOUR

A number of factors have been found to influence people's decisions to conform.

EXPOSURE TO DISSENT

Seeing other people resist a majority makes people realise that there is an alternative minority view, and this can reduce the likelihood of conforming behaviour.

Evidence: Asch (1956) found a few minutes' exposure could move people to a majority view but much more persuasion is needed to take on a minority view.

REACTANCE

People can 'react' against the majority view simply because that is the view most people hold. This might be a personality variable, since some people are more reactive that others.

Evidence: Pennerbaker and Saunders (1976) suggest that reactance is more likely if the majority view is perceived to infringe on personal freedoms and the view appears overly authoritative and aggressive.

GROUP UNANIMITY

If the opinion of the majority group is not unanimous it is easier to resist conformity.

Evidence: Asch (1956) found that just one other person in the group agreeing with the judgement of the true participant was enough to reduce conformity significantly.

PERSONALITY

Personality traits such as inferiority make people more likely to conform. People with fewer of these traits are more likely to resist conformity.

Evidence: The exact role of personality is not clear. Having these traits does not necessarily mean you will conform.

GROUP SIZE

Conformity increases with group size levelling off at six or seven and disappearing at 15 or 16.

A large majority has greatest impact in instances of informational social influence (where there is no objectively correct answer).

Evidence: Stang (1976). When there is a correct answer that an individual cares about, conformity is greatest with a majority of three to five; increasing the size of the majority has little effect.

GENDER

Females tend to conform more, particularly in face-to-face situations.

Evidence: Eagly and Charvala (1986). Whilst there were no gender differences in conformity amongst participants under 19 years of age, a difference did emerge in older participants.

Apply Your Knowledge

Most people do not smoke and overall the number of smokers is reducing all the time. However, the number of teenage girls who smoke is on the increase. Research has consistently shown that health-related messages and scare tactics are the least successful methods for curbing teenage smoking.

Using your knowledge of resistance to conformity, suggest one way that smoking in teenage girls could be reduced. (*3 marks*)

ASK AN EXAMINER

There are lots of reasons why a person might resist pressure to conform, and only a selection is presented here. The advantage for you of knowing several explanations is that you will be able to respond to the exam question flexibly. For example, if you are asked to explain why a person in a scenario might resist conforming, you will be in a better position to apply a more appropriate reason, thereby making it a better answer – you have responded directly to the question!

RESISTING CONFORMITY

Not everyone obeys all the time. Although 65% obedience in the Milgram study is impressive, this still leaves 35% who were *disobedient*. A number of factors have been found to influence obedience.

TECHNIQUE	EXPLANATION
Take responsibility	Disobedience becomes more likely as people begin to take responsibility for their actions.
Become more autonomous	Moving from an 'agentic' state to a more 'autonomous' state means that we are operating more autonomously, not as 'agents' of others. This means we can behave more disobediently.
Remove legitimate authority	If legitimate authority figures, such as the police or even the army, are removed it becomes easier for people to disobey as they become self-regulated.
Consider immediacy, strength and number	Immediacy, strength and number are the three factors influencing obedience as described by social impact theory. Separating ourselves from those who may try to make us obey, and surrounding ourselves with lots of like-minded disobedient people who we do not see as authority figures, will improve a person's ability to disobey.

The following factors are also important:

GENDER

Whilst Milgram found no gender differences in obedience, this may be a reflection of the methods used to test obedience.

Evidence: Kilham and Mann (1974) showed very low levels of obedience in female participants in the Milgram paradigm if asked to shock a woman. However, if asked to shock a man obedience rose much higher.

Sheridan and King (1971) found that many more women than men would shock a puppy when told to do so.

PERSONALITY

According to Adorno et al (1950), an authoritarian personality is intolerant of others, has strong personal beliefs, and is submissive and obedient to authority.

Evidence: Milgram (1974) identified participants with authoritarian personalities as ones most likely to obey orders and give the largest shocks.

ASK AN EXAMINER

If you think carefully about it, you will notice that explaining resistance to obedience *is closely related to* explaining why people obey! *Look at it this way for example – if people obey more when the authority is legitimate then removing this legitimacy will increase disobedience. The same logic applies to personal responsibility, agency and social impact. If you think of it this way, there is much less for you to learn!*

Apply Your Knowledge

When Mr Baily gives out homework, he finds that all his students hand it in. However, he has noticed that when his student teacher, Mrs Phillips, gives homework to the same students, some of the homework does not get returned.

Use what you have learned about how people resist pressures to obey to explain the behaviour of the students. (*4 marks*)

INDIVIDUAL DIFFERENCES AND INDEPENDENT BEHAVIOUR

The extent to which people engage in independent behaviour (i.e. they do not conform or obey) varies according to how they differ as individuals.

ASK AN EXAMINER

There are times in psychology when the same research can be used for a number of different purposes. We have a good example of this here. We looked earlier at gender and personality as explanations for independent behaviour, but they are also what psychologists refer to as individual differences. You might see the term 'individual differences' used in an exam question – don't worry, it is quite straightforward really. When we talk about individual differences in psychology we are normally referring to such things as gender and personality, so you can use the same information again.

INDIVIDUAL DIFFERENCES IN OBEDIENCE

GENDER

Whilst Milgram found no gender differences in obedience, this may be a reflection of the methods used to test obedience.

Evidence: Kilham and Mann (1974) showed very low levels of obedience in female participants in the Milgram paradigm if asked to shock a woman. However, if asked to shock a man obedience rose much higher.

Sheridan and King (1971) found that many more women than men would shock a puppy when told to do so.

PERSONALITY

According to Adorno et al (1950), an authoritarian personality is intolerant of others, has strong personal beliefs, and is submissive and obedient to authority.

Evidence: Milgram (1974) identified participants with authoritarian personalities as ones most likely to obey orders and give the largest shocks.

Apply Your Knowledge

Although it has always enforced a dress code, Albany School is having a few problems with the introduction of a school uniform. Although the majority of students wear the new uniform apparently without complaint, there are still some individuals who resist.

What have you learned from your study of social influence that could explain this independent behaviour? (*5 marks*)

INDIVIDUAL DIFFERENCES IN CONFORMITY

GENDER

Research suggests that females tend to conform more than males, maybe because females respond differently to males in face-to-face situations.

Evidence: Eagly and Charvala (1986) found that whilst there were no gender differences in conformity amongst participants under 19 years of age, a difference did emerge in older participants.

PERSONALITY

A number of personality traits have been associated with greater likelihood to conform, for example feelings of inferiority or need for approval. Therefore, people with fewer of these traits are more likely to resist pressures to conform.

Evidence: However, having these personality traits does not predict likelihood of conforming, therefore the exact role of personality in conformity is not clear.

THE INFLUENCE OF LOCUS OF CONTROL ON INDEPENDENT BEHAVIOUR

Locus of control refers to the sense of control that a person has over their life.

People with an *internal locus* of control feel that they have influence and control over their lives, tend to have confidence, security, positive outlook, and little need for approval from others. Because they have little need of approval from others, they are less likely to conform. They are also less likely to obey authority.

People with an *external locus* of control feel that they have little or no influence and control over their lives; things occur because of luck or fate. These people bear the opposite characteristics from those of internals. Because these individuals have a greater need for approval, they are more prone to normative social influence and hence are more likely to conform. They are also more likely to obey authority.

ASK AN EXAMINER

Although you could be asked a question in the exam on the influence of individual differences on independent behaviour (in which case you would write about gender, personality and locus of control), you could also be asked a question specifically on locus of control. Prepare for this! Learn what locus of control is and how it influences conformity and obedience.

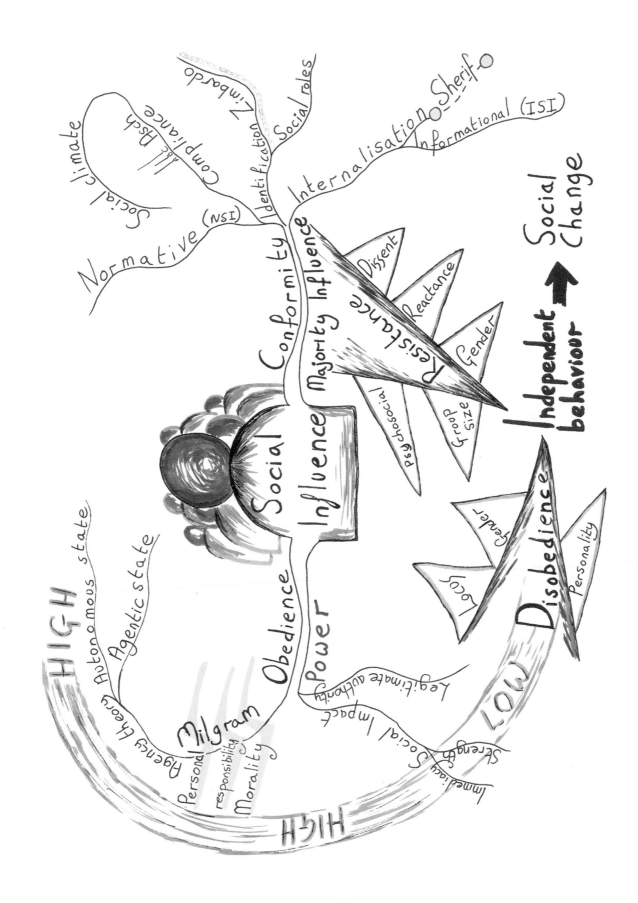

SOCIAL CHANGE

CONFORMITY AND JUSTICE

According to Nemeth (1986), people are more likely to conform when it is the easiest thing to do. In these circumstances, people may not fully listen to or consider the arguments of a minority group.

CONFORMITY AND INNOVATION

Whilst the conformist often does not consider alternative opinions, the non-conformist is more likely to show independent thinking. Non-conformists tend to have an internal locus of control; they are risk-takers and more effective problem solvers.

According to Martin and Hewstone (2003), this kind of innovative thinking is important in developing alternative opinion and stimulating social change.

MAJORITY INFLUENCE: MAINTAINING ORDER

A majority in society usually has *power*. This power is used to maintain the *status quo* (i.e. to keep things as they are), or at least to allow only gradual change on terms dictated by the majority.

The social system (controlled by the majority) creates roles for individuals that are very powerful. They carry with them expectations and exert pressure on people's thoughts, emotions and behaviour. Social roles are important in maintaining the power of the majority and sustaining the status quo.

Being a member of a majority can also result in *deindividuation* – where personal identity is lessened and you become more of a member of a group than an individual.

Zimbardo et al (1973) demonstrated in their prison study that powerful social roles created by the situation in which people find themselves can create strong pressures both to conform and obey authority figures.

Apply Your Knowledge

In 1955, Rosa Parks refused to give up her bus seat to another passenger. The passenger was white, and she was a black woman. In Montgomery, Alabama, at that time, she was obliged to make way for the white passenger. Her refusal began a campaign of civil disobedience. The action of this single woman lit a fuse in the black community.

How can research into social influence help us explain this example of social change? (*6 marks*)

Some topics you cover fit more readily into an extended written response question than others, and social change is one of these. Organise your thinking carefully with this one – use conformity, obedience and minority influence and be prepared to say what each one says about social change. Use research to support your points, and remember that using real-life examples can be a really effective way of demonstrating your understanding.

MAJORITY AND MINORITY INFLUENCE

Whether one social group influences another to bring about social change depends on a number of factors.

Social change can occur when a majority influences a minority because normative and informational social influence produce *compliance*.

Because majorities maintain the status quo, change is a relatively passive process and any social change is slow, e.g. change 'just happens' over time.

A minority can influence a majority. It is a slow process because members of the majority have to be convinced to change the way they think about something – *internalisation*.

Moscovici et al (1969) called this kind of social change *attitude conversion*.

HOW DOES MINORITY INFLUENCE OCCUR?

According to Moscovici, certain behavioural styles make the minority more effective in creating social change (in other words, creating conversion).

Consistency – a minority must be consistent and unanimous in its position. This gives the majority a signal that the minority is committed to its position, making the minority harder to ignore.

Confidence – this sends a message to the majority that the minority position is a serious one that demands attention.

Persuasiveness – the minority position must be convincing enough to persuade people to defect from the majority. This will be seen by many in the majority as a moral decision and will provide a model for the behaviour of others.

Research support
Moscovici et al (1969) had groups of six participants (two of whom were confederates) to judge colour slides as either blue or green. It was found that when the confederates consistently gave the wrong (minority) answer, they had some influence on the answers of the majority.

OBEDIENCE, POWER AND SOCIAL CHANGE

Power influences social change – it can be used to maintain the status quo, or it can be used to produce social change.

According to Turner (1991), for a social group to function effectively individuals must give up responsibility and defer to others of higher status. In effect, self-regulation is replaced by legitimate authority (the *agentic shift*), thus encouraging obedience to those in power.

BECOMING POWERFUL

According to Turner (2005), social groups grow to be powerful, i.e. the power of a social group develops

- People with a shared identity naturally gather together.

- The group grows by attracting others to join.

- As the group grows it gains authority and asserts power – for example, by controlling resources.

Check your knowledge

1 What is meant by the term conformity? (*2 marks*)

2 (a) Identify **two** types of conformity. (*1 + 1 mark*)
  (b) Describe **one** of the types of conformity identified in (a). (*3 marks*)

3 One type of conformity involves an individual accepting the opinion or behaviour of a group as part of their thinking. Name this type of conformity. (*1 mark*)

4 Explain how psychologists have investigated conformity. (*4 marks*)

5 Define the following terms:
  (a) Informational social influence. (*2 marks*)
  (b) Normative social influence. (*2 marks*)

6 (a) Identify **one** explanation of why people conform. (*1 mark*)
  (b) Outline **one** study that demonstrates the explanation identified in (a). (*4 marks*)

7 Give **one** criticism that has been made of research into conformity. (*3 marks*)

8 Outline **two** explanations of how people resist pressures to conform. (*3+ 3 marks*)

9 Outline **one** influence of individual difference on conformity. (*3 marks*)

10 Outline **two** explanations of how people resist pressures to obey. (*3+ 3 marks*)

11 Describe Milgram's research into obedience. (*6 marks*)

12 Give **two** explanations of why people obey. (*3+ 3 marks*)

13 (a) Give **two** ethical criticisms of Milgram's research into obedience. (*2+ 2 marks*)
  (b) Explain how **one** of the ethical criticisms given in (a) could be dealt with. (*3 marks*)

14 Outline **one** influence of individual difference on obedience. (*3 marks*)

15 What is meant by the term locus of control? (*2 marks*)

16 How does locus of control affect conformity? (*3 marks*)

17 How does locus of control affect obedience? (*3 marks*)

18 Explain what **one** aspect of social influence research can tell us about social change. (*4 marks*)

HOW SCIENCE WORKS

Think about normative social influence

We can demonstrate this type of conformity with a simple experiment

● Find a smallish jar and fill it with small dried peas or sweets.

● There are two experimental conditions:
In one condition, ask participants to publicly estimate the number of items in the jar – for example, whilst sat in class – and record their response.
In another condition, ask participants (preferably the same ones) for a private estimation.

● Write a set of standardised instructions for both conditions.

● Calculate the mean and standard deviation of estimates in both conditions and present these on a graph.

Things to consider

● What do the differences in standard deviations tell you about the effects of normative social influence?

● Why is it important that participants are naive about the aims of this study?

● What ethical issues need to be considered with studies such as this?

● This study used a repeated measures design. What are the drawbacks of such a design here?

HOW SCIENCE WORKS

Think about obedience research

Imagine that you are a researcher conducting a field experiment study into the effects of perceived authority in a real-life setting.

Your study involves using confederates – one in everyday clothes and the other in the official uniform of a police community support officer.

The confederate in everyday clothes is going to request that passers-by pick up a piece of litter from the ground. In one condition, they will be alone, whilst in another condition they will be accompanied by the police officer.

● The variable you are measuring is obedience. How are you going to operationalise this variable?

● Obedience research raises a number of ethical issues. Suggest how you would deal with the issues of deception and informed consent.

● Describe how you would control for the possibility of demand characteristics and investigator effects.

● One weakness of field experiments is that there is less control of extraneous variables. What extraneous variables will need to be controlled in this study?

● Describe one advantage of using a field experiment to investigate obedience.

The extended written response

Discuss the implications for social change of
research into social influence. *(12 marks)*

*It has been suggested that pressures to conform can prevent
social change. Nemeth says that it is often easier to conform
than not to, and one consequence of this is that people tend not
to listen to non-conforming arguments for social change. Strong
normative and informational social influences encourage people
to comply with the majority opinion, and this serves to maintain
the status quo.*

> The question asks for research into
> social influence, so this first
> paragraph contains just that – the
> role of conformity in maintaining
> the status quo.

*Support for the role of conformity comes from Martin and
Hewstone who point to the importance of non-conformity in social
change. Because it involves independent thinking, non-conformity
is likely to encourage alternative, innovative opinion, which is
essential for social change.*

> The next couple of sentences could
> be either descriptive or evaluative in
> reality – it depends on how they are
> said. Since a balance of description
> and evaluation is needed in these
> extended written responses,
> sometimes the opportunity to use
> something as evaluation has to be
> taken when it arises.

*The majority view in society is usually the powerful one and,
because of this social change, when it occurs, is likely to happen
slowly and perhaps without any actual conscious knowledge or
effort. One way in which power is maintained by the majority is to
create social roles that exert pressure on people to do what the
majority expects.*

> Another descriptive passage, but
> now focusing on a different aspect
> of social influence research.

*Evidence for the power of social roles comes from Zimbardo's
prison study. He found that participants who took the role of
prison guards quickly identified with their powerful social roles, as
did the participants who took on the role of prisoners.*

> To maintain the balance of description
> and evaluation, a very brief summary
> is provided of Zimbardo's study.
> Notice how brief this is – studies like
> Zimbardo's tend to get students
> carried away with unnecessary detail.
> In this exam, where there is very
> limited space, being drawn into such a
> detailed description would be very
> costly indeed.

Despite the power and influence of the majority, there is evidence that a minority can create social change. For example, the suffragette movement of the 1920s held a minority view that eventually became a majority one.

A real-life example like this can be an effective way to achieve two things: to demonstrate understanding and achieve evaluative marks through application. This example does the former, but might also be interpreted by an examiner as the latter.

This is supported by Moscovici, who claimed that social change occurs because of conversion, where the majority is influenced by the persuasiveness, confidence and consistency of a minority. His research showed that a consistent minority view could influence the majority one – for example, when it came to judging the correct colour of slides.

The final couple of sentences are evaluation, this time minority influence. There really isn't the space in this essay for long descriptions of research, so again very careful thought has to be given to saying lots with as few words as possible.

COMMENTS

This answer covers a number of aspects of social influence research, namely conformity, majority influence, social roles and minority influence. It is therefore more than addressing this aspect of the question. It is not always easy with questions like this to maintain that important balance between the knowledge/recall and analysis/evaluation skills, so particular care must be taken to write clearly and communicate these skills to the examiner. Make no mistake, this is a tough question to answer in so small a space, so careful planning is absolutely vital.

Though the question is clear in that research into social influence is required in the answer, the issue of social change is open to interpretation. It is not an easy term to define either, so probably the most effective way of demonstrating that you understand the concept is not only to use appropriate social influence research but also to include good historical examples in the answer. They need to be used carefully, however, as there is a risk that the answer will lose research focus and become anecdotal. Not many marks are awarded to anecdotal responses.

In The News

Student of human evil to speak at CSUMB

In his latest book, "The Lucifer Effect: Understanding How Good People Turn Evil," psychologist Philip Zimbardo examines what leads good people to perform evil acts.

His conclusion? It's not just a few bad apples.

"Of course, there are people who do bad things over and over again. But I don't believe people are born good or bad. They are born with potential to do good and evil," Zimbardo said. "It's the situations they are in that bring those qualities out."

He has criticized the Bush administration for its pre-emptive strike on Iraq and for creating an environment that led to the prisoner abuses at Abu Ghraib. In 2004, Zimbardo testified as a defense expert in the court-martial of Army Staff Sgt. Ivan Frederick, an Abu Ghraib prison guard, arguing that few people can resist the urge to become abusive in such environments without proper training and supervision.

"The whole point of my analysis is that in all these situations, what we do is we punish the perpetrators and we don't change the system," he said.

His fascination with the roots of evil, Zimbardo said, started when he was growing up in a South Bronx ghetto, the son of a barber and a housewife who didn't finish high school. While he watched some neighborhood friends go to prison and get tangled up in drugs, he was on track to go to college, unlike his parents and siblings. "If you grow up in a ghetto, what you have all around is evil. You have drugs. People doing bad things. Parents beating up their kids," he said. "And so my interest was in trying, always as a kid, to understand what was going on."

As a college freshman, Zimbardo nearly left psychology behind when he earned his only C in a beginning course, an ironic twist for a psychologist whose studies are now covered in any basic college psychology class. "It was the worst course I ever had," he said, laughing.

Persuaded by a friend to keep him company in an experimental psychology course in his senior year, Zimbardo realized he enjoyed running experiments and went to Yale University to become a psychologist.

In 1971, Zimbardo and other researchers simulated a prison in the basement of the Stanford psychology department, wanting to see how students would behave in such a setting with prisoner and guard identities. Palo Alto police officers who agreed to participate in the experiment arrested undergraduates who had also agreed to participate at their homes and took them to "prison," where other undergraduates acted as guards. Within six days, student guards had become so abusive the now-famous experiment had to be shut down prematurely.

"Our guards became sadistic and our prisoners became depressed and showed signs of extreme stress," according to a slide show documenting the experiment. While prisoners had the option to leave the experiment, most seemed to forget that they could do so. They told each other there was no way out, reinforcing their sense of imprisonment.

"A lot of the evil in the world is really about people in institutions," Zimbardo said, adding that his studies have applications to the ongoing gang warfare in Salinas.

"If you want to deal with gangs in Salinas, you wait until the kid does something bad and you put them in jail. But you know what? Someone will replace them," he said. Instead of putting gang members in jail, Zimbardo said, the focus has to be on changing what makes joining a gang appealing.

"That's a harder job. That's about changing whole systems. But unless you do that, stuff goes around and around and around," he said. "Putting people in prison is just a way to make most middle-class people more comfortable. There are an endless group of people who replace them."

Several years ago, he and about 200 students and faculty members walked out at graduation to protest an honorary degree given to Robert McNamara, defense secretary during the Vietnam War. "It was a statement that it is wrong of the university to honor someone who is an architect of war," he said. "In (McNamara's) recent memoirs, he says we knew the war was unwinnable. We kept it going for years before we left." Zimbardo's outspoken nature has never cost him a job, he said, but did, he feels, delay pay raises and promotions.

Zimbardo said he has made a choice recently to turn his focus from evil to study the nature of heroism, a topic that has been relegated to philosophical and theological circles and received little attention from psychologists.

He said he plans to start writing a curriculum to teach heroism in the classroom. "In every situation of evil, there is almost always some few who resist and rebel, who don't comply," he said. "They qualify as being heroic."

DANIA AKKAD
Monterey County Herald
(California), September 23, 2007

Stretch and Challenge

1 Zimbardo's most famous study is the Stanford Prison Experiment.
(a) What were the situational factors in this experiment that gave rise to the abuse by the prison guards?
(b) What are the implications of the study for social change?

2 Using the article and your knowledge of psychological research, identify ethical issues in Zimbardo's Stanford Prison Experiment.

3 'While he (Zimbardo) watched some neighbourhood friends go to prison and get tangled up in drugs, he was on track to go to college, unlike his parents and siblings.'
(a) Find another example in the article where Zimbardo demonstrates independent behaviour.
(b) Using your knowledge of social influence research, give one explanation for the example of independent behaviour in the quote.

4 Zimbardo claims that, no matter how many gang members you put in jail, there will always be someone to replace them. Using your knowledge of conformity, explain why some people go along with gangs despite the risks involved.

> ## Stretch and Challenge cntd
>
> **5** By saying that the focus on punishing gang members has to change, Zimbardo is expressing a minority view. What would Zimbardo have to do to turn his minority view into a view held by the majority?
>
> **6** 'In every situation of evil, there are almost always some few who resist and rebel, who don't comply.'
> Outline factors that contribute to resistance to obedience.

THE EXTENDED WRITTEN RESPONSE – ADDITIONAL QUESTIONS

1 Outline and evaluate explanations of independent behaviour in either conformity or obedience. (*12 marks*)

2 'Peer pressure may be regarded as an example of majority influence. When all your friends are drinking alcohol at a party, it is quite difficult to resist joining in.'

Why do we conform? (*12 marks*)

3 'Obedience can be seen as beneficial. However, sometimes people are urged by an authority figure to do things that are actually or morally wrong.'

Describe and evaluate Milgram's research into obedience. (*12 marks*)

Example answers to these questions can be found at www.askanexaminer.com

USEFUL WEBSITES

http://www.youtube.com/watch?v=DKivdMAgdeA
A film of Solomon Asch's conformity experiment. The narrator guides us through the research. Watch as the participants begin to conform.

http://amos.indiana.edu/library/scripts/autokinetic.html
This site provides a description and a podcast on the autokinetic effect, used by Sherif (1936) in his research on conformity.

http://changingminds.org/explanations/theories/social_impact.htm
A brief, clear description of Bibb Letane's (1981) social impact theory here. Use the links provided for more information.

http://technorati.com/videos/youtube.com%2Fwatch%3Fv%3DagRZnsiNb_E

A series of programmes and podcasts here based around Milgram's obedience studies. Spend a little time here. You'll find really interesting ideas relating to obedience and following orders in different walks of life.

http://www.drstanleymilgram.com

This site is organized and run by Thomas Blass, himself a well-known social psychologist. Here you'll find a large amount of really interesting information about Milgram's work.

http://www.nursesnetwork.co.uk/forum/index.php?showtopic=1263

This is a discussion board where nurses can discuss issues relating to their work. Here we find a really interesting posting about obedience and authority amongst nurses. Notice that this person refers to the work of Hoffling, which is often used as an example of obedience in a real-life situation.

http://changingminds.org/explanations/theories/reactance.htm

Here we find a really good explanation of reactance theory, where people actively seek to take part in forbidden behaviours. Once you've taken a look at this, have a look at the link below to a paper from Bushman and Stack.

http://sitemaker.umich.edu/brad.bushman/files/bs96.pdf

This paper from Bushman and Stack is tricky to read as it is aimed at professional researchers, but we know that many of you like to really stretch yourself. It shows how labelling something as 'forbidden' (for instance, using labels like 'parental advisory' on a CD) can actually make the CD sell more, because of a 'boomerang effect'.

http://www.youtube.com/watch?v=1KXy8CLqgk4

Watch a brief film of Zimbardo's prison experiment. Take a look at people's comments about the film on this page. It really is interesting how much this research can still surprise and shock people. It was conducted quite some time ago, but it's still relevant today.

http://www.lucifereffect.org/

Zimbardo's latest work is on what he calls 'the Lucifer effect'. It is concerned with trying to understand how good people turn evil. This site gives us a brief overview of the idea and the links here are very useful and informative, particularly about the theory surrounding the Stanford prison experiment and resisting authority and influence.

Section 6

Individual Differences –
Psychopathology
(Abnormality)

WHAT YOU NEED TO KNOW

Individual Differences is in Unit 2 of the specification. As you learn you are expected to develop your knowledge and understanding of Individual Difference, including concepts, theories and studies. This also includes a knowledge and understanding of research methods and ethical issues as they relate to this area of psychology. You also need to develop the skills of analysis, evaluation and application. Rather than just recall and reproduce information, you are expected to be able to apply your knowledge and understanding. The subject content is split into two parts:

Defining and explaining psychological abnormality

- Ways defining abnormality, together with their limitations:

    Deviation from social norms • Failure to function adequately • Deviation from ideal mental health

- Key features of the biological approach to psychopathology
- Key features of psychological approaches to psychopathology:

    Psychodynamic approach • Behavioural approach • Cognitive approach

Treating abnormality

- Biological therapies: *ECT • Drugs*
- Psychological therapies:

    Psychoanalysis • Systematic desensitisation • Cognitive behavioural therapy

DEFINING ABNORMALITY

Abnormality is a very difficult thing to define. There is no clear agreement about what constitutes abnormality or normality, but a number of attempts have been made to clarify the issue.

DEVIATION FROM SOCIAL NORMS

Norms are unwritten rules created by society to guide behaviour. Breaking these rules might be considered abnormal.

Limitations
1 Social and cultural norms change over time, therefore so does what is considered abnormal, e.g. homosexuality is now acceptable; in the 1970s it was a 'mental disorder'.

2 Social norms must be considered *in context*, e.g. judges wear wigs, and are 'normal' but if they wore one out of context (i.e. outside the courtroom), they would be considered 'abnormal'.

3 Who decides on the norms? Our western 'white' norms cannot always be sensibly applied elsewhere in the world, e.g. *talking to the spirit world* is not 'normal' here but maybe is in another culture.

ASK AN EXAMINER

There's no way round it, no short cuts – you need to know these three definitions really well. Here's one tip though, which might help you get maximum marks – use examples to clarify your answer. For example, if describing social norms, give an example of a behaviour that breaks social norms.

FAILURE TO FUNCTION ADEQUATELY

Sometimes people engage in behaviours that are somehow 'not good for them'. Relationships and day-to-day living may be difficult, e.g. anorexia nervosa is a maladaptive behaviour that can cause major disruption. It can be measured using the Global Assessment of Functioning (GAF) scale.

Limitations
1 Whether or not someone is failing to function can be a subjective judgement.

2 Some behaviours, although unacceptable, may not be maladaptive to the person, e.g. a 'happy' murderer is someone who is abnormal but not maladaptive. Maladaptive does not necessarily mean abnormal.

3 What is 'adequate' in one culture may not be in another, e.g. the kind of public mourning seen in some cultures might be seen as abnormal in others where such emotions are more controlled.

DEVIATION FROM IDEAL MENTAL HEALTH

If we can recognise what is *normal* then whatever fails these criteria is necessarily *abnormal*. Jahoda (1958) suggested six criteria for 'normality', or *optimal living*:

1 Positive view of self
2 Actualisation
3 Autonomy
4 Accurate view of reality
5 Environmental adaptability
6 Resistance to stress

Limitations
1 Very few people satisfy all these criteria, e.g. 'actualisation' is reached by few people in life.

2 The criteria are open to interpretation, e.g. what is *real* for one is not *real* for another – *reality* for a front-line soldier is very different from that of an accountant.

3 What is 'ideal' in one culture might not be considered 'ideal' in another, e.g. the criteria emphasise personal fulfilment, a value not always shared by non-Western cultures.

Apply Your Knowledge

Caroline reads her horoscope every morning, and spends lots of money regularly telephoning premium numbers to get updates. She does exactly what her horoscope says, and on some days she doesn't leave the house at all if she thinks that the horoscope is unfavourable.

(a) Use one definition of abnormality to explain whether or not Caroline is exhibiting abnormal behaviour. (*3 marks*)
(b) Give one limitation of the definition used in (a). (*3 marks*)

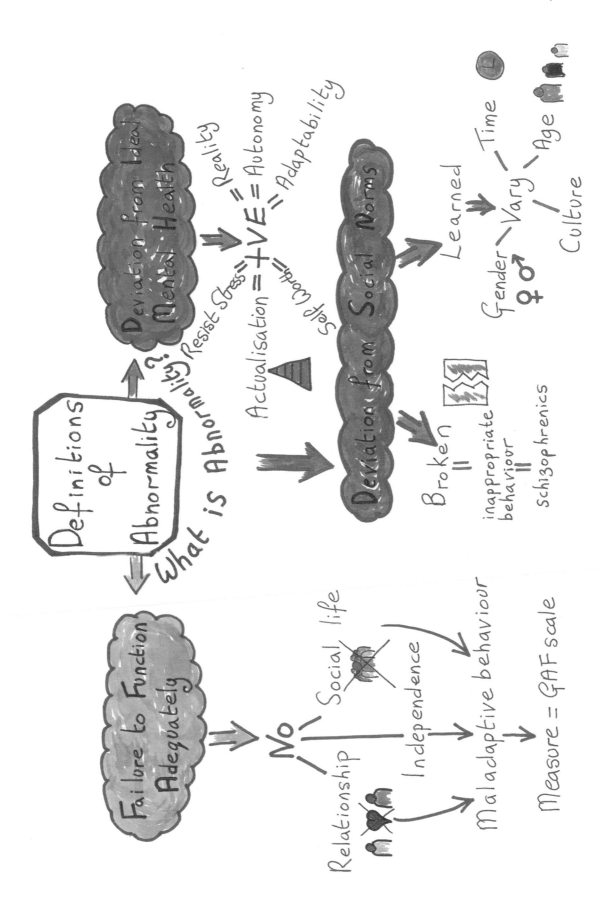

Definitions of Abnormality

What is Abnormality?

Deviation from Ideal Mental Health

Resist Stress = Reality
Actualisation = +VE = Autonomy
Self worth = = Adaptability

Deviation from Social Norms

Learned

Broken = inappropriate behaviour = schizophrenics

Gender ♀ ♂ — Vary — Time
— Age
Culture

Failure to Function Adequately

No — Social life
Relationship — Independence — Maladaptive behaviour
Measure = GAF scale

BIOLOGICAL CAUSES OF ABNORMALITY

Mental health problems are regarded as illnesses. Problems have their origins in a damaged or malfunctioning biology.

THE BIOLOGICAL APPROACH

INFECTION

● *Bacteria and viruses* can infect the brain, causing mental illness.

● Brown (2004) says that women who suffer with influenza during pregnancy may have children who develop schizophrenia later in life.

GENETICS

● We inherit mental illnesses in the same way we inherit physical characteristics.

● Holland et al (1988) show that identical twins (who share 100% of their genes) are both more likely to suffer with an eating disorder than non-identical twins (who share 50% of genes).

BIOCHEMISTRY

● *Neurotransmitters* are the chemicals that brain cells use to communicate.

● Imbalances in these are said to cause mental illness, e.g. schizophrenia is linked to an imbalance in a neurotransmitter called *dopamine*.

● Taking drugs can help correct such an imbalance.

BRAIN DAMAGE

● A blow to the head, interruptions to blood flow such as stroke, and growths such as tumours can cause behavioural problems.

● The type of problem depends on where the damage occurs.

The twins study – Holland et al (1988)

They wanted to know whether the susceptibility to suffer from anorexia nervosa was inherited.

How did they do it? They compared the rates of anorexia in identical (monozygotic, 100% shared genes) with the rates in non-identical twins (dizygotic, 50% shared genes). If anorexia occurred in both identical twins at a higher rate than in both non-identical twins, then this would suggest a genetic contribution.

What did they find? 56% of the identical twins both suffered with anorexia but only 5% of the non-identical twins both did. This shows that susceptibility to anorexia may well have a significant genetic component.

Take a closer look: ● Even though physically and genetically identical, monozygotic twins may have different experiences (some were raised in different countries!), making them different psychologically. Something other than genetics may influence the problem.
● Diagnosing anorexia is difficult. It is, for instance, similar to bulimia in some ways, so we cannot be certain the twins were anorexic.
● If anorexia was completely a genetic disorder, then monozygotic twins should share anorexia 100% of the time, but this was not the case. This means that extraneous variables were influencing the results.

BIOLOGICAL THERAPIES

Because abnormality is considered a symptom of some underlying biological problem, therapies focus on altering the physical state of the body.

DRUGS

● Can be *curative* (they cure the problem) or *palliative* (they suppress the symptoms).

● *Antipsychotics* are used in treating disorders like schizophrenia, where people may hallucinate or experience disturbed thoughts. These work by suppressing the neurotransmitter dopamine.

● *Antidepressants* are used to treat mood disorders such as depression, e.g. drugs such as Prozac increase the level of a neurotransmitter called serotonin.

● *Anxiolytics* reduce anxiety and include benzodiazapines such as Valium.

ELECTROCONVULSIVE THERAPY (ECT)

● This involves inducing convulsions by delivering brief electric shocks to the brain.

● It is not clear how it works, but is thought to improve symptoms by altering levels of the neurotransmitters serotonin and noradrenaline.

● Coffey et al (1991) say that those treated with ECT show no signs of brain damage at all, so it is deemed safe. Reid (2005) said that in rats shocks to the brain actually benefit survival of brain cells through stimulating the production of a protective protein.

DO BIOLOGICAL THERAPIES WORK?

● Tamminga (1970) – drug therapies effective in treating schizophrenia and do reduce some symptoms. Some patients though (40%) said that some symptoms were not improved.

● Lieberman (1998) – antidepressants do reduce the symptoms of depression.

● Rather than curing the problem, drugs can help to delay or reduce the severity of another episode, providing relief for the patient and making the problem more manageable, and giving opportunities for psychological therapies.

● Rey and Walter (1997) – 70% with severe depression find relief with ECT, but Schwartz (1995) says that 85% of those relapse, so the helpfulness of ECT is short lived for many.

ASK AN EXAMINER

Students sometimes struggle to get maximum marks when they are asked to describe the biological approach, but this is probably due to disorganised thinking than to any difficulty with the question. Make the connection with physical illness then say something about the four possible causes of mental illness – and if you want to make sure of your marks add an example here and there. Straightforward or what!

Apply Your Knowledge

Mark has not been feeling too good lately. He seems to be anxious all the time and can't seem to concentrate on important things like his family or work. His doctor has given him some pills to take and has asked to see him again in a month.

(a) What name is given to this sort of therapy? (*1 mark*)

(b) Assess the effectiveness of this kind of therapy. (*4 marks*)

ASK AN EXAMINER

An exam question could ask explicitly for drugs or ECT, so be sure to know something about each! If you get a general question on biological therapies, then write about both – it will be easier to get all the marks this way.

THE PSYCHOLOGICAL APPROACH TO PSYCHOPATHOLOGY

Mental health problems are not regarded as *illnesses* as such. Rather, problems have their origins in abnormal thoughts, feelings and behaviours. There are three psychological approaches to abnormality: *psychodynamic*, *behavioural* and *cognitive*.

PSYCHODYNAMIC CAUSES OF ABNORMALITY

This is most closely associated with Sigmund Freud. Our unconscious (the part of our mind that we are not aware of) drives our behaviour. Traumatic childhood memories and experiences can become part of our unconscious.

THE STRUCTURE OF THE PSYCHE

The mind (psyche) is influenced by three forces: the *id*, the *ego* and the *superego*. A healthy psyche is one in which the three parts are in equal balance. Abnormal behaviour is often the symptom of the unconscious conflict between these three forces.

PSYCHOSEXUAL DEVELOPMENT

Traumatic childhood memories can be 'repressed' and cause psychological problems later in life. We can become fixated at various stages during *psychosexual development*, causing abnormality in later life. Each psychosexual stage is associated with different kinds of behaviour:

Oral stage: oral traits, such as smoking, eating and drinking, particularly when stressed.

Anal stage: possible obsessions with cleanliness and order, or difficulty expressing emotions.

Phallic stage: anxiety and inadequacy. Problems with gender identity and moral understanding.

Genital stage: fixations from the early years become active and affect behaviour.

PSYCHODYNAMIC THERAPIES – PSYCHOANALYSIS

Psychoanalysis is a 'talking therapy' that aims to bring subconscious thoughts into consciousness. *Resistance* occurs when the client finds things hard to talk about. A 'cure' starts with *transference*, which is where repressed feelings and thoughts are projected onto the therapist.

SOME TECHNIQUES USED IN PSYCHOANALYSIS

Free association: client relaxes and speaks freely about whatever comes to mind to encourage unconscious thoughts to emerge.

Dream analysis: the therapist analyses the latent (symbolic) content of dreams to uncover unconscious wish fulfilment.

DO PSYCHODYNAMIC THERAPIES WORK?

● The therapies take a very long time and can be very expensive. They seek to identify the problem that is hidden, so judging effectiveness is very difficult.

● Grunbaum (1993) – therapy provides a *placebo effect*. It is *being treated* that helps, *not* the treatment itself.

● Eysenck (1952) – psychodynamic therapies do not work – recovery relates to *spontaneous remission* (or 'natural improvement'). Recovery rate of patients not in therapy was comparable to those in therapy.

● Freud's case studies, e.g. Anna 'O' and the 'Rat Man', demonstrate the effects of the unconscious on conscious behaviour and the success of psychodynamic therapy as a treatment.

ASK AN EXAMINER

Make sure that the cause of abnormal behaviour is clear in your answer – this is vital in order to get all the marks!

ASK AN EXAMINER

Psychodynamic theory can appear very daunting at first – lots of new ideas and ways of thinking about things. Don't worry about it though. You will never be offered more than 6 marks for describing the approach, so you are not expected to write a great deal. Organize your thinking – mention the assumption about the unconscious and childhood, something about the structure of the psyche and something about psychosexual development. 6 marks – easy!

Apply Your Knowledge

John is obsessively tidy. Whenever anybody visits his house and puts something down he immediately tidies it away. John doesn't realise he's doing this but his friends find it irritating.

Using the basic assumptions of the psychodynamic approach, explain the origins of John's problem. (*4 marks*)

THE BEHAVIOURAL APPROACH

Belief here is that all behaviour (normal or abnormal) is learned via *classical* or *operant conditioning*.

CLASSICAL CONDITIONING

We form an *association* between something in the environment (a *stimulus*) and a physical or emotional state (a *response*). For example, in the case of a phobia we *learn* to become afraid by associating the phobic object with fear.

OPERANT CONDITIONING

We learn through *reinforcement*. A reinforcer is anything that increases the likelihood of us repeating a behaviour. Simply put, if something is pleasurable we might do it again, if not we probably won't. For example, if dieting gains compliments from people (the *reinforcement*), we may continue to diet in order to continue the reinforcement and eventually generate an eating disorder.

BEHAVIOURAL THERAPIES – SYSTEMATIC DESENSITISATION

If a behaviour can be *learned* it can also be *unlearned*.

Systematic desensitisation

This is explained best through an example. For flying, it may look like this:

1 Imagine a situation where someone is afraid of flying. First, the person must learn relaxation.

Progressive relaxation		**Reciprocal inhibition**
The client learns relaxation and breathing control	**leads to** →	Anxiety response is inhibited as it is incompatible with relaxation

ASK AN EXAMINER

Systematic desensitization is much easier to remember than to write! Think about the hierarchy of fearful stimuli, and how you progress up it whilst in a relaxed state. It is easily applied to any question that is focused on someone being afraid of something, so be sure you can recognise one when you see it.

2 An *anxiety hierarchy* is identified. The client is gradually exposed to stimuli further up the hierarchy (more anxiety) until he or she can cope with the highest levels.

Photo of plane	Watching a plane fly	Being at an airport	Sitting on a plane	Flying!

Low ——————————————————————→ High

Anxiety level

DO BEHAVIOURAL THERAPIES (SYSTEMATIC DESENSITISATION) WORK?

- Yes, for some disorders – most effective treatment for 80–90% of simple phobias.

- It's a robust therapy – e.g. you don't have to experience a spider in real life for it to work! The thought is enough.

- Paul (1960) – compared systematic desensitisation with other therapies and found it the most effective in reducing public speaking anxiety.

- It is only really useful for problems where anxiety is an issue.

Apply Your Knowledge

Derek is afraid of dogs. He freezes in terror when he encounters one and doesn't go anywhere where there might be a dog.

How might systematic desensitisation be used to help Derek with his problem? (*4 marks*)

ASK AN EXAMINER

Make the contrast and understand it better! The cognitive approach focuses on thinking. This is quite different from the behavioural approach (behaviour) and the psychodynamic approach (unconscious drives).

THE COGNITIVE APPROACH

Abnormality results from faulty mental processes – *faulty cognition*.

Kendall (1993) – problems are caused by *distortions and discrepancies*.
Cognitive distortions: information is not accurately processed.
Cognitive deficiencies: lack of planning and thinking leads to an inappropriate solution.
Correct the *deficiency* or encourage greater *accuracy* and the problem can be helped.

BECK (1967) – THE COGNITIVE TRIAD

Depression is caused by a tendency in some people to interpret everyday events in negative ways. This is because of *cognitive error*, which leads to them feeling negative about themselves, the world and the future, which Beck called the *cognitive triad*.

Thinking about **themselves**
'I am a worthless person'

Thinking about **the world**
'All the problems in the world cannot be fixed'

Thinking about **the future**
'Everything is bound to get worse'

COGNITIVE THERAPIES – COGNITIVE BEHAVIOURAL THERAPY (CBT)

Helping a person to think differently can help overcome psychological disorders.

Step 1: *Understand the problem.* The client's thoughts are analysed to see how they affect the client.

Step 2: *Work out how to change the thoughts, feelings and behaviours.* Replacing negative feelings with positive ones. For instance, cars, planes or busy places may cause anxiety, but training can be done to replace anxious feelings with positive, fun feelings. The client may be required to take homework and practise.

At each session, the therapist reviews what has been done and the result. The length of therapy depends on the recovery rate of the individual.

DOES COGNITIVE BEHAVIOURAL THERAPY WORK?

- CBT is often favoured over other therapies because it aims to get rid of the problem, not just the symptoms.
- Evans (1992) – CBT at least as good as drug therapy in preventing a relapse.
- Keller (2001) – combination of CBT and drug therapy more effective than either therapy alone.
- Butler (2006) – effectiveness depends on the disorder. When the problem is severe, a combination of drugs and CBT is best, i.e. schizophrenics can experience 'thought disturbances' and it is only when drugs alleviate this that CBT can be used effectively.

Apply Your Knowledge

'Christmas shopping?! You've got to be joking!' said Hiro, 'I can't go into town with all those people everywhere. It's an absolute nightmare. No space to walk, all that noise. No way! I'm staying at home, there's no way I can ever go out into a crowd.'

How might Hiro's problem be overcome using a therapy from the cognitive approach? (*4 marks*)

Check your knowledge

1 Indicate on the table below which of the therapies are biological and which are psychological. *(5 marks)*

	BIOLOGICAL	PSYCHOLOGICAL
Psychoanalysis		
Electroconvulsive therapy		
Systematic desensitisation		
Cognitive behavioural therapy		
Drug therapy		

2 a) List **three** features of the biological approach to psychopathology. *(3 marks)*
  (b) Outline **one** of the features listed in (a). *(3 marks)*

3 Explain **one** weakness of the biological approach to psychopathology. *(3 marks)*

4 What assumptions does the behavioural approach make about the origins of abnormal behaviour? *(4 marks)*

5 Explain **one** weakness of the behavioural approach to psychopathology. *(3 marks)*

6 Give **three** key features of the cognitive approach to abnormality. *(2 + 2 marks)*

7 (a) Briefly outline the following definitions of abnormality:
    Deviation from ideal mental health *(3 marks)*
    Failure to function adequately *(3 marks)*
    Deviation from social norms *(3 marks)*
  (b) Give **one** limitation for each of the definitions outlined in (a). *(3 + 3 + 3 marks)*

8 Describe the use of the following biological therapies in the treatment of abnormality:
  (a) Drugs *(3 marks)*
  (b) ECT *(3 marks)*

9 Assess the effectiveness of biological therapies in treating abnormality. *(5 marks)*

10 How is psychoanalysis used to treat abnormality? *(4 marks)*

11 Describe how cognitive behavioural therapy is used in the treatment of abnormality. *(4 marks)*

12 Give **one** weakness of the cognitive approach. *(3 marks)*

13 Explain how systematic desensitisation is used in the treatment of abnormality. *(4 marks)*

14 Assess the effectiveness of any one psychological therapy. *(4 marks)*

HOW SCIENCE WORKS

A study investigating the effectiveness of treatments for fear of dental drilling found that people needed a mean number of 10.5 therapy sessions using systematic desensitisation and a mean number of 11.5 sessions using cognitive behavioural therapy.

(a) Use this graph paper to sketch an appropriate graph of this data. (*2 marks*)

(b) Name the type of graph you have drawn. (*1 mark*)

(c) What does this graph tell you about the effectiveness of the two therapies? (*2 marks*)

(d) Identify one ethical issue arising from this kind of research and explain how this could be dealt with. (*3 marks*)

(e) Outline how researchers might go about evaluating the effectiveness of drug therapy. (*3 marks*)

HOW SCIENCE WORKS

Think about the importance of social norms in defining abnormality

● Think up about five powerful social norms (for example, standing in a queue)

● Turn each into a Likert scale question about the extent to which breaking the norm is abnormal (for example, 'It is abnormal not to queue'. Do you agree or disagree on a scale of 1 strongly agree to 5 strongly disagree?).

● Identify a target population, decide on a sampling method and administer the questionnaire.

● Total the number of 4/5 and 1/2 responses and draw a graph of this.

Things to consider

● What does your graph tell you about the importance of social norms in defining abnormality?

● What could you have added to the questionnaire to gather qualitative data?

● What would qualitative data have added to your findings?

● What ethical considerations are important in research like this?

● Do you think that if you did the same thing again but with a different target population you would replicate your findings?

● You could investigate the importance of culture by including norms from other societies.

The extended written response

Describe and evaluate the cognitive approach to explaining abnormality. *(12 marks)*

According to the cognitive approach, abnormality results from faulty thinking. According to Kendall (1993) there are two kinds of faulty thinking that can lead to psychological problems. Cognitive deficiencies occur when a lack of sufficient thinking and planning affects behaviour in a negative way. Cognitive distortions occur when we don't process information accurately, leading to exaggerated thinking which affects everyday behaviour.

Some questions lend themselves to a 'describe first – evaluate second' approach, and this is a good example of that kind. The opening two paragraphs provide a description of the cognitive approach with as much detail as can be reasonably expected of a good candidate in the limited time and space of an exam. It is always possible to say more of course, or express things in a different kind of way, but don't use up too much space as you still have the 'evaluate' injunction to deal with!

According to Beck, there is a tendency to think negatively because of automatic cognitive error. These are very common in some people and lead to a tendency to interpret everyday events in negative ways. For example, some people might be overly critical of themselves because they only process the information which can be interpreted in negative ways. Beck used the idea of a cognitive triad to explain how cognitive errors lead to negative thinking about the world, self and the future.

The cognitive approach has been used to explain a range of psychological problems, but perhaps it has been most successfully applied to depression.

This is an evaluative point because it is showing application of knowledge. That is worth remembering – it can sometimes get you evaluation marks when all else fails!

It has also led to a number of effective therapies, for example, Cognitive Behavioural Therapy (CBT).

There is no need to describe CBT here – this is not an essay on therapy so too much detail on this would affect the focus of the essay.

CBT has been found to be particularly effective for treating depression and phobia. Evans et al found that CBT was at least as effective as drug therapy, and was even more effective when it was a combined treatment with drugs.

This is evaluation because criticism of the therapy is also a criticism of the approach on which it is based. A criticism is not necessarily negative – the previous few sentences made positive points about the cognitive approach and CBT. The next few sentences make several negative points, adding up to a fairly good balance between description and evaluation.

However, the cognitive approach has limitations. Whilst it offers an explanation for some forms of abnormality it cannot easily explain others. This limits its application in therapy, for example when someone has a severe problem thinking and talking about themselves, such as with schizophrenia. This means that sometimes the cognitive approach has to be combined with another approach. In the example of schizophrenia, a biological approach involving drug therapy might reduce extreme symptoms and make a cognitive approach possible.

These final few sentences provide several negative points which give the essay a sense of balance in evaluation. This balance between positive and negative evaluation can make an essay sound more reasonable, considered and thus, most importantly, effective. It is important to remember that, whilst being endlessly negatively critical of something rather than being balanced is easier, it is not necessarily the best way of appearing 'effective' in your evaluation.

COMMENTS

Straightforward describe-and-evaluate questions like this often lend themselves to an answer that is straightforward in structure. Here, a 'describe first – evaluate second' approach to answering the question was the easiest way forward. This way of answering essay-type questions is a good way of ensuring a balance between description and evaluation. By getting the description out of the way, all there is left to concentrate on is ensuring that you write in clearly evaluative ways. Both paper space and writing style can be managed easily.

You do not need masses of evaluation of the cognitive approach to evaluate it effectively. Overly brief or overly complex lists of criticisms of the approaches to abnormality have been avoided in favour of this technique – LEARN LESS, LEARN IT WELL, USE IT WISELY. You are far better off knowing less really well than trying to rote-learn rather meaningless material. The structure of this essay can be used as a template for other questions in this area – namely biological approach, behavioural approach and psychodynamic approach.

In The News

After research shows drugs don't work, can you REALLY beat depression by talking to a computer?

THE news that anti-depressants such as Prozac are no better than a placebo has caused consternation among patients with moderate depression and their doctors.

There is an alternative: cognitive behavioural therapy (CBT), a so-called 'talking therapy' designed to help alter negative thought patterns. It does help if you can get to see a therapist. Unfortunately, patients often face waiting up to 18 months for talking therapy treatment; it's estimated the health service needs another 10,000 therapists to meet demand.

The Government announced last week it was going to spend nearly £200 million on training therapists over three years. But that's a long wait for patients. In the meantime, there is another treatment for depression that is not only free of side-effects, but could be supplied to every GP practice in the country within a few months and at a fraction of the £300 million being spent every year on depression drugs, let alone

training therapists. Not only that, but it works. Indeed, two years ago, the National Institute for Health and Clinical Excellence (NICE) recommended it should be available to everyone in the country. The problem is, very few doctors know anything about it.

The 'wonder' treatment is CBT delivered via a computer. While this might sound impersonal and futuristic, there's good evidence that getting CBT from a computer is as effective as seeing a therapist. Recently, a study of computerised therapy by City University, London, found that three out of five depressed patients needed only eight weekly sessions to be cured.

The first thing CBT teaches you is that although you can't change what has happened, you can change how you feel and what you do about it. If you're depressed, you have lots of negative thoughts about yourself, how you are hopeless, how you never finish anything and so on. CBT helps you to explore

getting you to do practical exercises. For instance, asking how you would feel if your friends didn't turn up to meet you at the cinema as arranged. If you assumed it was because they didn't like you, it would prompt you to think of other reasons they might not have turned up, such as missing their train.

Once you are thinking and feeling differently about what's wrong, it's only a small step to start imagining the different actions you could take.

"Just setting them out makes them seem manageable. I got some useful ideas about how to deal with the negative thoughts I was always having about being so hopeless." This was in stark contrast to the kind of help Caroline, a 40-year-old manager at a dental practice, had from her doctor. "He gave me some pills, but they made it worse," she says. "Then he told me I'd get over it eventually and I'd have to live with it until then." Three years ago, Dr Peter Crouch, a GP in Swindon, became one of the first to offer the treatment. "We prescribe drugs at our practice as well," he says, "but I have noticed that the programme does seem to have a more lasting effect.

"Afterwards, even if a patient has had a bad experience that you'd expect to trigger depression, they often handle it much more effectively." And the flexibility of computerised CBT (cCBT) is a major benefit, he says. "For those with minor symptoms very few services can be delivered within a few minutes of consultation and in the patient's own home.

"It is also discreet – it allows a businessman who wants to keep his condition quiet to log on to the programme on his own computer." Swindon is one of the few health authorities that offers the therapy (through 30 GPs).

Barbara Stapleton, who works in mental health in Swindon, says she is amazed there hasn't been a proper push to make cCBT available. "The figures suggest it has cut GP visits and brought down drug prescribing," she says.

A NICE report estimated that making computerised treatment widely available would save £126 million a year. (The company behind the programme says it could get it to every GP for a total cost of £10 million). But so far the treatment is available in fewer than 5 per cent of English primary care trusts. Caroline lives in Manchester, where the local primary care trust does fund cCBT. "We're finding that when people are asked to rate their level of depression they reduce it by about half after following the programme," says Nicky Lidbetter, who has been helping patients use cCBT.

"If this was a cancer drug, imagine the hullabaloo with those kinds of improvement rates if it wasn't being given to people." The cost of an eight-week course of treatment is £65 per person. The cost of an eight-week course with a therapist is £750.

JEROME BURNE
Daily Mail (London), March
18, 2008

Stretch and Challenge

1 What impression does the article give about the effectiveness of drug treatment?

2 If you were to write a counter-argument to the view of drugs put forward in the article, what would you say?

3 A recent study of computerised cognitive behavioural therapy (cCBT) found that cure was possible after only eight weekly sessions. How does this compare with the concept of cure in psychodynamic therapy?

4 What aspects of Beck's cognitive triad can you identify in the article?

5 Explain why cCBT might only be accessible to certain people.

6 The goal of cognitive therapy is to focus on the patterns of thought and behaviour that are causing problems. Describe the techniques involved in CBT and consider ways in which it appears to differ from cCBT.

7 Using what you have learned about treatments for abnormality, assess the effectiveness of the cognitive approach to therapy.

THE EXTENDED WRITTEN RESPONSE – ADDITIONAL QUESTIONS

1 Discuss the biological approach to psychopathology. (*12 marks*)

2 Outline and evaluate two definitions of psychological abnormality. (*12 marks*)

3 Describe and evaluate one or more psychological therapies used to treat abnormality. (*12 marks*)

Example answers to these questions can be found at www.askanexaminer.com

USEFUL WEBSITES

http://www.freudfile.org/
The life and work of one of the most influential psychologists in history, Sigmund Freud.

http://www.makingthemodernworld.org.uk/learning_modules/psychology/02.TU.04/
This is a fantastic site. Have a poke about here and see what you can find out and learn about psychology and mental health. There are interactive components where techniques are explained and your opinions of them are recorded. There is a lot to do here, and a good deal of it is relevant to your examination.

http://neurophilosophy.wordpress.com/2006/12/04/the-incredible-case-of-phineas-gage/
The amazing story of Phineas Gage, whose abnormality was brought about by physical damage, a terrible accident at work, where a metal spike was driven through his head. Read all about it here.

http://www.youtube.com/watch?v=OmkiMlvLKto
This film tells the story of Clive Wearing, whose abnormality came about as a result of an infection.

http://www.apa.org/monitor/mar02/genetic.html
Here we find that whether someone suffers with anorexia is down to both their psychology and their physical make-up (genetics).

http://www.rcpsych.ac.uk/mentalhealthinformation/therapies/electroconvulsivetherapy,ect.aspx
Some questions and answers from the Royal College of Psychiatrists about the use of electroconvulsive therapy, a biological treatment for psychopathology.

http://www.nhsdirect.nhs.uk/articles/article.aspx?articleID=469#
Here, the National Health Service describes cognitive behavioural therapy.

http://www.socyberty.com/Psychology/Setting-Up-a-Systematic-Desensitization.52432
In this site, the steps for systematic desensitisation are described.

GET TO KNOW YOUR EXAM

AS level Psychology consists of two units, both assessed by a 1½-hour examination and each one accounting for 50% of the marks:

Unit 1 (PSYA1) – Cognitive Psychology, Developmental Psychology, and Research Methods.

Unit 2 (PSYA2) – Biological Psychology, Social Psychology, and Individual Differences.

This examination is designed deliberately to discourage rote learning of answers. The questions appear in a wide variety of formats, varying in the marks available and the skills they are assessing. The examination aims to assess three main skills. These are called *assessment objectives*, and they are:

1. Knowledge and understanding skills

These are assessed by questions that require you to recall knowledge. For example, you might be asked to select appropriate material and tick the relevant box, or you might be asked to give an outline of an explanation. The level of detail required will vary across questions according to the number of marks available.

2. Analysis, evaluation and application skills

These are about your understanding of things like strengths and limitations, and your ability to apply knowledge to new situations. You might be asked to evaluate something, or give a strength or a weakness. The level of detail required in your answers will vary according to the marks offered.

Every exam paper will have several examples of *analysis and application* questions. Examples of these are given throughout this book as Apply Your Knowledge questions, where you use your knowledge in unfamiliar situations. This is a good example of why rote learning is not an effective way of preparing for this exam. If you don't put the effort into developing a good understanding of psychology, you will struggle to get high marks in this type of question.

3. How science works skills

This refers to your knowledge and understanding of how psychology as a science works – basically, it is assessing your psychological research skills. Questions assessing these skills do not have their own separate section – all how science works questions are *contextualised*. This means that you will be required to demonstrate your knowledge and understanding in the context of a particular scenario given in the question. You will find examples of this kind of question in the Research Methods chapter.

How science works is mainly assessed in PSYA1, where it is has equal importance with the other skills. This means that your knowledge will be tested in the context of Cognitive Psychology and Developmental Psychology.

How science works is much less important in PSYA2, with only half as many marks allocated to it as in PSYA1. The type of question you will be asked will also be much more limited. Be sure to know about things like how studies were conducted, their advantages and weaknesses, problems of interpreting results and ethical issues associated with research.

In your own learning and research you might come across lots of jargon used to describe these skills – for example, they are often referred to as AO1, AO2 and AO3 skills (AO standing for 'assessment objective'). Ignore this stuff – you really don't need a detailed knowledge of what these skills are, and effort put into it is wasted. Your concern should be with learning about psychology. Your task is to answer the questions correctly, because in doing this you will in any case be demonstrating these skills. Examiners (and to some extent teachers) are the only people to whom this jargon really matters.

There is only one area of the exam where an awareness of assessment objectives is useful, and that is with *extended written response questions*. Why is it important here? Because, in these questions, two skills are being assessed and it is very important that you know how to write answers which effectively address these skills. Also, your responses to these questions will need an equal balance of skills in order to achieve all the available marks.

The extended written response question

These are sometimes referred to as 'essays'. They vary in demand from 8 marks to 12 marks and require you to demonstrate knowledge/understanding (AO1) and analysis/evaluation/application (AO2) skills in equal proportion. The more marks there are available, the more you are expected to write. With these questions, whilst it is important to know *what* to write, it is just as important to be aware of *how* you write it.

The knowledge and understanding skills are straightforward enough – this is where you demonstrate what you know about the topic in question. Quite simply, the marks you get for AO1 will depend on the extent to which your writing demonstrates accurate understanding and detailed knowledge. No waffle or confusion is allowed for the highest mark.

Many students find the analysis, evaluation and application skills a little trickier. Many kinds of knowledge count as AO2, for example criticisms of studies or theories, supporting evidence, alternative explanations. However, it is not enough that you include this material in your answer; you must include it *effectively*, i.e. it must *look* evaluative.

Certain key terms can help to 'trigger' AO2 marks by making it clear to examiners that you are being evaluative. For example, 'however', 'on the other hand', 'support for this', 'a criticism of this is' are all good words and phrases that will communicate your intentions to the examiner. This is why it is important to think about *how* you write – the examiner will not think for you and make helpful assumptions on your behalf. Think about what it is you are trying to achieve by writing something and if this is for AO2 marks then make sure that the examiner is aware of it by using appropriate triggers.

How the essay is structured depends on both your personal preference and the question. Some people think it is a good idea to write all the AO1 material first, then write AO2. There are certainly advantages in this approach – you can think very carefully about each skill in turn, and you can carefully gauge the amount of space devoted to each. Sometimes, however, it is effective to alternate the skills.

DOING THE EXAM

The examination questions are presented in a booklet with space available for you to write your answers. For each available mark you are given two lines on which to write your answer. Space, then, is very limited, so it is really important that you consider your answer carefully before you write. There are no options on the exam paper; all questions are compulsory.

Avoid waffle and error if at all possible. Gauge the detail in your answer according to the marks available. For example, more is

Mark scheme for 12-mark extended written response questions

AO1 Knowledge and Understanding	AO2 Application of Knowledge and Understanding
6 marks **Accurate and reasonably detailed** Accurate and reasonably detailed description of research that demonstrates sound knowledge and understanding. There is appropriate selection of material to address the question.	*6 marks* **Effective evaluation** Effective use of material to address the question and provide informed commentary. Effective evaluation of research. Broad range of issues and/or evidence in reasonable depth, or a narrower range in greater depth. Clear expression of ideas, good range of specialist terms, few errors of grammar, punctuation and spelling.
5–4 marks **Less detailed but generally accurate** Less detailed but generally accurate description that demonstrates relevant knowledge and understanding. There is some evidence of selection of material to address the question.	*5–4 marks* **Reasonable evaluation** Material is not always used effectively but produces a reasonable commentary. Reasonable evaluation of research. A range of issues and/or evidence in limited depth, or a narrower range in greater depth. Reasonable expression of ideas, a range of specialist terms, some errors of grammar, punctuation and spelling.
3–2 marks **Basic** Basic description that demonstrates some relevant knowledge and understanding but lacks detail and may be muddled. There is little evidence of selection of material to address the question.	*3–2 marks* **Basic evaluation** The use of material provides only a basic commentary. Basic evaluation of research. Superficial consideration of a restricted range of issues and/or evidence. Expression of ideas lacks clarity, some specialist terms used, errors of grammar, punctuation and spelling detract from clarity.
1 mark **Very brief/flawed or inappropriate** Very brief or flawed description demonstrating very little knowledge. Selection and presentation of information is largely or wholly inappropriate.	*1 mark* **Rudimentary evaluation** The use of material provides only a rudimentary commentary. Evaluation of research is just discernible or absent. Expression of ideas poor, few specialist terms used, errors of grammar, punctuation and spelling often obscure the meaning.
0 marks **No creditworthy material**	*0 marks* **No creditworthy material**

expected of you for 4 marks than 2 marks so be sure to give more.

Whilst thought and planning are really important in the exam, adequate preparation is essential *for* it. Limited time means that you don't have the luxury of endlessly pondering an answer. There is a 'rule of thumb' that always applies in exams – *the less well you know something the more time you have to spend thinking about it, and the more time you spend thinking the less time you have to spend writing*! Learn the material well and manage your time effectively.

In addition to your psychological knowledge, marks are also awarded in the exam for quality of written communication (QoWC). This refers to such things as legibility of handwriting, grammar, punctuation, spelling, and use of specialist terminology. QoWC, however, is assessed only in the extended written responses worth 12 marks.

As mentioned earlier, you don't need to worry about what skills you are demonstrating – JUST ANSWER THE QUESTION. If you do this appropriately, you will pass.

The examination itself asks questions using a range of different styles. These are simplified in the following table. Take a look at the practice exam papers – they contain examples of all the different kinds of exam questions you are likely to get. There are also examples of these questions throughout the book.

PLAN FOR SUCCESS – PREPARE FOR YOUR EXAM

The purpose of revision is to 'fix' the information in your mind so that you can remember it when you really need it – in the exam.

Revising is an individual thing – what works for you might not work for someone else.

What you can be sure of is that you cannot directly transfer to AS level revision habits learned doing GCSEs. You have to develop and change what you do, even if only slightly, because the skills required of you at AS level are different to those at GCSE.

The responsibility for revision is yours, the learner. A 'revision' session with a teacher is all well and good, but it really isn't revision – it is part of the preparation for *your* revision. There are no short cuts. Revision takes time, effort, planning and self-discipline *on your part*. It is the very best way to avoid the stresses of cramming, late nights and under-achievement.

Question Type	Examples of Question Styles
Knowledge recall questions	Tick correct boxes, recall an idea, outline or describe something.
Analysis and application questions	Applying knowledge of psychology to an unfamiliar situation.
Evaluation questions	Explain a weakness, assess, or give a strength of something.
Contextualised research method questions	Answer questions on research methods in a context provided by the question.
Extended written response questions	'Essay' questions, requiring an equal demonstration of knowledge/understanding and evaluation/application skills. There will be one 12-mark question in Unit 1 and at least one 12-mark question in Unit 2. There may be more questions for less marks in either or both units.

The first steps

The first steps begin well before you start revising.

Get yourself sorted – make sure that you have all the material you need (textbooks, notes, past exam papers, etc.). Just as important is getting rid of anything you *don't* need. What you want in your file is the essential stuff.

Organise yourself – organised notes help to organise thinking and organised thinking leads to efficient learning. Simple psychology! Straightforward things like using file dividers can really help to clarify what it is you have to do. Familiarise yourself with the specification. This will tell you what you need to know and how things could be ordered.

Remember, this examination is designed to be unpredictable so don't question-spot. Just because a question appeared recently does not mean it won't appear again in the very near future. Prepare well and prepare to learn everything.

Manage your time

Do not study all the time. It is important to strike a balance – too much work can be as bad as too little. Make sure that you find some time for fun and relaxation.

Spaced practice – revising for about 40 to 50 minutes with 10 to 15-minute breaks works for most people, but this will depend on your attention and concentration span. Do what works for you.

Keeping track – it is important to know what revision will involve, what you need to do and what has been done. Some kind of revision timetable is essential for recording this. After drawing up your revision timetable, indicate on it all the times when you can't revise, maybe with 'X'. For example, you might have a part-time job or other commitments.

You now know the time available to you for revision. The next step is to add what it is you have to learn, but remember – psychology might not be only exam that you have to revise for and that has to be built into the timetable too!

One good idea is to cover your least favourite (usually your toughest!) topics first, and at times when you know your concentration levels will be at their best. First is good because you may have to re-visit these 'tough' topics, so you need to leave yourself that opportunity. Build in a bit of flexibility, too – you never know what might happen to disrupt your revision schedule.

You must be realistic about your revision

Week No.			Date:	
	am		pm	
Mon	X	Privation	Day care	History
Tues	Msm	X	Geology	History
Wed	Wmm	Geology	X	X
Thurs	Ewt	Attachment theories	X	X
Fri	History	Memory strategies	Geology	Attachment disruption
Sat	X	X	Geology	History
Sun	Research methods	X	X	Geology

timetable. You are only fooling yourself if you are not honest about it. Discipline and motivation are important – there is no point writing up a revision timetable if you are not going to follow it!

It can be really useful to build in a system of rewards – this is operant conditioning in action! Do you have a can't-miss TV programme? Make it your reward for completing a revision task. (Be prepared to punish yourself too – if you don't complete your task you must have the willpower to resist 'rewarding' yourself anyway!)

The learning bit

Revision is an active process. Passively sitting and reading will do you little good. Both authors have had the experience of reading a chapter only to find that, almost immediately afterwards, they can't remember a thing they read! You may have had the same experience, and it tells us something very important – *learning* is about *doing*. If you want information to stick, then you have to use it and change it in some way. For example, don't just read, write notes. And when writing notes don't just copy out pages of text. Simplify things, enlarge key words, use colour, create diagrams, use images.

Practice exam questions

You should not go into the exam and be surprised by anything. Styles of question should be familiar, you should be familiar with the style of question and the skill of writing in a restricted/limited space, and especially writing to a given amount of time. The practice exam paper in this book is included to help you develop a sense of exam time, as well as give you valuable practice at answering exam questions.

Flashcards

Reduce your notes to essential key points. You can then put these key points onto index cards. You can find these in any stationers, or

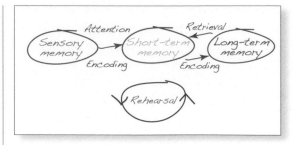

even cut out and make your own – 15cm x 10cm is a good size, and if you are making your own try to get different colour card.

Don't write too many words on each card – you should be able to glance at a card and get what you need quickly, not have to read through hundreds of words.

Vary the font – CAPITALISE, use colour, add diagrams and meaningful images, arrows and highlights. Only write on one side of the card, and try to stick to one topic per card. The cards can be carried around and reviewed in spare moments. We have lots and lots of 'spare moments' in a day – you can do an incredible amount of revision by not wasting these precious moments. And finally, as you use your flashcards you will find flaws in them, e.g. in the way that something is explained or written. Be prepared to revise them regularly – it is all part of the learning process.

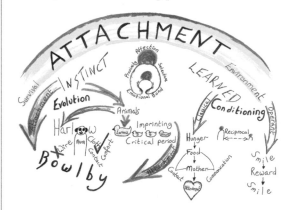

Mind maps™

Mind mapping is a really useful strategy for revision. This is because creating a mind map uses lots of different parts of your brain – you are using words, colours, images, spatial connections. A single, well-drawn mind map can take the place of pages of text. What is really important about mind maps, however, is something that is often overlooked – the thinking that goes into producing one. You really have to get to grips with the subject matter to produce a good mind map.

Mind maps make even complex ideas more understandable and memorable. They help to organise your thinking, making it easier to retrieve ideas. They will help you recognise the key ideas and concepts important for exam answers and, perhaps most importantly, tell you how ideas are meaningfully related to each other so that what you write makes sense.

Whilst there are several mind maps in this book, they are only there as examples – it is much, much better to plan and draw your own. Mind maps are easy to do, but not so easy to do well. As with anything else, practice makes perfect, and you will soon develop your own style. Take a look at the following websites for advice on how to produce good mind maps. If you prefer to use a book then the best we can recommend is *Mapping Inner Space: Learning and Teaching Visual Mapping* by Nancy Margulies. Some time spent following the advice of this book will soon turn you into an expert mind mapper!

USEFUL WEBSITES

http://www.aqa.org.uk
AQA is the exam board who manage this particular AS Level in Psychology – remember, you are doing Specification A. This website is where you will find things like the specification, past exam papers and mark schemes, and general information on the examination process.

http://www.bbc.co.uk/schools/studentlife/
Lots of good advice to be found here on things like revision and dealing with exam stress. There are also good revision timetables you can download, or use as a template for your own design.

http://www.thebrain.com/#-47
Personally, we like to see mind maps drawn by hand but if this is in any way difficult for you then fear not, help is at hand. You can get free software here to create mind maps on your computer! There are lots of different kinds of software out there so try out a few to see which suits you best.

http://www.mind-mapping.co.uk/mind-maps-examples.htm
As we've already said, we prefer hand-drawn mind maps. The ones in this book look pretty good, we think, but in case you need some more ideas on how to do it, take a look at some of these!

http://www.videojug.com/film/how-to-revise-successfully
This is a short film that gives you some useful revision advice. There are lots of things you can do to really develop your knowledge before an exam.

http://www.wikihow.com/Revise
A quick summary of things to remember when revising.

http://www.brainboxx.co.uk/a3_aspects/pages/Revision.htm
These pages set out the different skills you need when revising. Of course, by now you'll know all about memory techniques!

http://www.pe2000.com/anx-relax.htm
Learn to relax. It's a really useful skill, and is particularly important during all stressful times.

PSYCHOLOGY (SPECIFICATION A)   PSYA1

Unit 1 Cognitive Psychology, Developmental Psychology and
       Research Methods

Time allowed: 1 hour 30 minutes

Instructions

  Use black ink or ballpoint pen.
  Answer all questions.
  You must answer the questions in the spaces provided. Answers written in margins or on
  blank pages will not be marked.
  Do all rough work in this book. Cross through any rough work you do not want to be
  marked.

Information

  The maximum mark for this paper is 72.
  The marks for questions are shown in brackets.
  You are reminded of the need for good English and clear presentation in your answers.
  Quality of written communication will be assessed in question 9. Question 9 should be
  answered in continuous prose.

SECTION A – COGNITIVE PSYCHOLOGY AND RESEARCH METHODS

Total marks for this question: 4 marks

1 (a) Tick **two** of the boxes below to indicate which of the following concepts relate to the multi-store model of memory:

Sensory memory ☐
Articulatory loop ☐
Chunking ☐
Visuo-spatial sketchpad ☐

(2 marks)

1 (b) According to the multi-store model, what is the **capacity** and **duration** of short-term memory?

....

....

....

....

(2 marks)

Total marks for this question: 15 marks

2 It has been suggested that humans are not constantly vigilant and often simply don't remember details of events happening around them. To test this, psychology students conducted a study in a nearby town centre. Working in pairs, one student approached a passer-by and asked for the time. A few minutes later the second student approached the same passer-by and asked him or her to describe the person who had just asked the time.

2 (a) From what you know of eyewitness testimony, what would you expect the students to find?

....

....

....

....

....

....

(3 marks)

2   (b) State the aim of this study.

....

....

....

....

(2 marks)

2   (c) The students are conducting a field experiment. In the context of this study, give **one** advantage of a field experiment.

....

....

....

....

(2 marks)

2   (d) Why might it have been a good idea for the students to have conducted a pilot study?

....

....

....

....

(2 marks)

2   (e) What kind of sampling technique was used by the students?

....

....

(1 marks)

2   (f) How does a field experiment differ from a natural experiment?

....

....

....

....

(2 marks)

2   (g) Identify one ethical issue arising from this research and explain how the students
might deal with it.

....

....

....

....

....

....

(3 marks)

Total marks for this question: 8 marks

3   Discuss the influence of anxiety on eyewitness testimony.

....

....

....

....

....

....

....

....

....

....

....

....

....

....

....

(8 marks)

(Extra space) ....

....

....

....
....
....

Total marks for this question: 4 marks

4   One method developed in recent years to improve the amount of accurate recall from witnesses is the cognitive interview.

Outline what is involved in conducting a cognitive interview.

....
....
....
....
....
....
....
....

(4 marks)

Total marks for this question: 5 marks

5   Recently, Jenny was stopped by a lorry driver asking directions to a local factory. She was able to imagine the location and accurately describe the route.

5   (a) Use what you have learned about the working memory model to explain how Jenny was able to do this.

....
....
....
....
....
....

(3 marks)

5   (b) Unfortunately, the lorry driver did not have pen and paper handy. What memory improvement strategy might the lorry driver have used to remember Jenny's instructions?

....

....

....

....

(2 marks)

Turn over for the next question

SECTION B – DEVELOPMENTAL PSYCHOLOGY AND RESEARCH METHODS

Total marks for this question: 4 marks

6   (a) The following statements relate to attachment. Identify which two relate to Bowlby's theory of attachment.

Statement	Tick only the two that apply
Babies attach to one person in particular.	
Attachment develops because babies copy the loving and caring behaviour of the parents.	
Attachment develops in a fixed sequence.	
Babies become attached to the adult who feeds them.	

(2 marks)

6   (b) Give one criticism of the evolutionary perspective on attachment.

....

....

....

....

(2 marks)

Total marks for this question: 14 marks

7   The Strange Situation was for many years the standard way to assess the quality of a child's attachment. It has been suggested, however, that the Strange Situation lacks validity. For example, behaviour of children in the Strange Situation varies depending on which caregiver they are with at the time.

To investigate this, a psychologist conducted the Strange Situation test first with the mother, then with the father, and finally with the grandmother. Some of the results are summarised in the table below.

	% Secure Attachment
Child with mother	65
Child with father	50
Child with grandmother	65

7 (a) Use the graph paper below to sketch an appropriate graph for these results.

(2 marks)

7 (b) Write a suitable non-directional hypothesis for this study.

....

....

....

....

(2 marks)

7 (c) (i) What does the term 'validity' mean when used in the context of psychological research?

....

....

....

....

(2 marks)

(ii) Other than what is already mentioned above, give one other way in which studies using the Strange Situation may lack validity.

....

....

....

....

(2 marks)

7   (d) How could the psychologist go about assessing the reliability of her findings?

....

....

....

....

(2 marks)

7   (e) Use the findings in the table to evaluate Ainsworth's research into attachment types.

....

....

....

....

....

....

....

....

(4 marks)

Total marks for this question: 6 marks

8   Gowri has noticed that, since starting at the local nursery, her 3-year-old son Anil seems to be much more cooperative, sociable and confident.

8   (a) What aspects of centre day care might be encouraging Anil's social development?

....

....

....

....

....

....

(3 marks)

8   (b) What has research told us about the effects of day care on aggression?

....

....

....

....

....

....

(3 marks)

Total marks for this question: 12 marks

9   'Attachment is an important component in laying the foundations of a healthy individual. If it is disrupted in some way, there may be consequences for social and emotional development.'

Discuss research into the disruption of attachments.

Planning space

....

....

....

....

....

....

....

....

....

....

....

....

....

....

....

....

....

....

....

....

....

....

....

....

(12 marks)

(Extra space)...

....

....

....

....

....

END OF QUESTIONS

There are no questions printed on this page

PSYCHOLOGY (SPECIFICATION A)   PSYA2

Unit 2 Biological Psychology, Social Psychology
and Individual Differences

Time allowed: 1 hour 30 minutes

Instructions

Use black ink or ballpoint pen.
Answer all questions.
You must answer the questions in the spaces provided. Answers written in margins or on blank pages will not be marked.
Do all rough work in this book. Cross through any rough work you do not want to be marked.

Information

The maximum mark for this paper is 72.
The marks for questions are shown in brackets.
You are reminded of the need for good English and clear presentation in your answers.
Quality of written communication will be assessed in question 9. Question 9 should be answered in continuous prose.

SECTION A : BIOLOGICAL PSYCHOLOGY

Total marks for this question: 2 marks

1   Which two of the following concepts (A–D) relate to the pituitary-adrenal system? Tick the two correct boxes.

A Release of corticosteroids	
B Adrenal cortex	
C Adrenal medulla	
D Release of adrenaline	

(2 marks)

Total marks for this question: 4 marks

2   To everyone who knows her, Clare is Miss Sensible. She is patient, easy-going and tolerant. She doesn't come across as intense or competitive, and simply never does anything on impulse.

2   (a) From what you know of personality factors and stress, what type of behaviour does Clare demonstrate?

....

....

(1 marks)

2   (b) What has research shown about the link between stress and the type of personality shown by Clare?

....

....

....

....

....

....

(3 marks)

Total marks for this question: 4 marks

3   What is the relationship between stress-related illness and the immune system?

....

....

....

....

....

....

....

....

(4 marks)

Total marks for this question: 4 marks

4   Explain how psychologists have investigated workplace stress and identify one limitation of this kind of research.

....

....

....

....

....

....

....

....

(4 marks)

Total marks for this question: 10 marks

5   Rowena prefers to deal with stress by being prepared for it. For example, she knows that she finds driving stressful so she limits the amount of driving she does by taking the train whenever possible. Her friend Adrian, however, turned to his GP and has been prescribed some pills to help him deal with his stress.

5   (a) Identify the approach to coping with stress taken by Rowena.

....

....

(1 marks)

5   (b) Explain how drugs are going to help Adrian manage his stress.

....

....

....

....

....

....

(3 marks)

5   (c) State one disadvantage of Adrian's approach to stress management.

....

....

....

....

(2 marks)

5   (d) Outline one psychological method of stress management.

....

....

....

....

....

....

....

....

(4 marks)

Turn over for the next question

SECTION B : SOCIAL PSYCHOLOGY

Total marks for this question: 3 marks

6   (a) Identify the research method used by Milgram in his study of obedience.

....

....

(1 mark)

6   (b) Give one limitation of this method.

....

....

....

....

(2 marks)

Total marks for this question: 4 marks

7   Amil is a bit of a risk-taker. He thinks that in order to do well in business you have to have confidence in what you do and be independent and not worry too much about what other people think.

7   (a) What kind of locus of control does Amil appear to have?

....

....

(1 mark)

7   (b) How might Amil's locus of control influence his behaviour in a situation which requires him to conform?

....

....

....

....

....

....

(3 marks)

Total marks for this question: 5 marks

8 (a) Outline one study into conformity that demonstrates normative social influence.

....

....

....

....

....

....

....

....

(4 marks)

8 (b) Identify one ethical issue arising from this study.

....

....

(1 mark)

Total marks for this question: 12 marks

9 Discuss the influence of individual differences on independent behaviour.

Planning space

....

....

....

....

....

....

....

....

....

....

....

....

....

....

....

....

....

....

....

....

....

....

....

....

(12 marks)

(Extra space)..

....

....

....

....

....

SECTION C : INDIVIDUAL DIFFERENCES

Total marks for this question: 6 marks

10   Deviation from social norms is one definition of abnormality.

10   (a) What is a 'social norm'?

....

....

....

....

(2 marks)

10   (b) Give one example of how breaking a social norm might lead to the behaviour

being defined as abnormal.

....

....

....

....

(2 marks)

(c) Outline one other way of defining abnormality.

....

....

....

....

(2 marks)

Total marks for this question: 8 marks

11   Outline and evaluate the use of ECT in treating abnormality.

....

....

....

....

....

....

....

....

....

....

....

....

....

....

....

....

(8 marks)

Extra space ....

....

....

....

....

....

Total marks for this question: 6 marks

12   Karl is afraid of spiders. His fear completely dominates his life. Things have
become so bad that he has sought the help of a therapist.

12 (a) What assumptions would a therapist of the psychodynamic approach make about the cause of Karl's problem?

....

....

....

....

....

....

(3 marks)

12 (b) Karl decides to seek behavioural therapy. Explain how systematic desensitisation would be used to cure Karl of his fear of spiders.

....

....

....

....

....

....

(3 marks)

Turn over for the next question

Total marks for this question: 4 marks

13   Research was conducted comparing different treatments for fear of spiders.
        Effectiveness was measured by the number of therapy sessions needed until the
        client was able to hold a spider without fear. The results are presented in the graph
        below.

13   (a) What kind of graph is this?

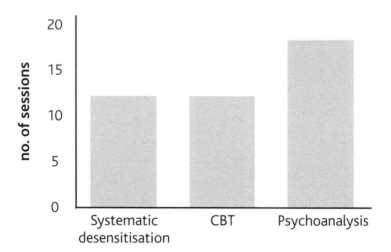

....

....

(1 mark)

13   (b) Using the graph, what conclusions could be made about the effectiveness of
        these therapies?

....

....

....

....

....

....

(3 marks)

END OF QUESTIONS

There are no questions printed on this page

Example Answers

There is often more than one way to answer a question and still gain maximum marks. The answers below are examples of answers you could give – please don't think that this is the only way of doing it! Ask An Examiner boxes provide you with extra guidance and advice. Also, please remember that we are offering thorough answers here – perhaps a little more than might be reasonably expected in an exam for maximum marks.

SECTION 1: RESEARCH METHODS

(p.13) 1. Ainsworth argues that whether an adult is secure or insecure in his or her adult relationship may be a reflection of attachment experiences during early childhood. To test this idea, researchers designed a study using self-report techniques.

ASK AN EXAMINER
Be careful not to make your answers too brief here – there are 2 marks on offer for each point so be sure to give enough detail that your answer is worth 2 marks!

(a) The study involved designing a questionnaire.
(i) Suggest two things that the researchers should have considered in the design of this questionnaire. *(2+2 marks)*

> What types of questions to ask (whether open or closed) and how the questions should be phrased (whether they create qualitative or quantitative data).

(ii) Give one weakness of questionnaire research. *(2 marks)*

> There is no guarantee that the answers participants give will be truthful.

(b) The researchers had their questionnaire printed in a local newspaper and invited readers to complete and return it.
(i) What name is given to this kind of sampling technique? *(1 mark)*

> Volunteer sampling

(ii) Outline one problem with this method of selecting participants.
(2 marks)

> The sample may not be representative of the population. Here the researchers are sampling from the 'people who buy the local newspaper' population so it may be biased.

(c) (i) **What is meant by the term 'quantitative data'?** (*1 mark*)

> The data are in the form of numbers.

(ii) **How would the questionnaire generate this kind of data?** (*1 mark*)

> It could ask for people to rate something on a scale of 1 to 5. The response would be a number so the data can be regarded as quantitative.

(d) **Suggest a question for inclusion in the questionnaire that would generate qualitative data.** (*2 marks*)

> What difficulties do you have forming relationships?

(e) (i) **What is a pilot study?** (*2 marks*)

> A small scale trial run of the study, carried out in order to check that the procedure does what it is supposed to.

(ii) **Why would it have been useful for the researchers to have conducted pilot study?** (*2 marks*)

> Self-report techniques like questionnaires need to be piloted in order to ensure that participants are interpreting the questions properly and that the questionnaire really is providing the data that is wanted. Problems can be ironed out and the questionnaire perfected before the real study.

An example of a very general response is given here. Lots of possible responses could be used here. For example, you could have focused on issues of reliability and validity, sampling of participants, demand characteristics and investigator bias.

(p.15) 2. The Great Holtodo has a world-renowned memory. He really is something special, and can remember the order of up to 500 cards that have been professionally shuffled. Holtodo claims that the key to his superb memory is taking regular exercise and drinking water derived only from melted Welsh snow. For some time now psychologists have been closely investigating Holtodo's amazing talents and claims.

(a) (i) What kind of study is this? (*1 mark*)

A case study.

(ii) State one weakness of the research method identified in (a). (*2 marks*)

Case studies relate usually to only one person, so generalizing the findings to others is difficult.

(iii) From what you know of strategies for memory improvement, how could Holtodo's memory for 500 cards be explained? (*3 marks*)

He may be using a mnemonic such as the method of loci to help him. He would do this by imagining a familiar place, like his house, or a familiar route he takes regularly. When he is given a card to remember he imagines it placed somewhere on his route, or in his house. When he needs to recall them he would imagine walking along his route, or through his house, identifying the cards along the way.

(b) The team designed a laboratory experiment to investigate the possible benefits to memory of drinking this special water. The results were recorded and placed in the table below:

Participant number	1 cup	2 cups	3 cups
1	10	13	12
2	13	15	25
3	9	9	30
4	12	15	17
5	4	8	12

(i) Identify the independent variable and the dependent variable in this experiment. (*1 mark*)

IV – Number of cups of water consumed

DV – score on memory task.

(ii) Identify the experimental design used here and give one limitation of this kind of design. (*3 marks*)

Repeated measures design: There could be problems because of order effects. These include practice and fatigue.

(iii) Identify one possible extraneous variable in this study. (*1 marks*)

Some participants may have eaten chocolate before they began the task and some may have skipped breakfast or lunch. It could be this that may have influenced their memory, not the water.

(iv) Assuming that they used the mean as a measure of central tendency, what would be an appropriate 'measure of dispersion' for these data?
(*1 mark*)

Standard deviation

You won't be asked to calculate a standard deviation in the exam, but you are certainly expected to know why and when you would use one! Prepare for this by understanding measures of central tendency and dispersion.

(v) What type of graph would you use to display these data? (*1 mark*)

A bar chart.

(vi) Write a short summary of the findings of this experiment. (*3 marks*)

In all cases, drinking 3 cups of water gives a better score on the memory test than drinking one or 2 cups of water. This would suggest that the water improves performance.

In some participants the effect was very large, rising from a score of 9 after one cup to 30 after 3 cups. In some participants the rise was not very large, for instance, rising from 10 to 12. This shows that there are individual differences here.

(p.16)   3.   Psychologists conducted a study into the quality of attachment relationship between children and their professional caregivers in a day care centre. The graph below shows their results.

(a) (i) What kind of correlation does this graph describe? (*1 mark*)

Positive

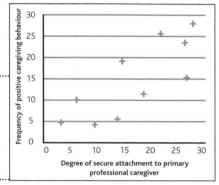

(ii) Identify the two variables measured in this study.
(*1 + 1 mark*)

Degree of attachment to primary professional caregiver, and frequency of positive caregiving behaviour.

(iii) What conclusions might the psychologists draw from the findings of this study? (*2 marks*)

The more positive care-giving a caregiver provides to the child, the more securely attached that child will become to its caregiver.

(iv) Within the context of this study, give one disadvantage of correlational research. (*2 marks*)

It does not indicate cause. The secure attachment might be due to something other than the amount of positive caregiving they had received

(b) From what you know of research into attachment, explain one difficulty that the psychologists might have encountered with assessing attachment type. (*2 marks*)

> Some researchers question how valid measures of attachment are. For example, it has been said that the Strange Situation only assesses attachment to the person a child is with at the time.

(c) Outline two ethical issues that arise in research involving children.
(*2 + 2 marks*)

> Protection: the child may become distressed, but should be protected from this at all times.
> Informed consent: the child is too young to understand the right to withdraw, or the true nature or motivation for the research.

(d) As part of the study, the psychologists interviewed the professional caregivers about their attitude towards centre day care.

(i) Give one advantage of conducting interviews as part of this research.
(*2 marks*)

> They can provide unexpected, and extremely rich and varied data that can also help inform future research.

(ii) Identify one potential problem with these interviews and suggest how this might be overcome. (*3 marks*)

> We do not know whether the caregiver answers correctly because there may be a bias within the procedure. For instance, they may want to answer honestly, but because this may damage their reputation, or the

reputation of others they may not do so. This can be overcome by interviewing them anonymously, or gathering the data anonymously, perhaps on a computer or over the internet.

(p.18)　4. It has been suggested that one important factor influencing the development of secure and insecure attachments is maternal sensitivity. To investigate this, a group of child psychologists conducted an observational study of maternal behaviour in a local mother-and-baby group.

(a) Suggest two behavioural categories that the researchers might have used in their observation. (*2 marks*)

Mother's positive emotions and mother's gentleness of behaviour.

It would be very easy to misinterpret the question here and lose marks. Look at what the study is about – it is about maternal behaviour. Your behavioural categories then should refer to the behaviour of the mother rather than the child.

(b) This study is a naturalistic observation.
(i) Outline one advantage of naturalistic observations in the context of studies like this. (*2 marks*)

It has high ecological validity – the behaviours observed occur naturally, they are not influenced by an artificial experimental situation.

(ii) It is important in such studies that participants remain unaware that they are being observed. Suggest two things that the researchers could have done to ensure that this was the case. (*2 marks*)

They could film the behaviour from behind a screen, or they could pretend to be one of the other mothers in the group. In each case the participants would not know they were being observed.

(c) How could the researchers have checked the reliability of the observations? (*2 marks*)

By comparing the observation scores of two
or more researchers. If there was agreement.

(d) Describe one method used by psychologists studying children to assess attachment type. (*3 marks*)

The strange situation. It is an 8 stage procedure
where observers record the child's responses to
the mother and the stranger at different points in
the procedure.
1 – Mother enters the room with the child.
2 – Mother responds when child wants attention.
3 – Stranger enters the room and approaches baby
slowly, mother leaves.
4 – Stranger encourages play. If child is distressed
procedure ends.
5 – Mother enters. Stranger leaves. Child settles
down and mother leaves child alone in the room.
6 – If child distressed, procedure ends.
7. – Stranger enters, step 3 repeated.
8 – Mother returns, stranger leaves.

ASK AN EXAMINER

This is a very detailed response – you wouldn't have to be this detailed for 3 marks. The main thing is to communicate in enough detail (e.g. three or four specific points) how the Strange Situation works. You could of course do something quite different, like describe the Attachment Q-Sort – the choice is yours!

(e) Outline one ethical issue that should have been considered by the psychologists. (*2 marks*)

Debriefing: After the procedure the mother should
be fully informed about the motivation for the
experiment, and the mother must be allowed to
ask any questions she may have.

(p.22)   5.   Maxi-cog is advertised as a scientifically proven way to promote mental alertness and performance naturally. Just two capsules a day will apparently lead to enhanced memory. Having failed to find this scientific proof, a team of psychologists set out to test the claims of Maxi-cog. They gave their participants the maximum daily dose of Maxi-cog and, for a period of two weeks, recorded their daily performance on a memory test. The results can be seen in the table below.

Participant number	No. of days on Maxi-cog	% Test score
1	0	20
2	0	12
3	2	24
4	4	39
5	5	46
6	5	40
7	8	50
8	6	56
9	12	34
10	14	76
11	15	45
12	13	76

(a) What does the data appear to show? (*2 marks*)

It appears to show a positive correlation between the number of days on Maxi-cog and performance on a memory test.

(b) What type of graph would you use to present these data?
(*1 mark*)

Scattergraph

(c) Suggest one way in which memory might have been tested in this study. (*1 mark*)

Participants could be asked to remember the order of as many cards as they can from a pack of shuffled cards.

(d) Write a suitable hypothesis for this study. (*2 marks*)

Taking Maxi-cog improves the percentage achieved on a memory test.

(e) Is this hypothesis directional or non-directional? (*1 mark*)

Directional

(f) Identify one potential investigator effect in this study and suggest how it might be eliminated. (*3 marks*)

The participant may know the researcher as their teacher or lecturer and may want to impress them or they may not like them and deliberately perform badly on the task. This could be eliminated by keeping the identity of the researcher secret, or using someone unknown to the participant to administer the Maxi-cog and collect the data.

(g) Identify one sampling method that might have been used in this study and explain how this could have been used to select participants for this study. (*3 marks*)

Volunteer sampling. The researcher could post a notice in their department asking for volunteers to take part, either for free or for a small fee.

You will often find that there is more than one answer to a question. Here, you could have chosen any sampling technique – you just had to make sure that you were able to explain how you use the one you chose!

(p.24)   6.   People often have difficulty carrying out more than one task at a time, especially when they are quite similar tasks. To investigate this, researchers presented groups of participants with telephone numbers to remember and recall. There were three people in each group.

Group 1 had to remember the number 01267976432 and they were presented with it in silence.
Group 2 had to remember the number 0756382496 and they had to listen to the experimenter talk whilst trying to remember the number.

(a) The hypothesis tested was: 'Less numbers will be recalled in the right order when the person listens to a conversation whilst trying to remember.'

(i) Is this a directional or non-directional hypothesis? (*1 mark*)

Directional

(ii) What is the operationalised independent variable? (*1 mark*)

Whether or not they listened to a conversation.

(b) Which type of experimental design is used in this experiment? (*1 mark*)

Independent samples.

(c) Identify a flaw in this experiment and explain how the investigator might have avoided it. (*3 marks*)

The numbers remembered by each group are different, the first number 01267976432 is easier to remember than the other number because it begins and ends with numbers in numerical order 012 and ends 432. It also looks a bit like a standard telephone number, which will be familiar to people. This could be avoided by making both groups try and remember the same number.

(d) The data are presented in the graph.

(i) What type of graph is this? (*1 mark*)

A bar chart.

(ii) What is the main finding indicated by the graph? ((*1 mark*)

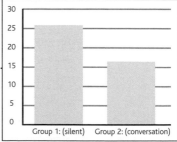

Those in the silent group were better at remembering than those who had to listen to the conversation.

(e) Use what you have learned about the working memory model to explain these findings. (3 marks)

The conversation interferes with the memory process because it uses the phonological loop that is also required in remembering the numbers. The phonological loop is part of the WMM. It contains the phonological store that is involved in the perception of all sounds, in particular speech. It is our 'inner voice' so when we try to remember numbers it is here that we 'speak' them to ourselves, and pass them to the articulatory loop for 'rehearsal'. This is why remembering in silence is better than remembering when listening to speech.

(f) This was a laboratory experiment. Using your knowledge of research methods, explain the value of such studies when investigating things that relate to 'real-life' experiences. (4 marks)

In the laboratory, behaviour is controlled carefully and so is artificial. Because of this lab experiments are said to lack ecological validity. Also, you can't use a lab experiment to investigate everything. Sometimes you have to investigate naturally occurring behaviour, so the use of the lab is limited. It is also possible that biases and demand characteristics can be easily introduced in the lab and these are often extremely hard or impossible to get rid of. This can influence the relationship between the IV and DV and so damage the validity and reliability of the experiment.

MATHS EXPERTS MAKE THE BEST POOL PLAYERS. AN INVESTIGATION INTO THE RELATIONSHIP BETWEEN MATHS ABILITY AND POOL-PLAYING ABILITY
(Answers from p.28)

Aim: The aim of this research is to see whether people who are good at maths are also good at playing pool.

Be clear. Just say what it is that you are doing.

This is a directional hypothesis. A non-directional hypothesis might be; 'There is a relationship between people's ability at maths and their ability at playing pool.' If you are not sure what might happen, but you think something might, then choose a non-directional hypothesis.

Hypothesis: People who are good at maths are also good at playing pool.

Design: This is a correlational design.

We are comparing one variable with another. Whenever we do this, we are engaging in a correlational design.

The independent variable: Here we will vary the type of task given. We'll need a pool-playing task and a maths task.

In a correlational design, we don't change something and see how it affects the performance on a task, we vary the task itself.

The dependent variables: Performance on the different tasks.

So we'll need to write down a score for each participant. One for the pool-playing task, and one for the maths task.

Possible extraneous variables: They are doing the task twice, so practice may influence their performance, or they may get tired. We can control for this by making half the participants do the pool-playing task first, and half the maths task first.

We are counterbalancing for order to ensure that practice or fatigue do not influence our results.

Operationalising the variables: We need two tasks. The maths task can be a list of simple sums. We'll get participants to answer them as fast as possible, and measure how many they got right in one minute. The pool-playing task is trickier. We can set up one shot at a time, and count how many times the person pots the ball in a row before missing.

How about 'number of balls potted in one visit to the table' or you could replace 'pool' with 'snooker' and measure 'top break'.

Getting organised: We'll need a stopwatch for timing a minute for the maths test, and a nice long series of sums written on a piece of paper. We'll need a pool table, and a piece of paper for recording data. A couple of people for a pilot will do (ask some friends) and an opportunity sample of people hanging about the common room will do.

The rule is make sure you've got everything to hand that you need.

SHHH-I'M TRYING TO WORK!: AN INVESTIGATION OF WHETHER PEOPLE REMEMBER THINGS BETTER IN SILENCE THAN WHEN THEY ARE LISTENING TO SOMEONE TALKING. (Answers from p. 30–31)

Aim: The aim of the research is to see whether memory is better in silence than when listening to a person talking.

It really is that simple. What's the point. What are you doing this for?

This is a directional hypothesis. A non-directional hypothesis might be 'people's memory is different when remembering in silence than when remembering when listening to someone talking'.

Hypothesis: People are better at remembering in silence than when listening to someone talking.

We could have chosen an independent samples design where we had two groups. One in silence, one where people listened to someone talking, or a matched pairs design, like an independent samples design, but with people in each group 'matched' as much as possible. Each design has good and bad points. (Look back to Research Methods to remind yourself if you're unsure!)

Design: This will be a repeated measures design. Each person will do the task once in silence and once when listening to someone talking.

The independent variable: 'Condition' – whether listening to speech or remembering in silence.

This is the thing that you are varying – you have control over whether the person does the task in silence or not.

This is the thing that you are measuring – the thing that depends on the independent variable. 'What score will they get on the task? It depends on whether they were listening to someone talking or not.' See?

The dependent variables: Score on the memory task.

Possible extraneous variables: They are doing the task twice, so practice may influence their performance, or they may get tired, so I'll control for that by making some people do the task in silence first then when listening to someone speaking, and some people do it the other way around. I'll counterbalance the order.

Practice and fatigue are both possible sources of confounding variables. Randomising, or better still counterbalancing order, are the way to deal with them!

Operationalising the variables: Independent variable (speech or no speech): I'll record some speech from the TV or radio onto a computer to play to the participants. When they do the task in silence I can just turn the sound off. Dependent variable: I'll give people a list of words to remember, showing participants one word at a time, each word for one second. I'll test them for how many they can remember.

There are often many ways to operationalise. You could use any number of memory tasks or ways of recording and presenting sounds

Getting organised: I'll need a stopwatch for timing the presentation of the words, a piece of paper for recording how many words are remembered, a computer for recording and playing the sounds and a room where I won't be disturbed while the research is in progress. I need a couple of people for a pilot (I'll ask my two friends) and I'll advertise for participants (that's a volunteer sample) with the promise of tea and a biscuits!

The rule is make sure you've got everything to hand that you need.

SECTION 2: COGNITIVE PSYCHOLOGY – MEMORY

(p.41) 1. 'The number you require is 04963532146, thank you for calling.' When you call directory enquiries to request a telephone number you often forget to have a pen and paper handy.

The question asks you to use your knowledge of the MSM, so you are expected to use this theory in your answer! You will earn few marks if it is not clear that ideas and concepts from the MSM are being applied.

Using what you have learned from the multi-store model of memory, how might you improve your chances of remembering the number correctly? *(3 marks)*

> According to the MSM, the capacity of STM is limited to 7+/−2 items. A telephone number longer than this is more than STM can hold. However, STM could hold more if the information was chunked. If the number was converted into three chunks – for example, 0496 3532 146 – then this would be within the capacity of 7+/−2 chunks and would be more easily remembered.

There is more than one way to answer this question. You could, for example, talk about rehearsal, in which case you could talk about maintenance, keeping the phone number in mind by repeating it over, or committing it to LTM through elaborate rehearsal.

(p.45) 2. Kelly talks all the time. In fact, her friend Sophie wonders if she ever stops! Whenever they sit together in class Sophie has trouble following what the teacher is saying, or concentrating on her written work.

Use what you have learned about the working memory model to explain Sophie's problem. *(3 marks)*

> Our working memory has difficulty performing two tasks successfully at the same time when they require the use of the same component. Listening to Kelly requires the phonological loop too. Unfortunately, attending to the teacher and doing written work also requires Sophie to use the phonological loop, which gives rise to her difficulties.

> *You are not asked to write loads here, but questions like this are tough because they really test your understanding. There are lots of things you could say here to gain marks, but for just 3 marks be concise, watch your limited space and make sure you are clearly using the WMM in your answer.*

(p.45) 3. Sally struggles to cope with mental arithmetic of more than a few steps and digits. No matter how hard she tries she gets lost and has to start again.

Use ideas you have learned from the working memory model to explain Sally's problems with mental arithmetic. (*4 marks*)

> Doing mental arithmetic is quite a complicated process needing a few components of working memory. She is probably using her articulatory loop to repeat numbers and her visuo-spatial sketchpad to hold an image of the numbers in her mind. Sally is asking a lot of her working memory, given that it has a limited capacity. It could also be that particular components are required to do too much – for example, whilst verbally holding one sum in memory it would be very difficult for Sally to work verbally on the step.

> *Notice here that specific components of working memory are being referred to in the answer. You need to make it clear how WMM explains Sally's problem, and this is the most effective way of doing it. You are being offered 4 marks here – it is only reasonable for examiners to expect a little detail!*

(p.46) 4. It seemed like any other day for Kevin, working at the petrol station. That is, until a customer pulled out a shotgun and robbed his till. As Kevin told the police officer, he was terrified and thought he was going to die.

What has research told us about the effect that Kevin's anxiety during the robbery might have on his reliability as an eyewitness? (*5 marks*)

> *The question asks for 'research'. This is a general term and does not necessarily mean that you have to include named studies.*

> Research suggests that Kevin's recall may be affected by his anxiety. Loftus et al

monitored the gaze of participants being shown a robbery and found that they tended to focus on the gun used. This is called 'weapons focus'. The violence of an event can also cause anxiety and influence recall. Loftus and Burns found that participants who had seen a non-violent version of a crime recalled more detail than those who had viewed a violent version. However, other studies based on real experiences of crime have found little evidence for anxiety reducing the accuracy of recall.

ASK AN EXAMINER

Of course, there is much more you could say here, but you must remember that there is limited space in which to write. This response is concise and the research follows logically from the opening sentence.

(p.47) 5. 76-year-old Irena was walking through town with her 7-year-old granddaughter when they heard a loud 'smash!' A car had driven through a shop window, and they watched as two men loaded up their vehicle with electrical goods and drove off.

ASK AN EXAMINER

The question doesn't ask you to write specifically about children or the elderly (and it never would). It is asking you about age, so this could be a good opportunity to show what you know about both, making it easier to get all the marks. In the answer however we demonstrate how easy it is to gain maximum marks just by using research on the elderly!

(a) What has research told us about the reliability of the testimony of these eyewitnesses? (5 marks)

Memory is not a constant thing – it changes with age. At 76, Irena would be considered elderly, and research with this age group has found that their memory is more susceptible to misleading information. Coxon and Valentine suggest that poor recall is more likely to be because of a less complete memory than increased suggestibility. Research

by Searcy et al suggests that if Irena is
called to identify the criminals in a line-up
then she is more likely than someone much
younger to make a false identification.

(b) **What technique might police officers use to ensure that the testimony of Irena is as accurate as possible?** (*1 mark*)

The cognitive interview

(p50)   6.   During the interview of a witness to a serious crime, the police officer encourages the witness to report everything that comes to mind regarding the experience. She also encourages the witness to imagine and explain how the events might have appeared to another observer.

(a) Outline **two other** techniques that the police officer should use to ensure that she is doing the cognitive interview correctly. (*2 + 2 marks*)

The police officer could try to recreate
as close as possible the mood and environment
during which the event occurred; for example
by asking the witness to think back and imagine
how he or she felt. This is called 'reinstating
the context'.

     Another thing the police officer could do
is ask the witness to change the sequence
when recalling events; for example, reversing
the order. This might help to jog memory and
reveal a few more details. This is called
'change sequence'.

> **ASK AN EXAMINER**
> Note that a name for the technique is given here, though there was already enough written in the description of it for 2 marks. If 3 marks each were available then naming the technique would get you the third mark. If in doubt, always give a little more detail if you have the space – it is a good way of ensuring you get the marks you deserve.

(b) Give **one** limitation or **one** strength of the cognitive interview. (*2 marks*)

Relatively brief training in the cognitive interview can result in improvements in witness recall; for example Geiselman et al found that 35% more information can be obtained in this way.

(p.52) 7. The twins each had 12 items from the shopping list to buy and each decided to use a different method of remembering the items.

(a) Identify two different strategies for improving memory that the twins might have used. (*2 marks*)

Method of loci and narrative chaining.

This answer is the most straightforward way to deal with the question. However, any strategy for improving memory would be a legitimate answer here. This means that you could have used more general aspects of memory, such as organisation, retrieval cues and state-dependency – as long as for part (b) you can explain how you would use them to improve memory for a shopping list!

(b) Explain how one of the techniques identified in part (a) would be used to remember the shopping list. (*3 marks*)

With method of loci you would imagine a familiar place, such as your home, and take a mental 'walk' around it. Items from the shopping list would be 'left' at various memorable locations. When you want to remember items, you once again take this mental 'walk', and as you pass them where they were left you will 'remember' them.

You had lots of options here, but care needed to be taken with selecting our techniques because part (b) was linked to part (a). There is no point naming something in (a) that you are going to struggle with explaining in (b)! Read all parts of a question carefully before starting to answer it.

SECTION 3: DEVELOPMENTAL PSYCHOLOGY – EARLY SOCIAL DEVELOPMENT

(p.64) 1. Mary has noticed that her young baby does things to attract her attention, such as babbling, smiling and crying.

How does the evolutionary perspective on attachment explain these behaviours? (*4 marks*)

The baby is displaying instinctive signalling behaviours. Things like crying and smiling are social releasers which encourage the mother to care for the infant. This is important for the infant because without the care and attention of a caregiver during the early years it would not survive. Forming an attachment gives newborn infants a survival advantage over those that do not.

The evolutionary perspective is quite broad and involves explanations of animal and human behaviour. The approach taken here with this example answer is a very general evolutionary one. You could do equally as well being more specific, for example by focusing on human evolutionary behaviour and the theory of John Bowlby.

(p.65) 2. **You have been invited to give a talk to the local mother-and-baby group. Using ideas from Bowlby's theory of attachment, what advice might you give the mothers about how they could form a strong mother—child bond?**

(*4 marks*)

This question is trickier than it might first appear. It isn't asking for a general description of Bowlby's theory – it requires you to carefully select from his theory those ideas which relate to forming a strong attachment.

Bowlby said that an infant must form an attachment to one main caregiver, usually the mother. Care needs to be consistent, meaning that she needs to ensure that she does not do anything to disrupt the attachment, for example by leaving the child in the care of someone else. The mother also has to give responsive and sensitive care for a successful attachment to develop.

There is so much more you could say here, but look at the question and the space you have available. You have to be really focused and write only that which directly addresses the question. Waffle quickly takes up space needed for meaningful words which will earn you the marks. Every word counts!

This means that the mother needs to respond appropriately to social releasers.

(p.66) 3. Marion provides most of the care for her son, Joseph – feeding, comforting and playing with him. She has noticed that, whilst he is happy to spend time with his dad, Joseph seems most content when he is with her.

Use your knowledge of the learning theory of attachment to explain Joseph's behaviour. (*4 marks*)

Because Marion is providing the main care for her son, Joseph has associated his mum with the satisfaction of primary drives, such as hunger and thirst. She has also become associated with other pleasurable things, such as comfort and security. This learning is called classical conditioning. Whilst dad provides care, it is Marion who is more strongly associated with need satisfaction. Therefore, Joseph prefers her company.

You could also have explained Joseph's behaviour in terms of operant conditioning, where Joseph finds the presence of mum more reinforcing than dad. Given the limited space however, it would be quite a challenge to give an account of both classical and operant conditioning without very careful planning.

(p.68) 4. Andrea has noticed that her two sons are quite different. When she gets home from work the first thing Sam does is run to her and give her a great big hug, whilst she has to go to find Rob to make sure he is okay. When a plumber came to the house the other day Sam was fine with him, but Rob wouldn't stop crying and appeared scared.

(a) Identify:

(i) The type of attachment shown by Rob. (*1 mark*)

You could be more specific and identify the type of insecure attachment shown by Rob, but for 1 mark there really isn't any need. Keep that one for when more marks are available and therefore more detail is needed in your answer!

Insecure

(ii) The type of attachment shown by Sam. (*1 mark*)

Secure

The Strange Situation is not the only way of assessing attachment, so you don't have to use it in this answer. Indeed it is used less and less these days in favour of less stressful and more reliable methods such as the Attachment Q-Sort (AQS). So you have options!

(b) Explain how the type of attachment shown by each child could be assessed. (*4 marks*)

> The Strange Situation could be used. This is a standardised test which takes place in a laboratory setting. It is a sequence of three minute episodes involving the child, mother and a stranger. Each child would experience a series of introductions, separations and reunions. Researchers would discretely observe and rate the reactions of the children, for example separation anxiety shown when the mother leaves the room. Depending on the behaviour they would be classified as either Type A, Type B or Type C.

You would quickly run out of space if you tried to write every detail of the Strange Situation. Just summarise it and no more, making sure that you include enough detail for 4 marks. If you've learned the various sequences then that's great, but watch your space! If you know anything at all about the Strange Situation this is an easy one to get marks on.

(*p.72*) 5. A psychologist intends to conduct cross-cultural research into attachment and has moved with her family from Britain to Japan. She is having problems finding a nursery place for her 8-month-old baby.

(a) Use what you know of culture and attachment to explain the problem of finding a nursery place. (*2 marks*)

> It is part of normal child-rearing practice in Japan for the mother and child to be rarely apart for the first 12 months. This means

that there is little demand for this type of
child care so it is hard to find a place.

(b) Explain the difficulty that the psychologist might have using the Strange Situation in her research. (*4 marks*)

The Strange Situation was developed in the
West and therefore reflects that particular
culture's values and customs. It might also
be unethical, given the distress it causes
some children, and Japanese children in
particular because of the high rate of Type C
attachments. Rothenbaum et al believe that
some of the most basic ideas in attachment
theory, like the sensitivity, secure base and
competence hypotheses, are culturally biased,
making any conclusion from research like this
suspect.

(p.74)   6.   'Would the mother of Maddy please come to the customer services desk where she will find her lovely little girl.' A 2-year-old girl has got lost in supermarket.

(a) What type of attachment is Maddy most likely to have? (*1 mark*)

Secure

Notice here that even if you got part (a) wrong, you could still get full marks for part (b) as long as what you wrote is relevant to the answer in (a). This is quite a common approach in the exam – the examiners want to give you every possible chance to earn marks. Read the question very carefully!

(b) Outline the attachment behaviour you might expect from Maddy if she had the type of attachment you identified in (a). (*3 marks*)

The number of marks available indicates the kind of answer an examiner is looking for. Part (b) is a good example of how the same kind of question could appear but for different marks. In this case, the easiest way to gain marks is to give one bit of detail for each mark.

Maddy would be most likely to show distress on separation from her mother, but would be happy and easily comforted at reunion. Maddy would be most happy to engage with strangers when mother is present.

ASK AN EXAMINER

The focus in this example answer was on cross-cultural problems of using the Strange Situation. You could also have included in the answer anything which pointed out difficulties with the Strange Situation, for example reliability and observer bias.

(p.75) 7. 'Operation Pied Piper' involved children being evacuated from six British cities deemed vulnerable to German bombing. In September 1939, 1.9 million children gathered at rail stations not knowing where they were going or if they would be split from brothers and sisters gathered with them.

From what you have learned about attachment, assess the possible effects of this experience on the children involved. *(4 marks)*

Bowlby claimed that a child must form an attachment to a mother or mother substitute during a critical period between 6 months to 2½ years of age. Any disruption to this attachment would cause social and emotional problems later in life. One possible effect is affectionless psychopathy. The effect of the evacuation would however depend on the degree of the disruption – e.g. on the ages of the children involved and whether or not they received care from a genuine mother substitute.

(p.76) 8. Russian institutions are bursting with children abandoned at birth. They now total more than 600,000 children and are defined by the state as being 'without parental care'.

What might be the long-term effects of this kind of early experience?

(4 marks)

> Research suggests that early institutionalisation can have long-term effects. Adoption out of institutions can undo early experience, with children adopted earlier faring best. Rutter et al reported the progress of a group of adopted children now 11 years old. They suggest that, whilst children adopted when younger than 6 months showed no obvious ill effects, those adopted between 6 and 42 months of age continued to show negative effects of this early experience.

A research approach has been taken with this answer, with the focus largely on the findings of the ERA studies. It would be perfectly okay to focus on other research, such as Tizard and Hodges, or indeed on a more general description of the long-term effects of institutionalisation.

(p.80) 9. Having taken a short career break Sinita has to return to work. She needs to put her 1-year-old son into a day care centre.

(a) What should Sinita be looking for in a good quality day care centre?

(3 marks)

> Well-trained staff, lower enrolments so that there are good child-carer ratios and plentiful materials.

You are not being assessed for quality of written communication here – that only happens in 12-mark extended written responses. Don't worry about not writing in lengthy grammatical sentences – just answer the question in enough detail to get the marks!

(b) What benefits could there be for the child's social development?

(3 marks)

> Good quality day care centres have been associated with children having more friendly interactions with others (e.g. less arguing and conflict), being more independent, cooperative and confident.

(p.82)   10.   An educational psychologist is conducting research using primary school children. He has noticed that one child, Lucas, is particularly disruptive. School records show that Lucas attended a day care centre.

(a) What might the psychologist assume about Lucas's experience of day care? (*3 marks*)

> Some research suggests that the more time spent in day care, the more disruptive behaviours, such as aggression, are shown in later school years. The psychologist might assume that Lucas spent quite a lot of time in child care from an early age.

(b) Explain how the psychologist might research the effects on children of day care. (*4 marks*)

> The psychologists could set up an observational study of children in day care centres. They could be observed for things like friendly and unfriendly behaviour, general social skills, play and interaction with adults. Their behaviour might be compared to observations of other children who do not attend day care. If the long-term effects of day care are being investigated, then further studies would have to be conducted with the same children. Their behaviour at two or more different points in time could be compared to see if the quantity of care is an important factor.

Part (b) is just a wide-open question. There is so much to write that the real challenge is giving as much detail as possible in as few words as possible. What you don't want to do is spend ages describing one process and then end up with quite a narrow response. The key to success with this type of question is to have a good understanding of research methods.

(p.84) 11. A child psychologist has been asked to give advice to a company which wants to set up a good quality day care centre.

(a) From what you know of the implications of research into attachment for child care practices, what advice might she offer? (*3 marks*)

> Early attachment relationships have a major influence on social development, so non-parental child care should be designed to minimise risk of attachment disruption. Too much day care and day care too early in life should be avoided if possible. Well qualified staff that can provide good quality continuous care to fewer children will reduce threat to attachment.

(b) From what you know of the implications of research into day care for child care practices, what advice might she offer? (*3 marks*)

> A number of factors have been shown to be associated with good quality day care. For example, lower adult-child ratios which enable carers to give children individual attention, better qualified staff and lower staff turnover so as to maximise quality of care, and plentiful space with lots of stimulating materials.

ASK AN EXAMINER

Watch out! This is a tricky question. Part (a) is asking specifically about attachment and part (b) is asking specifically about day care. This means that you must be specific and focused with your answers. The two parts are asking quite different things, but it is very easy to get them mixed up, which would cause you to lose marks.

SECTION 4: BIOLOGICAL PSYCHOLOGY – STRESS

(p.95) 1. The athletes at the start of the race take their marks and prepare for the sound of the starter's pistol. 'BANG!' they're off!

(a) Identify one physical feeling that tells the athletes that they are feeling stressed. (*1 mark*)

> The heart is beating faster and harder.

For part (a) you could mention any of the feelings that people get when they are feeling stressed – dry mouth, 'butterflies' in the stomach, etc. Another way to answer part (b) is by describing the sympathomedullary pathway, since both of these are activated in the body's response to stress. Doing BOTH however is a little over the top! There are only 4 marks available and there is limited space on the exam paper.

(b) Explain how the physical feeling you identified in part (a) was generated by the body's response to stress. (*4 marks*)

> The physical feelings are caused by the pituitary-adrenal system being activated. This involves a part of the brain called the hypothalamus getting the body ready for action. It does this by sending a signal to the pituitary gland causing it to release ACTH. This hormone is detected in the bloodstream by the adrenal cortex, which in response, releases more hormones called corticosteroids. It is these hormones which cause the physical feelings.

(p.97) 2. Jason always seems to have a cold at exam-time. Just his luck!

Why might Jason be prone to colds around exams? (*4 marks*)

> Examinations are a time of stress. Research has shown that stress can reduce the effectiveness of the immune system, which is important in protecting us from infection and disease. For example, Kiecolt-Glaser et al

found that the immune systems of medical students were affected by the stress of doing exams. An immune system which is being suppressed by stress is going to have difficulty fighting off infections from things like the cold virus, making us more likely to become ill.

(p.99) 3. Two men meet every morning walking their dogs and exchange greetings. One day, one of the men does not turn up. His friend later finds out that the man has suffered a heart attack.

Using what you have learned from studying stress in everyday life, what might make one man less likely to suffer with coronary heart disease (CHD) than another? (4 marks)

Personality is a factor which might make one man less likely to suffer CHD than another. According to Friedman and Rosenman, people with Type A personalities are more likely to suffer from CHD than people with Type B personalities. Type A people tend to be overly competitive, intense and driven. In their study they found that 70% of men who developed CHD were Type A individuals.

ASK AN EXAMINER

This question can also be answered by using the concept of the Hardy personality, rather than Type A/Type B. In this case, people who are less likely to have CHD are those who have the 3-C's. Outline the 3-C's, point out that they provide a 'buffer', and if you like you can support your point with a piece of research – e.g. Weiss found that people who score higher on the Hardiness Test show least stress-related symptoms.

(p.100) 4. Tom shares an office with John, a young new employee. John regularly listens to music, and talks on the telephone with his colleagues and friends constantly.

(a) Identify one workplace factor that might be affecting Tom. (1 mark)

A noisy environment.

Although the question is clearly directing you towards identifying noise as a stressor for Tom, it would be okay to identify another environmental stressor and explain that. For example, John might be being affected by high office temperature. It is still creditable that you have identified a potential environmental stressor and understood the impact it is having on Tom.

(b) Explain why the factor you have identified in part (a) might lead to Tom experiencing stress. (*3 marks*)

> Work often involves some level of concentration. Things in the working environment which prevent concentration can be frustrating because they prevent you getting the job done. This is stressful. Noise is one example of something in the workplace that can prevent concentration and therefore cause stress.

(*p.102*) **5.** Linda has had a lot to put up with lately. Not only did her close friend pass away, but she lost her job just before Christmas. Now she isn't looking forward to her forthcoming holiday very much.

What has research into the effects of life changes told us about the likely effects of these events on Linda's future health? (*5 marks*)

> According to Holmes and Rahe, life events such as those experienced by Linda, could lead to ill-health. They devised a scale called the SRRS containing 43 different life events, each one with an 'impact' rating. The score for each life event experienced was added up, and the higher the score the more likely a person was to suffer illness. For example, a total score over 300 meant an 80% chance of developing physical illness in the following year. Sarason et al however argue that the impact of a life event depends on whether the event is

perceived as positive or negative. For Linda, whilst both Christmas and taking a holiday might cause disruption, they may be positive experiences for her which might go some way towards counteracting the negative experiences of losing a friend and her job.

(p.103)

6. Some psychologists say that our experience of the annoyances and irritations of everyday life are better predictors of health and well-being than major life events.

> (a) What name is given to these annoyances and irritations of everyday life? (*1 mark*)

Daily hassles.

> (b) Outline the problems of using measures of these annoyances and irritations as predictors of health and well-being. (*4 marks*)

The relationship between hassles and health is correlational, so it is difficult to be certain about cause and effect. Also, measuring the effect of hassles involves thinking about past events, and research has shown that this kind of remembering is unreliable. Perhaps the biggest problem though is that there are individual differences in interpreting hassles – a hassle to one person might not be a hassle to another. This directly influences the impact of any particular hassle.

ASK AN EXAMINER

This is an example of how important it is to directly answer the question given, not write what you want to. You might be tempted here to describe the Hassles and Uplifts scale, but this would not really gain you any marks since the question asks you about problems of using scales like this. You have limited space in which to write your answer, so it is really important to avoid irrelevant material – which won't earn you marks – and get right to the point.

(p.105) 7. Julia has a brother serving overseas in the armed forces. She is very worried about his safety. In fact, she feels anxious all the time and is having difficulty concentrating on anything.

Outline emotion-focused methods of coping that Julia might use in dealing with her stress. (5 marks)

There a number of emotion-focused approaches that Julia might take. She might put up psychological barriers called defence mechanisms to block out the stress. On the other hand she might reappraise the situation, that is, think about it differently which will have the effect of changing the way that she feels. Another thing that Julia could do is tackle her physical feelings of arousal directly, perhaps by exercise or relaxation training. People in these situations often turn to drugs to reduce arousal. These could be recreational drugs such as alcohol and tobacco, but could also be drugs prescribed by her doctor. Drugs such as benzodiazepines reduce the physical symptoms of stress, and in Julia's case should allow her to get on with other things in her life. Julia doesn't have to take one or other emotion-focused approach however. It is common for people to do several at once or even switch between them.

ASK AN EXAMINER

Notice here that you are not simply being asked to say what emotion-focused methods of coping are — you need to shape your answer to a context here. This is a common type of exam question, so be sure to read the question carefully and demonstrate your knowledge and understanding by responding to the question set.

ASK AN EXAMINER

This answer takes a rather broad approach to the question. You could however choose to be more focused and apply one technique in more detail. Arousal reduction is probably the best choice in this case because there is most to write about. Physiological methods of stress management such as drug therapy are basically arousal reducing emotion-focused approaches to the problem of stress, so this entire area is opened up to you for inclusion in your answer.

SECTION 5: SOCIAL PSYCHOLOGY – SOCIAL INFLUENCE

(p.116) 1. Zach really doesn't like horror films, but all his friends do. Whenever they go to the cinema together they always choose to watch a horror film.

(a) What type of conformity does Zach's behaviour demonstrate? (*1 mark*)

> *Compliance*

(b) Outline the findings of one study which demonstrates this type of conformity. (*4 marks*)

> *Asch found that 75% of his 123 participants gave what they knew to be wrong answers at least once on a line judgement task. Because participants knew the answer to be wrong but still conformed, they were showing compliance. On trials where there was an unambiguous difference in the lines, nearly two thirds of participants did not conform, suggesting that the pressure to conform is not so strong that people can't resist it.*

Asch is the obvious study to use here as an example of compliance, though other studies are relevant, for example Crutchfield. If the scenario indicates that you should write about identification, then Zimbardo's prison study would be the example of research to use.
Notice here too that the answer is very focused on findings because it is what the question asks for! Detail about procedures is unnecessary and won't earn you any marks. Keep your answer focused!

(p.117) 2. Everyone seems to think that Emma is funny – she makes people laugh with her jokes. Except Kate. Kate doesn't think that Emma is funny at all. She still laughs at her jokes though.

Use what you have learned about why people conform to explain Kate's behaviour. (*4 marks*)

Remember! Explain is different from types. Take care with the question wording and don't confuse this! Types = I.C.I. and explain = I.N.S.S.

Kate is demonstrating a kind of social influence called normative social influence. This means that people conform because of a need they have to be accepted as a member of a group. The need for acceptance and approval from her group means that Kate goes along with the group norm – that Emma is funny – and engages in behaviours which allows her to 'fit in'.

There is often more than one possible reason for someone conforming, and it is up to you to choose which one best explains the scenario you are presented with. In this case, you are clearly being directed towards normative social influence. Although it is actually more difficult to do, you could make social impact theory work here too.

(p.119) 3. At the start of the experiment the participant met a man called Mr Wallis, who was then hooked up to a shock generator. Mr Wallis was in fact a confederate. The participant sat in another room and tested Mr Wallis on word pairs. When he got one wrong, the participant was to give him an electric shock. This increased from 15 to 450 volts as more incorrect answers were given. There was no actual shock given. A pre-recorded sound played, indicating Mr Wallis in varying degrees of pain, until after 315 volts there was silence. Another confederate called 'Mr Williams', wearing a lab coat, encouraged the participant to continue.

(a) Identify one ethical issue which arises from this research. (*1 mark*)

Deception

(b) Suggest how you might deal with the ethical issue identified in (a).

(*3 marks*)

Deception can be most simply dealt with by fully disclosing the nature of the study before hand. In other words, don't lie! Unfortunately, doing this will often make a study impossible to do. In this case, some deception might be acceptable, provided that participants are fully informed about the study after the event and given the opportunity to withdraw their data.

The scenario in this question is clearly describing Milgram's study. Whilst there are lots of ethical issues arising from Milgram's research, the question is asking you to engage with the scenario. Two ethical issues emerge from this most clearly – deception and protection from harm. Remember, answer the question in front of you – if you have to engage with the content then do so!

(p.120)   4.   A researcher used a confederate to ask passengers on a train to give up their seat, even when there were other seats available. This request was refused. However, when the confederate made the same request accompanied by a train guard, it was granted without argument.

Use what you have learned from your studies of obedience to explain the behaviour of the passengers. (*4 marks*)

> One explanation for the behaviour of passengers is legitimate authority. When the passenger's request for a seat was refused it was possibly because they were not seen as having any legitimacy. However, the train guard is a credible authority figure giving the request greater legitimacy. People are more likely to obey when there is legitimate authority.

There are lots of ways to answer this question. For example, instead of explaining obedience you could explain the disobedience, or you could even use a mixture of both. The important thing is that you are clearly answering the question using your knowledge of obedience.

(p.121)   5.   Most people do not smoke and overall the number of smokers is reducing all the time. However, the number of teenage girls who smoke is on the increase. Research has consistently shown that health related messages and scare tactics are the least successful methods for curbing teen smoking.

Using your knowledge of resistance to conformity, suggest one way that smoking in teenage girls could be reduced. (*3 marks*)

> There is a very strong normative social influence amongst teen girls – the peer pressure to smoke is very strong. By exposing teen girls to dissent, i.e. to peers who do not smoke, then this both

reduces exposure to the majority view and

provides an alternative, minority one.

> **ASK AN EXAMINER**
>
> Whilst there are a number of explanations for why people resist conformity, they don't all apply equally to scenarios. You have to think through all the explanations you have learned and carefully select one that best fits the scenario. This kind of question is not easy, and you will only succeed if you have done the hard work – learning!

(p.122) 6. When Mr Baily gives out homework he finds that all his students hand it in. However, he has noticed that when his student teacher, Mrs Phillips, gives homework to the same students, some of the homework does not get returned.

Use what you have learned about how people resist pressures to obey to explain the behaviour of the students. (*4 marks*)

It is possible that students are in an
autonomous state when Mrs Phillips is
present, which is more likely to happen if they
do not see Mrs Phillips as an authority figure.
Autonomy is more likely to result in
disobedience. Another possibility is that the
students do not see Mrs Phillips as having
legitimacy, therefore she is easier to disobey.

> **ASK AN EXAMINER**
>
> As can be seen here, your answer can contain a mix of several possible explanations. It is important that you write in enough detail to get all the marks, and sometimes this involves a response like this. Remember though that you have limited time and writing space so plan and think about your answer.

(p.123) 7. Although it has always enforced a dress code, Albany School is having a few problems with the introduction of a school uniform. Although the majority of students wear the new uniform apparently without complaint, there are still some individuals who resist.

What have you learned from your study of social influence which could explain this independent behaviour? (*5 marks*)

Some individuals might resist wearing school
uniform because they have a strong internal

locus of control. They feel that they have more control over their environment, and have greater confidence and security in what they do. On the other hand, perhaps the independent behaviour could be explained by high reactance – pupils are not wearing the school uniform because wearing it is what they are expected to do. Another possibility is that the individuals most closely identify with the minority who don't wear uniforms than the majority who do.

ASK AN EXAMINER

Look at the number of marks on offer here. Whilst it might be possible to give one detailed explanation for the independent behaviour, the question clearly allows any number of explanations. It is often easier to get marks by taking a broad approach to answering the question rather than focusing on just one thing.

(p.126) 8. In 1955, Rosa Parks refused to give up her bus seat to another passenger. The passenger was white, and she was a black woman. In Montgomery, Alabama, at that time, she was obliged to make way for the white passenger. Her refusal began a campaign of civil disobedience. The action of this single woman lit a fuse in the black community.

How can research into social influence help us explain this example of social change? (6 marks)

This example of social change could be explained in a number of ways. Research has shown that views held by a minority can influence those held by the majority. In this case, the minority was the black community and power was held by the majority white population. Moscovici called this kind of social change 'conversion'. He argued that a number of things make the position of a minority, such as that represented by Rosa

Parks, more effective. These are consistency, where the minority maintains its position demonstrating commitment, confidence which sends a signal to the majority that the minority view demands attention, and persuasiveness where the minority arguments are good enough to attract members of the majority.

There are a number of approaches you could take with this question but the most obvious is the one taken here. The question clearly points to minority influence, although it would have been easy to apply the concepts of legitimate authority, disobedience and conformity.

SECTION 6: INDIVIDUAL DIFFERENCES – PSYCHOPATHOLOGY (ABNORMALITY)

(.138)   1.   Caroline reads her horoscope every morning, and spends lots of money regularly telephoning premium numbers to get updates. She does exactly what her horoscope says, and on some days she doesn't leave the house at all if she thinks that the horoscope is unfavourable.

(a) Use one definition of abnormality to explain whether or not Caroline is exhibiting abnormal behaviour. (*3 marks*)

According to the failure to function adequately definition Caroline's belief in horoscopes is affecting her day-to-day living and therefore the behaviour is maladaptive. There is nothing wrong with believing in horoscopes, but Caroline's belief has maybe gone too far in that many aspects of Caroline's personal life are being affected.

You could have written about deviation from social norms or ideal mental health here just as well to gain the marks. Sometimes questions direct you to an answer, sometimes, as here, they are wide open to several possible responses.

(b) Give one limitation of the definition used in (a). (*3 marks*)

> *The failure to function definition cannot be used in the same way in different cultures. What is adequate functioning in one culture might not be in another. For example, different cultures have different ways of grieving so that a 'normal' way of grieving in one culture might be viewed as 'abnormal' in another.*

(p.141) 2. Mark has not been feeling too good lately. He seems to be anxious all the time and can't seem to concentrate on important things like his family or work. His doctor has given him some pills to take and has asked to see him again in a month.

(a) What name is given to this sort of therapy? (*1 mark*)

> *Drug therapy*

(b) Assess the effectiveness of this kind of therapy. (*4 marks*)

> *Drug therapies have been shown to be effective for a range of mental health problems, for example many schizophrenics experience fewer extreme symptoms after taking antipsychotic drugs. Also, antidepressant drugs have been shown to reliably reduce symptoms of depression with only mild side effects. However, some people do not respond to drugs, or drugs provide only temporary relief. Drugs can sometimes also be made more effective when they are combined with psychological therapies.*

(p.143) 3. John is obsessively tidy. Whenever anybody visits his house and puts something down he immediately tidies it away. John doesn't realise he's doing this but his friends find it irritating.

Using the basic assumptions of the psychodynamic approach explain the origins of John's problem. (*4 marks*)

> The psychodynamic approach assumes that our unconscious drives our behaviour. John's obsession with tidiness has a number of possible origins. It may be a symptom of an unconscious conflict between the three psychic forces – the id, ego and superego. On the other hand, it might have more to do with some traumatic childhood experience that has become part of his unconscious but is still influencing behaviour.

ASK AN EXAMINER

You don't have to be very specific here – for example, explaining exactly how the conflict between the id, ego and superego results in obsessive tidiness would be too much. The same applies for traumatic childhood experiences. It is enough to recognise, and try to apply to the scenario if necessary, three things – the importance of unconscious forces guiding behaviour, the role of traumatic childhood experience, and the conflict between the id, ego and superego. You won't ever be offered more than 6 marks for describing or applying the psychodynamic approach, and this is a good way of organising your thoughts in order to get all the marks available.

(p.144) 4. Derek is afraid of dogs. He freezes in terror when he encounters one and doesn't go anywhere where there might be a dog.

How might systematic desensitisation be used to help Derek with his problem? (*4 marks*)

> The first step for Derek is to create with the therapist an anxiety hierarchy. This is a list of dog-related stimuli ranked from the least to the most frightening. The next step is progressive relaxation training. This is important to the therapy because of reciprocal inhibition – that is, when Derek is taken one step at a time through the hierarchy he cannot be anxious

and relaxed at the same time. Eventually Derek
will learn to associate relaxed rather than
fearful feelings when confronted with the stimuli.

(p.145)   5.   'Christmas shopping?! You've got to be joking!' said Hiro, 'I can't go into town with all those people everywhere. It's an absolute nightmare. No space to walk, all that noise. No way! I'm staying at home, there's no way I can ever go out into a crowd.'

How might Hiro's problem be overcome using a therapy from the cognitive approach? (*4 marks*)

The first step for Hiro and the therapist
would be an analysis of thoughts, behaviours
and feelings in order to uncover those that are
unrealistic or irrational. The next step would
then be to work out how to change these
unwanted thoughts using various strategies.
For example, Hiro may be encouraged to engage
in mental exercises which aim to replace
negative and unhelpful thoughts about crowds
with more positive and realistic ones.
Eventually the new ways of thinking become
integrated into everyday life and the symptoms
which brought Hiro to therapy will diminish.

Unit 1 Cognitive Psychology, Developmental Psychology and Research Methods

SECTION A – COGNITIVE PSYCHOLOGY AND RESEARCH METHODS

Total marks for this question: 4 marks

1   (a) Tick **two** of the boxes below to indicate which of the following concepts relate to the multi-store model of memory:

Sensory memory   ✓
Articulatory loop
Chunking   ✓
Visuo-spatial sketchpad

(2 marks)

1   (b) According to the multi-store model, what is the **capacity** and **duration** of short-term memory?

capacity – 7 +/– 2 items of information

duration – about 18+ seconds without rehearsal.

(2 marks)

Total marks for this question: 15 marks

2   It has been suggested that humans are not constantly vigilant and often simply don't remember details of events happening around them. To test this, psychology students conducted a study in a nearby town centre. Working in pairs, one student approached a passer-by and asked for the time. A few minutes later the second student approached the same passer-by and asked him or her to describe the person who had just asked the time.

2   (a) From what you know of eyewitness testimony, what would you expect the students to find?

Students will probably find that people have a poor memory for the person who stopped them for the time. We have a reconstructive memory which means that we don't recall exact details of events but a version based on logic and guesswork.

(3 marks)

2   (b) State the aim of this study.

The aim of this study is to investigate in a real-life setting how much people remember of events that have happened a short time before being asked to recall.

(2 marks)

2   (c) The students are conducting a field experiment. In the context of this study, give **one** advantage of a field experiment.

Because the study is taking place in a natural environment the behaviour of the participants should also therefore be natural and unaffected by the study.

(2 marks)

2   (d) Why might it have been a good idea for the students to have conducted a pilot study?

A pilot study would have told the students whether or not they have designed their study well. For example, how they approached participants, and how participants are questioned about their memory of events.

(2 marks)

2   (e) What kind of sampling technique was used by the students?

Opportunity

ASK AN EXAMINER

1 mark, one word – simple!

(1 marks)

2   (f) How does a field experiment differ from a natural experiment?

A field experiment involves manipulating the independent variable, but in a natural experiment the changes in the independent variable occur naturally.

(2 marks)

2 (g) Identify one ethical issue arising from this research and explain how the students might deal with it.

One ethical issue arising is confidentiality. This could be dealt with by assuring the participants that they will remain anonymous – they will not be identifiable from the responses they give the researchers.

(3 marks)

Total marks for this question: 8 marks

3 Discuss the influence of anxiety on eyewitness testimony.

Anxiety is a sense of worry or unease that would normally arise when witnessing a criminal event. Loftus et al suggested that the presence of a weapon causes anxiety and this makes EWT more unreliable. They found that P's who watched a film of a crime tended to focus their gaze on the weapon used in the robbery, and were less able to identify the robber than other participants who had seen a similar film but without a gun. According to Mitchell however, the weapon in such films does not cause anxiety but distracts attention away from the culprit because of its novelty, and it is this that affects eyewitness reliability.

(8 marks)

Any question above 6 marks requires an extended written response and thus needs both descriptive and evaluative content. Notice here how 'trigger' words (e.g. 'however') are used to tell the examiner when the answer is being evaluative.

(Extra space) Loftus and Burns made their P's watch a film of a crime, some watching a version with a very violent scene. They found that P's who saw the non-violent version recalled much more detail of the crime than those who had witnessed the more violent version. According to Loftus and Burns, the anxiety caused by the violent scene disrupted the storage of other details. It has been argued however that the findings of such research are to some extent due to artificial experimental situations used in the research. This is backed up by the findings of more naturalistic

research for example, Yuille and Culshal found that witnesses to a real life violent crime do not seem to have their recall of events affected by the aniety which the event must have caused.

Total marks for this question: 4 marks

4   One method developed in recent years to improve the amount of accurate recall from witnesses is the cognitive interview.

Outline what is involved in conducting a cognitive interview.

The cognitive interview uses four techniques:

1. 'Reinstate the context' means that the interviewee needs to be returned in their mind to the situation or context in which the event occurred.

2. 'Change sequence' involves requiring the interviewee to recall events in all sorts of different orders. For example, they might be asked to recall events in reverse order.

3. 'Change perspective' requires the witness to recall events from another perspective, for example another observer of the event.

4. 'Report everything' means that the eyewitness is encouraged to report everything, regardless of how fragmented or irrelevant it might seem.

(4 marks)

ASK AN EXAMINER

There is much more written here than is needed for 4 marks, but you have really guaranteed your marks by being thorough.

Total marks for this question: 5 marks

5   Recently, Jenny was stopped by a lorry driver asking directions to a local factory. She was able to imagine the location and accurately describe the route.

5   (a) Use what you have learned about the working memory model to explain how Jenny was able to do this.

In describing directions Jenny was using several components of the working memory model. In imagining the location she would have been using the visuo-spatial sketchpad, which can be thought of as our 'mind's eye'. In explaining the direction, Jenny was using the phonological loop, in particular the articulatory loop which deals with verbal material.

(3 marks)

5 (b) Unfortunately, the lorry driver did not have pen and paper handy. What memory improvement strategy might the lorry driver have used to remember Jenny's instructions?

The driver might have used narrative chaining. This would involve him building the route described by Jenny into a story, which would then be easier to remember.

(2 marks)

SECTION B – DEVELOPMENTAL PSYCHOLOGY AND RESEARCH METHODS

Total marks for this question: 4 marks

6 (a) The following statements relate to attachment. Identify which two relate to Bowlby's theory of attachment.

Statement	Tick only the two that apply
Babies attach to one person in particular.	✓
Attachment develops because babies copy the loving and caring behaviour of the parents.	
Attachment develops in a fixed sequence.	✓
Babies become attached to the adult who feeds them.	

(2 marks)

6 (b) Give one criticism of the evolutionary perspective on attachment.

It is debatable whether or not the rules of behaviour which apply to simpler animals such as monkeys and geese apply to humans. Humans are highly developed intellectually and emotionally, making us much more complex.

(2 marks)

Total marks for this question: 14 marks

7 The Strange Situation was for many years the standard way to assess the quality of a child's attachment. It has been suggested, however, that the Strange Situation lacks validity. For example, behaviour of children in the Strange Situation varies depending on which caregiver they are with at the time.

To investigate this, a psychologist conducted the Strange Situation test first with the mother, then with the father, and finally with the grandmother. Some of the results are summarised in the table below.

	% Secure Attachment
Child with mother	65
Child with father	50
Child with grandmother	65

7   (a) Use the graph paper below to sketch an appropriate graph for these results.

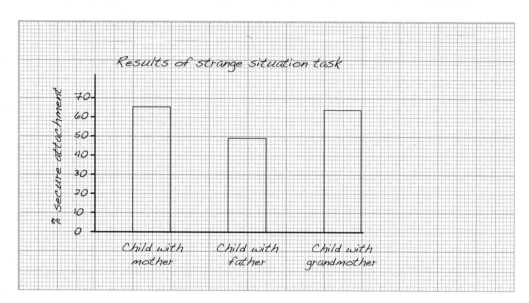

(2 marks)

7   (b) Write a suitable non-directional hypothesis for this study.

The behaviour of an infant in a Strange Situation will vary depending on which caregiver they are with at the time.

(2 marks)

7   (c) (i) What does the term 'validity' mean when used in the context of psychological research?

Validity refers to whether or not a test actually tests what it claims to.

(2 marks)

(ii) Other than what is already mentioned above, give one other way in which studies using the Strange Situation may lack validity.

The Strange Situation is only a 'snapshot' of behaviour and it might take place when the infant is feeling unwell or is in a bad mood. In this case, the Strange Situation would not be measuring attachment.

(2 marks)

7   (d) How could the psychologist go about assessing the reliability of her findings?

Reliability could be assessed by repeating the study – if the results are similar then the findings are reliable.

(2 marks

7   (e) Use the findings in the table to evaluate Ainsworth's research into attachment types.

This might seem like a tough question – it is asking for a number of skills, i.e. reading a table and using the content to evaluate something else. The question is made a lot easier however if you remember that evaluation does not have to be negative.

The finding of 65% secure attachment is in line with what Ainsworth would predict. That the rate of secure attachment is the same for mother and grandmother supports the validity of the Strange Situation since critics argue that this should vary with the caregiver. Where it does vary is with fathers. It could be that mothers and grandmothers are more sensitive caregivers, which is why there are more secure attachments with them.

(4 marks)

Total marks for this question: 6 marks

8   Gowri has noticed that, since starting at the local nursery, her 3-year-old son Anil seems to be much more cooperative, sociable and confident.

8   (a) What aspects of centre day care might be encouraging Anil's social development?

Research has shown that good quality day care can enhance social development. This involves children being given some independence, with less direct contact and guidance during play from the carer.

Also, Anil probably isn't spending too much time in day care.

(3 marks)

Don't get carried away here! You could write loads on day care, but there are only 3 marks each for questions 7(a) and 7(b) and limited space in which to write. Think carefully about what you need to say for 3 marks before you begin to write, or you could easily run out of space.

8   (b) What has research told us about the effects of day care on aggression?

According to Vlietstra, full-time day care is more likely to result in aggressive behaviour than part-time day care, suggesting that too much day care can have negative consequences. This is supported by Haskins, who found that aggressiveness was more likely in children who started day care earlier in life.

(3 marks)

Total marks for this question: 12 marks

9   'Attachment is an important component in laying the foundations of a healthy individual. If it is disrupted in some way, there may be consequences for social and emotional development.'

Discuss research into the disruption of attachments.

Look at the question! This is asking you about disruption of attachment, NOT failure to form attachment or institutionalisation. Disruption refers to attachment being formed but broken, so if you write about those other things your answer will be WRONG.

According to Bowlby, if an infant experiences disruption to an attachment then it would suffer both emotionally and socially later in life. This is called the maternal deprivation hypothesis. Bowlby supported his theory with his own research on juvenile delinquents. He found that of the juvenile thieves reported to be 'affectionless psychopaths' 86% had experienced early attachment disruption. For Bowlby, this was evidence that early disruption can lead to later problems. However, this research was correlational, so it is not proving that early disruption cause delinquency. Also, the data about early attachment experience was gathered retrospectively, so might not be reliable. Other research appears to contradict Bowlby's hypothesis. For example, Freud and Dann studied the development of a group of six children rescued from a Nazi concentration camp. They spent their early life in the absence of adults to provide care. They all suffered attachment disruption but Freud and Dann reported that they had no social/emotional problems later in life.

According to Stovall and Dozier being placed in foster care means that children experience a serious disruption to their attachment relationships, and that this kind of separation can lead to a variety of problems, such as withdrawal and depression. The age at which fostering occurs appears crucial. This is supported by Tyrrell and Dozier. They interviewed foster parents about attachment-related difficulties and found that, although there were some problems with children placed after 6 months, the greatest problems were reported with children placed after 12 months. These children were more likely to have insecure attachments.

Another cause of attachment disruption is premature birth. Premature babies are very immature so do not show the normal social releasers needed to encourage and maintain contact with the mother. Also, medical complications usually require an extended stay in hospital, separated from regular contact with the mother. This attachment disruption should cause greater problems in pre-term than full-term infants. This is supported by Plunkett et al who found a higher percentage of insecure attachments in pre-term infants compared to full-term infants. This is further supported by Minde who found that many pre-term infants assessed as securely attached at 12 months were reassessed as disorganised at 4 years. Such studies however have methodological problems, for example the reason for premature birth or developmental 'lag' are not taken into consideration. According to Goldberg, when these factors are considered there is no clear evidence of any long-term attachment problem.

(12 marks)

END OF QUESTIONS

Unit 2 Biological Psychology, Social Psychology and Individual Differences

SECTION A : BIOLOGICAL PSYCHOLOGY

Total marks for this question: 2 marks

1   Which two of the following concepts (A–D) relate to the pituitary-adrenal system? Tick the two correct boxes.

A Release of corticosteroids	✓
B Adrenal cortex	✓
C Adrenal medulla	
D Release of adrenaline	

(2 marks)

Total marks for this question: 4 marks

2   To everyone who knows her, Clare is Miss Sensible. She is patient, easy-going and tolerant. She doesn't come across as intense or competitive, and simply never does anything on impulse.

2   (a) From what you know of personality factors and stress, what type of behaviour does Clare demonstrate?

Type B behaviour

(1 mark)

2   (b) What has research shown about the link between stress and the type of personality shown by Clare?

Research has shown a link between personality types and stress-related illness, particularly heart disease. It has suggested that Type B personalities are less likely to suffer heart problems, although when they do get them they are more likely to die from them.

(3 marks)

Total marks for this question: 4 marks

3   What is the relationship between stress-related illness and the immune system?

Notice here that the question is not just about stress and the immune system (which gives you many things to say) but about stress-related illness. Your answer needs to focus on this to get all the marks.

> Research has shown that stress can reduce the effectiveness of the immune system. It is not uncommon for example to see an increase in coughs and colds in students around exam time. Kiecolt-Glaser et al found reduced levels of lymphocytes in university medical students after exams compared to levels measured before, suggesting that the stress of exams made the students more vulnerable to illness.

(4 marks)

Total marks for this question: 4 marks

4   Explain how psychologists have investigated workplace stress and identify one limitation of this kind of research.

(4 marks)

This appears to be quite a complicated question! You have to do TWO things – for most of the marks you have to explain the how of research in this area. You could treat this as a methodology question – it is the tougher option however and since this is NOT the research methods paper you may not have the knowledge yet to do this. The easiest way to answer such questions is the approach taken here – describe the method of a study you have learned!

> In researching workplace stress Johansson et al measured stress-related hormones (such as adrenaline) and stress-related absenteeism in finishers at a sawmill (a high-pressure job). These were compared with the same measures from other workers in 'low risk' jobs in the factory. One problem with this kind of research is that it is correlational, therefore it is difficult to establish a causal relationship between stress and work.

(4 marks)

Total marks for this question: 10 marks

5   Rowena prefers to deal with stress by being prepared for it. For example, she knows that she finds driving stressful so she limits the amount of driving she does by taking the train whenever possible. Her friend Adrian, however, turned to his GP and has been prescribed some pills to help him deal with his stress.

5   (a) Identify the approach to coping with stress taken by Rowena.

Problem-focused coping

(1 mark)

5   (b) Explain how drugs are going to help Adrian manage his stress.

Stress involves a physical response and drugs will reduce these symptoms of stress. If the symptoms are no longer there, then Adrian should no longer feel stressed. The most common prescribed drugs for stress are benzodiazepines, which work on the brain to affect naturally occurring chemicals to lessen tension and nervousness. Other drugs called beta-blockers work to reduce stress symptoms by lowering heart rate and blood pressure.

(3 marks)

You could if you wish restrict your answer to detailed descriptions of the actions of either benzodiazepines or beta-blockers. Remember though that you are only getting 3 marks for your efforts, so don't go over the top.

5   (c) State one disadvantage of Adrian's approach to stress management.

It has been argued that Adrian's approach does not treat the cause of his problem, only the symptoms. The problem remains, but his stress is being 'masked' by the drug.

(2 marks)

5   (d) Outline one psychological method of stress management.

Stress inoculation training (SIT) is a form of cognitive behavioural therapy which has three phases. First there is conceptualisation, where the client is encouraged to change the way they think about stress. Next comes skills training, where the client is taught various ways of coping with stress, such as relaxation techniques. Finally, there is application and follow-through, where the client takes what she has leaned to the real world.

(4 marks)

SECTION B : SOCIAL PSYCHOLOGY

Total marks for this question: 3 marks

6   (a) Identify the research method used by Milgram in his study of obedience.

Laboratory experiment

(1 mark)

6   (b) Give one limitation of this method.

Because the setting is artificial, laboratory experiments can produce unnatural behaviours in participants.

(2 marks)

Total marks for this question: 4 marks

7   Amil is a bit of a risk-taker. He thinks that in order to do well in business you have to have confidence in what you do and be independent and not worry too much about what other people think.

7   (a) What kind of locus of control does Amil appear to have?

Internal locus of control

(1 mark)

7   (b) How might Amil's locus of control influence his behaviour in a situation which requires him to conform?

People with a strong internal locus of control believe that they have control over their lives; they tend to be confident and have a positive outlook. Because of this they are less likely to be swayed by informational and normative social influences.

(3 marks)

Total marks for this question: 5 marks

8   (a) Outline one study into conformity that demonstrates normative social influence.

Asch wanted to know whether majority group pressure is strong enough to cause individuals to answer questions wrongly when the correct answer was obvious to them. In a line judgement task, ps had to say which of three lines was the same size as a 'test' line.

All six other people in the group were confederates instructed to give the wrong answer. Asch found that 74% conformed at least once.

(4 marks)

When asked to outline a study be sure to organise your thinking. You will never be offered more than 6 marks so therefore keep it simple – give a little of the main detail about what they were doing and why, what they did and what they found out. This will get you all the marks!

8   (b) Identify one ethical issue arising from this study.

Deception

(1 mark)

Total marks for this question: 12 marks

9   Discuss the influence of individual differences on independent behaviour.

Whether or not someone is obedient or someone conforms is likely to be affected by a number of things, not least a person's disposition or personality. A key aspect of personality related to independent behaviour is locus of control. This refers to the extent to which an individual feels that they are in control – are they themselves in control or are they being controlled? If a person feels that they are in control they are said to have an internal locus of control. Alternatively, people who feel that things are beyond their control are said to have an external locus of control. Research supports the idea that people with an internal locus of control are less likely to conform and are less likely to obey authority figures. It is suggested that this is because they have this strong sense of personal control over their decisions and fate. Other aspects of personality have been associated with independent behaviour. For example, because not everyone conforms it has been suggested that this independent behaviour is due to personality differences. It has been suggested that high conformity is associated with sense inferiority, need for approval and self-blame.

However, researchers have not been able to identify a personality type which would allow us to predict who is most likely to conform. It seems that, if there are personality characteristics associated with conformity, they are highly influenced by aspects of the situation, such as type of task, making them unpredictable. Personality has also been linked to individual differences in obedience. It appears that some people are more likely to obey than others. This is supported by Milgram, who argued that individuals with an authoritarian personality are more likely than others to obey orders from authority figures. These people are generally intolerant of others and submissive to authority. He suggested that, in his electric shock studies, those participants who gave the highest shocks were more likely to have this personality type.

(12 marks)

> **ASK AN EXAMINER**
> A lot more could be put into this answer – for example, gender could be considered an important individual difference. However, in the limited space and time allowed a decision was made during planning of the response to stick to personality. This is what planning is all about – use your planning space to make sure that you use what space and time you have effectively! If you feel you can do more, then feel free to do so – as long as you planned to do it!

SECTION C: INDIVIDUAL DIFFERENCES

Total marks for this question: 6 marks

10   Deviation from social norms is one definition of abnormality.

10   (a) What is a 'social norm'?

Unwritten rules created by society to guide behaviour.

(2 marks)

10   (b) Give one example of how breaking a social norm might lead to the behaviour being defined as abnormal.

There are age-based norms which dictate what is expected of people of different ages. For example, we would not expect an adult to have a child's tantrum.

(2 marks)

(c) Outline one other way of defining abnormality.

Sometimes people engage in behaviours which are somehow 'not good for them', in which case they are failing to function adequately and therefore abnormal.

(2 marks)

Total marks for this question: 8 marks

11   Outline and evaluate the use of ECT in treating abnormality.

ECT is a method of causing convulsions by passing electrical current through the brain. A shock of less than one second is delivered by electrodes placed on one or both sides of the head to an anaesthetised patient. There might be about six treatments in all over a two or three week period. It is most commonly used in cases of severe depression. One problem with ECT is that it is not clear exactly how it works. There is a concern that symptom reduction is due to the damage it causes to the brain. However, Reid suggests that ECT might actually benefit the brain by improving survival of brain cells. ECT does not work for all people and it is not clear why this is the case. Rey and Walter say that up to 70% of patients with severe depression are helped by ECT.

(8 marks)

Total marks for this question: 6 marks

12   Karl is afraid of spiders. His fear completely dominates his life. Things have become so bad that he has sought the help of a therapist.

12   (a) What assumptions would a therapist of the psychodynamic approach make about the cause of Karl's problem?

A psychodynamic therapist would assume that the origin of Karl's problem lies in his unconscious. His fear might be the symptom of an unconscious conflict between three forces – the id, the ego, and the superego. It could also originate during early experience, particularly during psychosexual development.

(3 marks)

12   (b) Karl decides to seek behavioural therapy. Explain how systematic desensitisation would be used to cure Karl of his fear of spiders.

Karl would be taught to relax, since you cannot be relaxed and fearful at the same time. A hierarchy of fearful stimuli would be created and, whilst in a relaxed state, Karl would progress up it. Initially Karl might have a simple drawing of a spider in the room, but eventually he might actually hold a spider.

(3 marks)

Total marks for this question: 4 marks

13   Research was conducted comparing different treatments for fear of spiders. Effectiveness was measured by the number of therapy sessions needed until the client was able to hold a spider without fear. The results are presented in the graph below.

13   (a) What kind of graph is this?

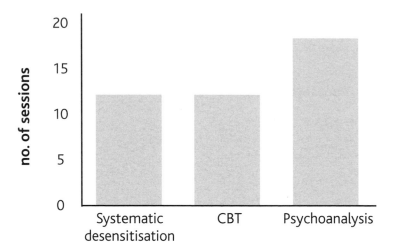

Bar chart

(1 mark)

13   (b) Using the graph, what conclusions could be made about the effectiveness of these therapies?

It could be concluded that there is no difference in the effectiveness of systematic desensitisation and CBT, as measured by number of treatments until 'cure'. Whilst psychoanalysis took more therapy sessions, it still achieved a satisfactory result and cured clients of their fear of spiders. It might well be that psychoanalysis is most effective based on some other criteria, such as being less likely to have clients develop the same phobia again.

(3 marks)

END OF QUESTIONS

ASK AN EXAMINER

Examiners are not out to trick you — they are more interested in seeing what you can do, not what you can't. This is a straightforward bar chart which directs you towards two straightforward conclusions. The answer offered here is a little 'embellished' — it has added a third sentence which, whilst not essential, demonstrates a good grasp of the subject matter.

GLOSSARY

A

Acronym
A method of improving a memory for something that takes the first letters of items to be recalled and forms them into an *acronym*. An example is ROYGBIV for the colours of the rainbow: red, orange, yellow, green, blue, indigo, violet.

Age of witness
The accuracy of the memory of an event (the *eyewitness testimony*) may be influenced by the age of the witness. The accuracy of the elderly or children may be questionable.

Agency theory
Milgram's theory for why people obey authority figures. It includes descriptions of *autonomous state* and *agentic state*.

Agentic state
Part of *agency theory*. The *agentic state* is where individuals feel that they have diminished responsibilities for their actions because they are the 'agents' of others.

Aggression
Intentional or unintentional harm directed towards others. Whether *day care* generates an increase in aggressive behaviour in children is unclear.

Aims
The *aims* of a research project describe the reason for carrying out the research. They indicate what the research intends to investigate or find out.

Ainsworth
Mary Ainsworth is a major thinker in the area of *attachment*. She was instrumental in designing the *Strange Situation*, an experimental technique for investigating attachment type in children.

Antidepressant
Drugs used to treat mood disorders, particularly depression.

Antipsychotic
Drugs used to treat symptoms of psychotic disorders such as schizophrenia, including hallucinations and disturbed thinking.

Anxiety
The physical tension associated with feeling stressed. A factor that may influence the accuracy of an eyewitness.

Anxiolytic
Drugs used to treat feelings of anxiety, common examples of which are benzodiazapines.

Anxious/avoidant attachment
A type of *insecure attachment*. Children explore less, show little distress on separation and are not very nervous around strangers. Also known as *Type A*.

Anxious/resistant attachment
A type of *insecure attachment*. Children show great distress when separated from the caregiver and ambivalence on reunion.

Articulatory loop
Part of the *working memory model*. Often referred to as the 'inner voice', it is the verbal rehearsal system in the memory.

Attachment
An emotional bond between the child and the principle caregiver.

Autokinetic effect
An optical illusion used by Sherif (1936). If you stare at a spot of light in a darkened room it will appear to move. He had participants in groups estimate how far they thought the spot had moved in an investigation of *conformity*.

Autonomic nervous system

Part of the *peripheral nervous system* that deals with physiological processes that ordinarily we do not consciously control, such as breathing and heartbeat. It has two components: the *sympathetic branch* and the *parasympathetic branch*.

Autonomous state

Part of *agency theory*. *Autonomous state* is where individuals who feel independence assume responsibility for their own actions.

B

Behavioural approach (to psychopathology)

A *psychological approach*. Like all behaviour, abnormal behaviour is learned, through *classical conditioning*, *operant conditioning* and *social learning*.

Behavioural category

When engaging in any observation, categories of behaviour are decided upon for observing and recording. *Behavioural categories* might include things like 'aggression towards peers' or 'aggression towards carers' in a study where children's behaviour is being observed.

Benzodiazepines

Drugs used in the control of *stress*. They work by affecting levels of *neurotransmitters*.

Beta-blockers

Drugs used in the control of *stress*. They work by directly lowering heart rate and reducing blood pressure.

Biological approach (to psychopathology)

Mental health problems are regarded as illnesses with identifiable symptoms, origins and treatments.

Biological therapies

Therapies designed to alter the physical state of the body. These include *electroconvulsive therapy* and *drug therapy*.

Bowlby

John Bowlby applied the principles of imprinting to the human infant–caregiver relationship and is regarded as the major thinker in the study of human attachment.

British Psychological Society (BPS)

The professional body that governs the professional activity of psychologists in Britain.

C

Capacity

The size of part of memory. The capacity of *long-term memory*, for instance, is hard or even impossible to estimate. The size of *short-term memory* is significantly smaller than that of *long-term memory*.

Case study

A detailed investigation, usually of a single individual with a particularly interesting or unusual psychological problem. An example of a *case study* includes Freud's Anna O.

Central executive

The part of the *working memory model* that controls or 'supervises' activity.

Classical conditioning

Learning happens because we learn associations between things. For instance, Pavlov said that the dogs in his experiments associated the sound of footsteps with the stimulus of food. When they heard footsteps they began to salivate in anticipation of food. A similar relationship between stimuli and responses might be said to happen when infants and caregivers become attached.

Code of ethics

What should and should not be done to ensure that research is carried out ethically.

Cognitive approach (to psychopathology)

A *psychological approach*. Abnormality results

from faulty internal cognitive (thinking) processes.

Cognitive behavioural therapy (CBT)
A *psychological therapy* within the *cognitive approach to psychopathology*. It aims to identify errors and distortions in thinking that give rise to problems and help clients to find alternative ways of thinking to overcome them.

Cognitive deficiency
A lack of appropriate planning and thinking that can negatively affect behaviour. For example, if someone gets lost in a city centre, he or she may never try to find a way around that city again by using a map, or organising the directions properly. Instead the person will give up and stay away from the place.

Cognitive distortion
This occurs when our cognitive system does not accurately process the information it receives. For instance, a phobia of snakes may lead someone to see a worm as 'huge' and frightening.

Cognitive interview
A technique employed by the police to carefully help a witness recall the events of an often stressful event or experience.

Cognitive triad
According to Beck, depressed patients typically think negatively about themselves, the world and the future; the three things make up the *cognitive triad*.

Collectivist culture
A culture in which the importance is placed on the group as a whole, not the individual. Examples include Japan and China.

Compliance
Where we conform even though attitudes and opinions have not changed. Lasts for as long as group pressure exists.

Condition
A word used in research methods to describe different manipulations of the *independent variable*.

Conformity
The act of altering one's behaviour to match more closely the behaviour of a majority of others.

Content analysis
A method of data collection that takes information from the content of things like newspapers, magazines, television programmes or recorded conversations.

Continuity hypothesis
The idea that the benefits of a *secure attachment* in infancy continue to show themselves in later life.

Correlation
A technique used to show whether two variables are related. A *positive correlation* includes the relationship between the amount of time spent revising and exam mark (the more revising you do, the better your mark will be) and a *negative correlation* might be the number of DVDs purchased from your savings and the amount of money in your savings account.

Correlation coefficient
A statistic that describes the correlation data. It varies between -1 and +1. A *positive correlation* has a correlation coefficient of between 0 and +1. A *negative correlation* has a coefficient of between 0 and -1. A *zero correlation* will have a coefficient of 0. Coefficients closest to 1 are strongest.

Corticosteroids
A number of different *hormones* that have specific effects on the body, such as encouraging blood clotting, or the water-salt balance in the body, etc.

Culture
All the things that make our society what it is, including laws, social *norms* and customs.

D

Daily hassles
The small annoyances or irritations of everyday life, such as missing the bus, or losing one's keys.

Day care
The act of caring for children during the day while carers are at work. Often this takes place in nurseries, with friends or with older relatives like grandparents.

Demand characteristics
Things in the conduct of a study that give participants some idea of how the researcher wants them to respond.

Dependent variable
The thing that the researcher measures that depends on the *independent variable*. For instance, if the research is concerned with how fast we can run while carrying different weights, then the *independent variable* might be the different weights; the thing that depends on this (the *dependent variable*) is the running speed, and it is this that the researchers record as their data.

Deprivation
Where there was once an *attachment* that has now been broken.

Deviation from ideal mental health
A definition of abnormality. The person who is regarded as 'abnormal' does not achieve Jahoda's (1958) criteria for optimal living. It focuses on recognising normality rather than abnormality.

Deviation from social norms
A definition of abnormality. The person who is regarded as 'abnormal' does not adhere to the *norms* laid down by his or her society.

Directional hypothesis
A *hypothesis* that sets out a particular 'prediction' of what the research will find. For instance, the hypothesis that 'girls are better at science than boys' is directional: it predicts that girls will get higher scores in science tests than boys will. Sometimes called a one-tailed hypothesis.

Disruption of attachment
The breakdown, or interruption, of the *attachment* process. The term 'deprivation' is sometimes used to mean the same thing.

Distress
A negative kind of *stress* – stressors that we feel we cannot cope with.

Dream analysis
A method used in *psychoanalysis* where the therapist interprets a client's dreams. The content of the dream is regarded in psychodynamic therapy as having meaning, since it is in dreams that hidden unconscious thoughts are freely expressed.

Drugs
A *physiological method of stress management* that involves taking medication to reduce the physical symptoms of *stress*. They include *benzodiazepines* and *beta-blockers*.

Drug therapy
A *biological therapy* where medication is prescribed that may be palliative (the symptoms of abnormality are suppressed) or curative (the mental health problem is cured).

Duration
The length of time that a memory can be held in part of the memory system. The duration of *short-term memory*, for instance, is very brief, only seconds long, but the duration of

long-term memory is significantly longer, and potentially limitless.

E

Electroconvulsive therapy (ECT)
A *biological therapy* where a voltage large enough to bring about a convulsion, or fit, is passed across the brain.

Emotion-focused coping
An approach to coping with *stress*, also known as 'avoidant' techniques. The person finds relief from the symptoms of stress by employing defence mechanisms, reappraising the situation and reducing arousal levels.

Encoding
Organising memory for storage. The phrase 'committing something to memory' refers to 'encoding'. It is used to describe changing information in memory into a form usable to different kinds of memory.

Endocrine system
A system of glands that control many biological functions and affect a wide range of behaviours by using chemicals in the bloodstream called *hormones*.

Episodic memory
Our memory of episodes in our lives. For instance, the first time we swam in the sea.

Ethical issues
Issues that must be considered in the design of research if it is to be regarded as ethically sound. These include issues of informed consent, deception, debriefing, the right to withdraw, confidentiality and protection from harm.

Eustress
A positive kind of *stress* that is healthy for us.

Evolution
An approach developed by Charles Darwin from an earlier idea. It describes how species develop over generations and evolve to live in the world around us, and cope with the demands placed upon them by their environment. The mechanisms by which we do this include *natural selection* and the principle of *survival of the fittest*.

Evolutionary perspective (attachment)
One way in which we can think about *attachment* that takes the evolutionary viewpoint. That is, it has survival value.

Experimental design
The process of designing experiments, that is, whether or not the same or different participants are used in all *conditions* of the experiment. There are a number of different general design options open to the researcher, each with their own strengths and weaknesses, e.g. *repeated measures* design.

Experimental method
A description of how research is carried out in psychology.

External locus of control
When a person feels that events are beyond his or her control.

Extraneous variable
Things other than the *independent variable* that might influence the *dependent variable*. These need to be avoided or controlled at all costs.

Eyewitness testimony (EWT)
The report of what happened in a crime, or an event by someone who has seen or witnessed it.

F

Failure to form attachment
A situation in which a child does not form an *attachment*. If this happens the child experiences *privation*.

Failure to function adequately
A definition of abnormality. The people who are regarded as 'abnormal' engage in activities that are seen as somehow 'not good for them'. Their behaviour is self-defeating. Day-to-day living, involving seeing others, having relationships, and holding down a job is difficult.

Field experiment
Research that involves the direct manipulation of *variables* in a natural environment, i.e. not in a laboratory.

Fight or flight response
The stress response evolved to allow us to deal with a problem or run away from it. This is the fight (deal with it) or flight (run away from it) response.

Free association
A method used in *psychoanalysis* where the therapist attempts to access the subconscious. Words are presented to the client, who replies with the first word that comes to mind. An example might be 'carrot' associated with 'rabbit'. The responses of the client allow the therapist to draw conclusions about the client's subconscious.

G

Gender
Whether someone is male or female. This can influence a range of behaviours – for example, the likelihood of conforming or resisting *obedience*.

General Adaptation Syndrome (GAS)
A theory developed by Hans Selye in the 1940s that helps us understand how stress may lead to illness. Selye found a similar pattern of physical responses in animals regardless of the nature of the stress they were experiencing. This pattern is the *General Adaptation Syndrome (GAS)*.

Graph
A visual, pictorial method of presenting data.

Group unanimity
If the group in the majority are not seen as holding a unanimous view (they are seen as being divided with some believing one thing, others something else) then their influence over those in the minority to conform will be weakened.

H

Hardy personality
The personality of people who seem to live with high levels of stress but do not seem to suffer obviously as a consequence. Kobassa (1979) says that the hardy personality has three characteristics. These are commitment – they have drive and purpose in their lives, control – they see themselves as being in control, and challenge – they regard problems as challenges to be overcome.

Hormones
Chemicals released into the bloodstream by the *endocrine system* that travel rapidly to different parts of the body. Some have a general effect on the body, some influence specific organs or glands.

Hypothesis
The *hypothesis* is central to research. It is a formalised version of the *aims* of the research and is set out as a statement that the research attempts to test. It may be *directional* or *non-directional*.

I

Identification
Conformity occurs because we want to be more like those in the group influencing us. Conformity lasts as long as the influencing group remains attractive.

Immune system
The mechanism in the body that provides a defence against infections.

Imprinting
According to Konrad Lorenz, *imprinting* is the act of *attachment* but applied to animals. Lorenz famously worked with imprinting in geese.

Independent behaviour
Refers to resistance to authority figures (*obedience*) or group pressures (*conformity*).

Independent groups
Also known as independent samples. An *experimental design* whereby *participants* are allocated to different groups. Each group does something slightly different in the experiment, and the performance of the different groups is then compared.

Independent variable
The *variable* manipulated by the researcher. Ideally, the only thing you want to influence is the *dependent variable*.

Individual differences
The things that make people different from one another. This may include the study of such things as *personality*, *gender* and abnormality.

Individualist culture
A culture in which the importance is placed on individual success and achievement rather than the group as a whole. Examples include the United States and Great Britain.

Informational social influence
Conformity may be influenced by the information available to us. For instance, looking at what others are doing can significantly influence whether we comply or not.

Insecure attachment
There are two types: *anxious/avoidant* and *anxious/resistant*.

Institutionalisation
Care that takes place in an institution, such as an orphanage.

Internal locus of control
When a person feels that he or she is in control of events.

Internalisation
The most permanent form of *conformity* where the group opinion is accepted as a belief.

Inter-rater reliability
A comparison of two or more observations of the same event to see if there is consistency.

Interview
A method of data collection whereby a researcher asks a participant questions. The interview can take a number of forms – for example, may be structured or unstructured.

Investigator effects
A situation in research where an investigator unintentionally encourages a participant to behave in a certain way.

L

Laboratory experiment
Research that is carried out in controlled conditions in a laboratory. Typically in psychology, a laboratory is a quiet room where people will not be disturbed and where sights and sounds can be carefully controlled.

Learning theory
An explanation of *attachment* based on the principles of learning, including *operant* and *classical conditioning* and *social learning*.

Legitimate authority
People are more likely to obey people whom they regard as having *legitimate authority*. These people might include the police, doctors, or maybe even teachers and lecturers!

Life changes
Alterations and events in our lives that may be stressful, including house moves, job changes, etc.

Locus of control
An aspect of *personality* whereby we see ourselves to be either in control of events (*internal locus of control*) or at the mercy of other outside forces (*external locus of control*). People are usually somewhere between the two extremes.

Long-term memory
Part of the *multi-store model of memory*. A longer term store where memories are kept until needed. When they are needed they are passed to the *short-term* store before recall.

M

Majority influence
The influence over a smaller number of people by a larger, more powerful group.

Matched pairs
Like an *independent groups* design, but members in each of the groups are matched (for age, gender, etc.) with people in the other groups. The best example of matched pairs is to use identical twins.

Maternal deprivation
A theory put forward by *Bowlby*. If an infant does not form an *attachment* to its mother or a true mother substitute within six months to two-and-a-half years then it will suffer social and emotional problems later in life.

Mean
A *measure of central tendency*. The sum of all the values divided by the number of values that there were.

Measure of central tendency
A *summary statistic*. The 'average' value. There

are three averages: the *mean*, the *mode* and the *median*.

Measure of dispersion
A *summary statistic* that describes how spread out the data are.

Median
A *measure of central tendency*. When the data are put in order, smallest value to largest value, or largest to smallest, the median is the 'central number' if there are an odd number of values. If there are an 'even' number of values then the media is the mean of the two numbers in the middle.

Memory improvement technique
A method employed to help memory perform better.

Method of loci
A *memory improvement technique* where items to remember are 'left' in different locations around an imaginary building or route. Imagining travelling this route or walking through the building helps us recall the items we had 'left' there.

Milgram
Stanley Milgram designed a series of experiments in the early 1960s to investigate *obedience* to authority.

Minority influence
The influence over a larger group of people by a smaller less powerful group.

Misleading information
Information that encourages witnesses to recall events in ways in which they did not happen. For instance, asking 'You did see a young boy in a white hooded top didn't you?' may lead the memory of the witnesses and encourage them to answer 'yes' even though they had not seen such a person.

Mode

A *measure of central tendency*. The most common value in the data set. If there are two numbers that are equally common, then we say that there are two modes, bi-modal. If there are more than two numbers that are equally common then we can say that the data are multi-modal.

Model (of memory)

A theoretical representation of memory. A model helps us visualise how memory might work. Once we have a model of memory, we can use research to test how good the model is. You often see phrases in research like 'this supports the working memory model' or 'this finding is what would be predicted by the multi-store model'.

Monotropy

The attachment of an infant to a single main caregiver.

Multiple attachments

Schaffer and Emerson (1964) showed that while some infants have a primary attachment figure, many form *multiple attachments* to more than one figure. Some children seem to have no preferred attachment figure.

Multi-store model

Originally from Atkinson and Shiffrin (1968) but described in part by William James as far back as 1890. Memory is described in three parts: *sensory*, *short-term* and *long-term*.

N

Natural experiment

A little like a *field experiment* but in this case variables are not manipulated. Rather, researchers take advantage of naturally occurring changes to observe natural behaviour. For instance, if a town changes its city centre roads to one-way then the behaviour of road users before and after the change (a naturally occurring change) can be monitored.

Natural selection

A central principle of *evolution*. Animals produce many young, but not all can survive. Those that do because of cunning, strength, etc., are 'naturally selected' to pass on their genetic material to the next generation.

Naturalistic observation

A technique whereby behaviour of people in their natural environment is observed.

Negative correlation

A *correlation* that suggests that as one *variable* increases the other decreases. For instance, the amount of DVDs purchased and the amount of money in our bank account: the more DVDs we buy, the less money we have left.

Nervous system

A system of billions of *neurons* communicating using *neurotransmitters*. Divided into two parts, the central nervous system (CNS) and the *peripheral nervous system* (PNS).

Neurons

Specialised nerve cells that make up the *nervous system*.

Neurotransmitter

A chemical used in transmitting information between *neurons* in the brain, examples of which include dopamine and serotonin. Imbalances in *neurotransmitters* may lead to abnormal feelings or behaviours. Addressing imbalances using *drug therapy* can reduce symptoms of mental health issues.

Non-directional hypothesis

A *hypothesis* that does not set out a precise 'prediction' of what the research will find. For instance, the hypothesis 'ability at science depends on whether you are a girl or a boy' is *non-directional*, because it does not predict that girls will be better or worse than boys, rather it states that there will be a difference between the genders. Sometimes called a two-tailed hypothesis.

Normative social influence
Conformity may be influenced by our basic need to be accepted as a member of a group.

Norms
Unwritten social rules that regulate behaviour.

O

Obedience
A direct form of *social influence* where people do as they are told by an authority figure.

Observational method
A research method that involves observing people, usually in their natural environment, and systematically recording what they say and do.

Observational technique
A data-gathering technique used in a number of different research methods.

Operant conditioning
Learning happens because we are rewarded (or reinforced) for our behaviour or the way we feel or because we are punished for it. For instance, a child may learn that smiling is rewarded by loving kind words so he or she may repeat the behaviour more often.

Operationalise
To make something measurable. For instance, if our *dependent variable* is 'memory score' then we can operationalise it by saying 'memory score on a ten-item list'.

Opportunity sampling
A method of *sampling* whereby *participants* are chosen to take part because they are convenient. An example might be asking people who happen to be sitting in a local cafe.

P

Parasympathetic branch
The part of the *nervous system* that returns the body to normal after an emergency has passed.

Participant
One who takes part in research.

Peer relations
Relationships with people of our own age and group.

Peripheral nervous system
Part of the *nervous system* that consists of all the *neurons* that lie outside the brain and spinal cord. Some of these neurons make up the *autonomic nervous system*.

Personality
A collection of characteristics, or traits, that make us who we are.

Pilot study
A brief version of the full research that is quicker, perhaps less controlled, and involves fewer participants. The pilot experiment is useful to 'iron out' any unforeseen problems, and also gives the researchers an idea of what might happen. Sometimes researchers may change their design or their *hypothesis* because a *pilot study* has suggested that they should.

Phonological loop
Part of the *working memory model*. An auditory store, containing a phonological store (the 'inner ear') and an *articulatory loop* (the 'inner voice').

Physiological methods of stress management
Methods of managing *stress* that work by reducing the physical symptoms of the stress. They include the use of *drugs*.

Pituitary-adrenal system (PAS)
Also known as the hypothalamic pituitary-adrenal (HPA) system. A biological system involving the higher brain centres (cortex, etc.), the hypothalamus, the pituitary gland and the adrenal cortex. Information passed through the system results in the release of *corticosteroids* when *stress* is detected. This gives rise to the various symptoms and feelings of stress.

Positive correlation
A *correlation* that suggests that as one *variable* increases so too does the other. For instance, amount of food eaten is positively correlated with how full we feel: the more food eaten, the more full we feel.

Privation
The situation where a child has never had the opportunity to form a close *attachment*.

Problem-focused coping
An approach to coping with *stress*, also known as 'approach' techniques. The person finds relief from the stress by treating it as a problem to be solved. He or she may do this by employing methods of anticipatory coping and by seeking social support.

Procedural memory
Our memory of how to do things – for example, how to make a cup of tea.

Progressive relaxation
A technique where people learn how to relax the tension in their muscles that accompanies their feelings of *anxiety*. It is often part of *systematic desensitisation*, a behavioural therapy for abnormality.

Psyche
In the *psychodynamic approach to abnormality*, the *psyche* is the name given to 'the mind'.

Psychoanalysis
A *psychological therapy* within the *psychodynamic approach to psychopathology*. Developed by Freud in the 1890s, the therapy can involve dream analysis or free association. The goal of the therapy is to reveal unconscious, hidden thoughts that hold the origin of the person's abnormality.

Psychodynamic approach (to psychopathology)
A *psychological approach*. The mind (*psyche*) is seen as being influenced by powerful and changing (dynamic) unconscious forces. Most closely associated with Sigmund Freud.

Psychological approach (to psychopathology)
Mental health problems, resulting from abnormal thoughts, feelings and behaviours which have their origins in our psychology.

Psychological method of stress management
A problem-focused method of coping with stress. The principle one is *cognitive behavioural therapy*, an example of this being *stress inoculation training*.

Psychological therapies
Therapies that are based on the assumptions of *psychological approaches to psychopathology*. These include *psychoanalysis*, *systematic desensitisation* and *cognitive behavioural therapy*.

Psychopathology (abnormality)
The study of *individual differences* that is focused on explaining, diagnosing and treating mental health issues.

Psychosexual development
Freud said we go through stages in our early development, which he called *psychosexual development*. These include (in order) the oral stage, the anal stage, the phallic stage, the latency stage and the genital stage. Experiences during this period can influence our behaviour as adults.

Psychosocial identity
When we see ourselves as belonging to a social group, and this membership then influences our behaviour. For example, Mugny (1980) says that we are more likely to resist conformity if the minority group is one that we regard ourselves as belonging to in some way.

Q

Qualitative
Research that focuses on collecting data in the form of opinions.

Quantitative
Research that generates data in the form of numbers.

Questionnaire
A 'pen and paper' or, more often than not these days, an 'online' selection of different types of questions, the answers to which allow researchers to address the aims of their research.

R

Random sampling
A method of *sampling* whereby all participants in a population have an equal chance of being selected to take part in the study. An example might be random generation of names by a computer or 'drawing names out of a hat'.

Range
A *measure of dispersion*. The simplest measure, given by subtracting the largest number in the set from the smallest.

Reactance
A situation where we change our views and take up a position opposite to that which might be expected. We might react if someone tells us what to do or think and take a deliberately opposing view.

Reciprocal inhibition
In *systematic desensitisation*, the client's stress response to a stimulus becomes inhibited because it is incompatible with another behaviour. For instance, if the client is in deep relaxation, and the stressful stimulus is brought to mind, then the usual feeling of anxiety is inhibited because one cannot feel anxious and relaxed at the same time.

Reconstructive memory
We don't store exact records of events in memory. This means that when we recall information, we change it – for example, according to logic and common sense. Memories that are reconstructed might therefore not resemble the actual event.

Rehearsal
Repeating information that we want to remember. *Rehearsal* allows us to re-enter the information into the *short-term memory*, so we hold on to it for longer and maybe make it permanent.

Reinforcement
In *learning* theory, something that increases the likelihood of a behaviour occurring again.

Reliability
Another name for *consistency*. A reliable study is one that, if repeated, would return the same result. In *observational* research where different people 'rate' behaviours, you might measure *inter-rater reliability* so as to check whether the different researchers agree with one another.

Repeated measures
An *experimental design* in which each participant takes part on more than one occasion. Results are a comparison of the person's performance under each of the *conditions*. For instance, if the experiment aimed to investigate whether running speed is influenced by the amount of weight carried,

the *independent variable* would be 'weight carried'. Under a *repeated measures* design each person would run carrying one 'weight' then the same person would run carrying another 'weight' and so on.

Retrieval
The act of 'remembering' something that had been committed to memory. When people say 'I seem to recall…' they are in the act of *retrieval*.

Retrieval cue
Something that helps you retrieve information from memory. For instance, a photograph of a castle may help you recall a holiday you once spent where you visited the castle in the picture.

S

Sampling
The act of choosing participants to take part in a study.

Scatter plot
Another name for a *scattergram*.

Scattergram
Also known as a *scatter plot*. A graph that plots a person's score on one variable on one axis, and their score on another value on the other axis. The *scattergram* is used to depict *correlation* data.

Secure attachment
A *secure attachment* is one where a child in the *Strange Situation* explores his or her environment, shows distress when separated from the mother, greets the mother warmly on her return and is outgoing and friendly with strangers when the mother is present. It is the most common form of *attachment*. Also known as a *Type B attachment*.

Secure-base hypothesis
According to attachment theorists, a secure attachment means having a secure base that

provides them with a sense of protection and comfort.

Self report
A method of collecting data from people where the participants present the information themselves, such as in a *questionnaire* or an *interview*.

Semantic memory
Our general knowledge memory. For instance, whether a dog is a mammal.

Sensitivity hypothesis
Ainsworth argues that *secure attachment* patterns result from sensitive and responsive caregiving.

Sensory memory
Part of the *multi-store model of memory*. Very short duration indeed. Passes information to *short-term memory*.

Separation anxiety
An infant's suspicion and possible fear at the approach of someone unfamiliar (a 'stranger').

Short-term memory
Part of the *multi-store model of memory*. Short duration of between 5 and 9 (7+/-2) items according to Miller (1956). Passes information to and receives information from *long-term memory*.

Social change
Changes in society. These can often come about because of the actions of individuals or small groups of people.

Social development
Our early experiences as infants that may influence a range of behaviours including our *personality*, emotions and *aggression*. The effect of social development on later life as well as how social development is affected by interactions with others are both important.

Social impact theory
Developed by Latane (1981), the theory says that behaviour is influenced by a combination of the number of people present, the perceived status or expertise of individuals, or the physical closeness of others.

Social influence
The study of how social situations influence how we feel, think and behave.

Social learning
An explanation of learning that says that we learn through a process of observation, modelling and imitation.

Social readjustment rating scale (SRRS)
A scale designed by Holmes and Rahe (1967) to measure the effects of life events on health. The higher the score on the SRRS, the greater the likelihood of suffering from subsequent physical illness.

Social releaser
The behaviours of an infant that encourage the main caregiver to stay close, and provide protection and sustenance. These include crying, smiling and gurgling.

Standard deviation
A *measure of dispersion*. Calculated using a mathematical formula, it describes the 'average' distance that each value in the data is away from the *mean*.

State-dependency
The emotional or physical state you were in when you stored a memory acts as a *retrieval cue*. Returning to that state can help you recall the memory.

Strange Situation
A procedure for investigating *attachment* type in children, developed by Ainsworth and Bell (1970) but used subsequently by many researchers.

Stranger fear
An infant's fear or anxiety of a stranger.

Stress
Stress is the body's way of responding to some demand placed on it. Some stress is positive, it motivates and drives us – this is *eustress*. When we cannot cope with stress because it is either too much, or too little (leading to boredom and apathy), it is called *distress*.

Stress inoculation training (SIT)
A *psychological method of stress management*. A form of *cognitive behavioural therapy*, developed by Michenbaum (1972), it aims to reduce *stress* by helping people to think differently about it.

Stress management
The control of *stress*. Methods can be either *physiological* or *psychological*.

Stress-related illness
Exposure to *stress* can influence our physical functioning and lead to a stress-related illness.

Summary statistics
Numbers that include a *measure of central tendency* and a *measure of dispersion*, which provide a useful summary of the data.

Survival of the fittest
An evolutionary measure of how good you are at passing on your genetic material to the next generation.

Sympathetic branch
The part if the *nervous system* that arouses the body in an emergency.

Sympathomedullary pathway
A biological system involving the higher brain centres (cortex, etc.), the hypothalamus, the *autonomic nervous system* and the adrenal medulla. Information passed through the system can result in the release of adrenaline and noradrenaline when stress is detected.

Systematic desensitisation

A *psychological therapy* within the *behavioural approach to psychopathology*. A therapy based on *classical conditioning* designed to reduce feelings of *anxiety*. A person is taught relaxation techniques, then the therapist exposes him or her to increasingly more stressful stimuli, in an *anxiety* hierarchy, at each stage helping the client to relax and cope. Eventually the client is able to cope with the focus of the anxiety alone.

T

Table

A method of presenting data or summary statistics as numbers in an organised grid.

Type A attachment

Another name for *anxious/avoidant* type of *insecure attachment*.

Type A behaviour

A personality described as having an excessively competitive drive, being impatient and hostile, expressing themselves with fast movements and rapid speech. A very 'intense' person who is more likely to suffer with coronary heart disease than a *Type B* person.

Type B attachment

Another name for *secure attachment*.

Type B personality

A person who compared to a *Type A* person is described as being less competitive, less hostile, more patient, easygoing and tolerant. *Type B* people express themselves with slower speech and slower movements than Type A people and they are less likely to suffer from coronary heart disease.

Type C attachment

Another name for *anxious/resistant* type of *insecure attachment*.

Type D attachment

Also described as an *insecure*, or disorganised/disoriented *attachment* by Main and Solovan (1990). This is a mixture of *Type A* and *Type C* attachments identified in the *Strange Situation*.

Types of attachment

The *attachments* formed between children and their caregivers can differ. They can be described as *insecure* or *secure*.

V

Validity

If the research investigates what it says it investigates then it is said to be *valid*. Similarly, if a tool used in research is valid then it measures what it is supposed to. For instance, a technique for measuring *attachment* is the *Strange Situation* and is regarded as valid for that. Using a thermometer to measure attachment is not valid.

Variable

Something that is changed or controlled in research. These include *extraneous*, *independent* and *dependent variables*.

Visuo-spatial sketchpad

Also known as a 'scratchpad' and referred to as the 'inner eye'. The visual and spatial version of the *articulatory loop*. Information is dealt with by visually organising it. Can be thought of as mental rough paper.

Volunteer sampling

A method of *sampling* whereby *participants* volunteer to take part, perhaps by responding to a notice requesting volunteers.

W

Word-length effect

The tendency to immediately recall short words better than long words.

Working memory model

Baddeley's model of memory, the

components of which include the *central executive*, the *phonological loop* and the *visuo-spatial sketchpad*.

Workplace stress
Issues in our workplace that may lead to *stress*, including workload, environment and the amount of control we have over our work.

Z

Zero correlation
Correlation data that suggests that there is no relationship between the two *variables* at all. For instance, the number of apples on an apple tree, and the amount of time you spend watching TV.

Index

Image credits

NEW 2008 AQA 'A' SPECIFICATION

Crown House Publishing Limited
www.crownhouse.co.uk

A2
LEVEL

Psychology

Nigel Holt
and Rob Lewis

THE STUDENT'S TEXTBOOK

ISBN 978-184590100-4

NEW 2008 AQA 'A' SPECIFICATION

Crown House Publishing Limited
www.crownhouse.co.uk

A2
LEVEL

Psychology

Nigel Holt
and Rob Lewis

THE STUDY GUIDE

ISBN 978-184590101-1